MR CARRY ON

THE LIFE AND WORK OF PETER ROGERS

★

MORRIS BRIGHT & ROBERT ROSS

BBC

Published by BBC Worldwide Ltd,
80 Wood Lane, London W12 0TT

First published 2000

ISBN 0 563 55183 6

Commissioning Editor: Ben Dunn
Project Editor: Rebecca Kincaid
Picture Research: David Cottingham

Set in Ehrhardt
Printed and bound in Great Britain by Butler & Tanner Ltd, Frome and London
Jacket and plate sections printed by Lawrence-Allen Ltd, Weston-super-Mare

Contents

Introduction
The Biggest Cult in Comedy!

The moment one hears those two magical, all-encompassing words –
Carry On – a wealth of comic information whizzes round the brain.
In an instant, you may think of that raucous, lusty laugh of Sid James;
the impossibly flared nostrils and elongated vowels of Kenneth
Williams; the boyish bemusement behind the National Health specs of
Charles Hawtrey; or the ever popping bra of Barbara Windsor.

You may think of the bombastic medical authority of Hattie Jacques;
the shifty eccentricity of Peter Butterworth; the muscles of Bernard
Bresslaw; the sexually charged cry of 'Cor!' from Kenneth Connor; or
the youthful naive adventures of Jim Dale.

You may think of the multi-layered character parts of Joan Sims;
the cheek-puffing laddish attitude of Terry Scott; or the clumsy facial
twitching of Jack Douglas.

You may think of the galaxy of comedy stars and character players
who peppered the films, from Leslie Phillips, Ted Ray, William Hartnell and
Bernard Cribbins in the early days, through to international players
such as Phil Silvers and Elke Sommer. There was also Jon Pertwee, Liz
Fraser, Frankie Howerd, Harry H Corbett, Bob Monkhouse, and
countless other talents who joined forces with the established team
to create a seemingly never-ending, never-flagging line of comedy
classics.

Of course, the series did end and did flag, and not all the entries
were classics, but a national identity was played out within the confines
of these saucy, winking, carnivalesque entertainments; a national identity that has withstood the test of time, political correctness and changes
in attitudes. The *Carry On*s now have a permanent place in the hearts
of an entire nation.

The story of *Carry On* started with the economically made *Carry
On Sergeant* in 1958. It was a warm-hearted, feelgood film, which Peter
Rogers, the producer, recalls was 'an instant success with the audiences,
but not with the critics'. Peter's relationship with the critics was almost

as sticky as his relationship with the British Board of Film Censors (now the British Board of Film Classification) but, ironically, it was the tabloids rather than the quality papers that were snooty about his cheerful comedies: 'It is amusing to recall that when the critics were at us, it was the popular press who were more anti than the quality press. Dilys Powell and C A Lejeune were very kind because they realized what the films were.'

What the films were, was a collection of corny old gags, tightly reined in by expert scriptwriters – Norman Hudis for the initial six films and Talbot Rothwell for most of the remaining – and an unsurpassable assembly of top acting talent who could play this light, frothy slapstick with a healthy injection of innuendo.

Ironically, perhaps, the one man who seemed to be forgotten in all this glorious comic delight was Peter Rogers himself. In true cliché terms, he was painted as a *Citizen Kane*-like figure, hiding away in his own polished Xanadu of great wealth and bad jokes. The truth, however, could not have been further from this image of refined aloofness. Contrary to popular belief, Peter was constantly on the set and heavily involved in the nuts and bolts of music composing, scripting and editing for his magnum opuses over a 20-year period, though it would take a series of tragic events and commercial dealings to bring the man who had always been part of the legend of 'A Peter Rogers Production' out into the public gaze.

For a man with no family of his own, the *Carry On* series was certainly Peter's one and only baby. When that baby reached the age of 21, and flew the nest, leaving nothing but the critical and commercial failure of *Carry On Emmannuelle* as a reminder, Peter's little universe started to crumble. The one thing that saved it was an astonishing re-evaluation of the *Carry On* films – and the *Carry On* cult was born.

Emmannuelle was not so much a bad film as a badly timed one. Four years had passed since the seductive Sylvia Kristel had seduced the entire world with her flamboyant bed-hopping antics. As a result, the *Carry On* treatment looked tired and dated in comparison with the full-on nudity of Robin Askwith's *Confessions* ... movies, and the various copycat drop-'ems for ageing comedy character actors during the late 1970s.

If *Carry On* had lost its way, at least it never totally lost its dignity. However, with the onset of full-on raunchiness requiring a smattering of old-timers – even *Carry On* legends Jack Douglas and Peter Butterworth played along with the new system for *What's Up Nurse?* – by

1977 the end was, most certainly, nigh. Besides, with the death of Sid James – the undisputed head of the *Carry On* 'family' – on 26 April 1976, the *Carry On*s had, in effect, lost their leading light as far as the general public was concerned.

In 1979, when plans for a further romp, *Carry On Again Nurse*, were shelved due to lack of interest from backers and distributors, Peter Rogers complained, 'There is money in the crap that I make, but they don't seem to see it!' Despite seeming to pre-empt Gerald Ratner's throwaway, empire-ruining comment, Peter was far from shooting himself in the foot with this remark. His comedy films had been labelled as crap for many years, and he decided he may as well join in with the insults.

Crap or not, he knew the films pleased the public and they had made him a fortune. The classic film industry joke after a private press screening of the 1975 film *Carry On Behind* was, 'I know why Sid James isn't in this picture. He was sick on the morning they made it!' Although it was good-natured, affectionate ribbing, the joke spoke volumes and the label stuck. The days for *Carry On* at the box office seemed numbered.

Television, however, was a different story. Gradually, throughout the mid to late 1970s, the classic films in the *Carry On* series became regular, popular and, above all, cheap time-filling material for television stations desperate to keep costs down. As a result, the glory days of Sid James and Kenneth Williams, battling through the Roman Empire, the French Revolution and a medical ward, became as much a part of the family tradition as chocolate eggs at Easter and turkey at Christmas. The deaths of Peter Butterworth, in 1979, and Hattie Jacques, in 1980, heaped still more emotive affection on these familiar favourites from a past era.

'Hip' and 'happening' show-business personalities were happy to express their love for the *Carry On*s and, into the cool and trendy late 1980s, even the alternative brigade who had branded the cheeky cherub Benny Hill as a sexist disgrace embraced the *Carry On* tradition as part of their own history of influences and heroes. Ben Elton, Rik Mayall, Hale and Pace, and Harry Enfield all went on record as fans. Leslie Phillips was invited to guest star in the *Comic Strip Presents* film, *Oxford*; Kenneth Connor cropped up in *Blackadder the Third*; and Barbara Windsor became the Queen Mother of comedy for a fresh-faced aggressive generation.

In 1987, Video Collection International unveiled an affordable and comprehensive collection of 13 *Carry On* titles from the classic days of Rank, while a get-together at Barbara Windsor's Amersham pub recruited *Carry On* director Gerald Thomas and stars Bernard Bresslaw, Terry Scott, Jack Douglas and Anita Harris for a promotional binge. Plans were announced for a new film – *Carry On Texas* – and new talent such as Lenny Henry, Victoria Wood and Russ Abbot were cited as possible replacements for those team members who had departed stage left.

Big screen spoofs of *Neighbours* and medical dramas were promised, but quickly abandoned. Television specials were always being discussed, and press releases continually emerged from the Pinewood office of Peter Rogers and Gerald Thomas. Amazingly, even after the deaths of Kenneth Williams and Charles Hawtrey in quick succession during 1988, the *Carry On* legend refused to lie down and die. If anything, the loss of the camp core of *Carry On* comedy brought the series even more cult clout in the modern age.

In these early days of *Carry On* fandom, one man stood above all others as the purveyor and protector of good old-fashioned smut. That man was Jonathan Ross. His Channel 4 chat programme, *The Last Resort*, mixed American-style panache with English eccentricity to form the perfect blend of wisecracks, funny remarks and sharp suits. The set was frequently littered with photographs of Sid James and the classic *Carry On* crew. Even more crucially, Jim Dale, Barbara Windsor and Frankie Howerd were high profile guests. Ross himself never failed to plug the films in one shape or another, and his biggest regret was deciding against inviting Kenneth Williams on to the show in late 1987. By April the following year, it would be too late.

In 1989, Harry Enfield's parody of the British film industry, *Norbert Smith – A Life*, brought together Barbara Windsor, Jack Douglas and Kenneth Connor for a brief clip from the nuclear-campaigning epic *Carry On Banging*, while, in January 1990, Andy Medhurst included the series (via *Carry On Nurse* and *Carry On Cabby*) in his National Film Theatre celebration of lowbrow comedy.

In December of that year, the films won their first award of note – the very first Jester Award for Lifetime Achievement in Film Comedy. The producer and director were on hand, along with Kenneth Connor, Bernard Bresslaw, Barbara Windsor and Liz Fraser, to accept the honour from Sir John Mills. The new boys – from Jonathan Ross and

Arthur Smith to Julian Clary and Rory Bremner – joined forces with Frankie Howerd and Barbara Windsor for the BBC Radio 4 *Loose Ends* Christmas Special ... *Carry On Up Yer Cinders*, while in May 1991, Peter Rogers once again announced plans for a series of television *Carry On*s.

It was only a matter of time before something came of all this interest and, in the end, it came in the shape of Jim Dale and Jack Douglas struggling against a tide of bad vibes in *Carry On Columbus*. Not quite the disaster it could have been, the film proved once and for all that the thought of a *Carry On* reunion was always going to be much better than the actuality. But, instead of sinking the good ship *Carry On* forever more, the new movie scored highly at the box office, injected even more fresh interest in the series, and even fired a deep-down affection for the films in usually ultra-cool detached critics. Typically, though, *Columbus* was branded as awful, weak and unfunny compared with those classic adventures with Sid James and Charles Hawtrey.

The turning point for the elevation of Peter Rogers to cult status came in 1993, when Peter and Gerald Thomas were invited to contribute a Pinewood tour of *Carry On* locations and memories to the BBC documentary series, *Hollywood UK*, celebrating British film of the 1960s.

However, 1993 was also a tragic year for the *Carry On* series. Not only did they lose character player Victor Maddern – familiar from films such as *Carry On Constable* and *Carry On Cleo* – and beloved unforgettable team members Bernard Bresslaw and Kenneth Connor, but Peter Rogers also lost his friend, partner and director of 42 years, Gerald Thomas.

Gerald, the architect of *Carry On* – the man who had overseen every production under budget and on time – had gone: Peter had lost his right arm, and the *Carry On*s could never be the same again.

Yet, as a result of Gerald's death, Peter was forced to accept invitations to openings, interviews and showbiz bashes. These had always been Gerald's forte, but Peter's *Carry On* baby was going through a second childhood and someone needed to 'front' them.

The *Carry On*s had literally become a vital, vibrant and ageless part of the British way of life, but it was one crucial year, 1995, which finally sealed their fate as the ultimate in classic comedy nostalgia. From 11 August to 31 August 1995, the Barbican Centre, that most respected home of British art and culture, did the almost unbelievable and held a retrospective season of *Carry On* films. Although it neglected to include the commercially released compilation, *That's Carry On,* in the season, the Barbican's endorsement of these much-debated corny classics opened up floodgates, which several acidic critics have been desperately trying to close ever since.

At last, however, narrow-minded individuals who had felt it uncool to laugh at Sid James and the gang could come out of the closet and admit their long-standing admiration for *Carry On*s. Intellectuals began to write on the merits, subplots and social history of the series, laddish magazines energetically embraced the new-lad image of *Carry On* smut, sauce and scantily clad chicks, and even that bastion of British broadcasting – the BBC 9 O'Clock News – featured a wry mention of the Barbican season.

Speaking to the *Evening Standard* in August 1995, Peter Rogers typically played down the season. Reeling with pretend shock at the prospect, he exclaimed, 'What a punishment. Even the Marquis de Sade couldn't have devised a worse torture. Yet, while the vintage self-deprecating bluff was firmly in place, behind closed doors the producer swelled with pride.

A gala screening of *Carry On … Up the Khyber* – the jewel in the *Carry On*s' crown, and Peter's personal favourite – heralded the start of the season at which die-hard fans could part with 30 quid to purchase the Khyber Pass – a ticket covering all 30 films on offer - and even KP Nuts marked the event with an extensive poster campaign. All across London, one could see Sid James chuckling, Kenneth Williams looking aghast or the delightful sight of Charles Hawtrey with a bag of KP's finest, uttering the immortal slogan, 'My nuts are chilli!'

Suddenly it was 'hip' to quip – and the definitive reference book, *The Carry On Companion*, by Robert Ross, effortlessly slipped out with perfect timing to a very favourable reaction. Academics used it and *Carry On* star Jack Douglas immediately called it 'the *Carry On* Bible!' It had been 10 years in the making and covered a decade of sea change in popular culture which was quite extraordinary.

Music Collection International launched its range of *Carry On* talking books – using the soundtrack of the film with additional narration from Patrick Allen, Peter Gilmore and even Joan Sims – while that purveyor of finger-on-the-pulse comic investigation, ITV's *Funny Business*, recruited Jack Douglas, Fenella Fielding and the author of *The Carry On Companion* to hotly debate the films' many qualities.

Six *Carry On* novels were written by Norman Giller, and yet another announcement for the 32nd *Carry On* picture was set to cast the incongruous pairing of the Chuckle Brothers and Ben Elton. But rumours, counter-rumours, and even the death of team member Terry Scott, could not stop the unstoppable march of *Carry On* to the absolute heart of the nation. The ultimate celebrations, however, were reserved for 1998 and the majestic 40th anniversary party.

Greetings cards, boxer shorts, T-shirts, bookmarks, phonecards, first-day covers and a wealth of other merchandise swept the stores. Pinewood Studios was host to a 40th anniversary plaque unveiling, as well as marking the individual contributions of Sid James, Kenneth Williams, Charles Hawtrey and Hattie Jacques. Beloved favourites Jack Douglas, Leslie Phillips, Barbara Windsor, June Whitfield, Lance Percival and Liz Fraser were among over 35 *Carry On*ers who joined Peter Rogers at this ultimate tribute to his priceless series of films.

It was very much a day of celebration, but, at the very end of his emotive speech, Peter touched on a sore point and made a joke about it. Remembering his loyal group of actors with great affection, he said cheekily, 'I loved them all dearly and would do anything for them except pay them more money!' It was the comment of a producer who had made a fortune and who had often been branded a mean man. Indeed, one *Carry On* character actor, spotting the cameras in place to record the day for the official 40th anniversary documentary, *What's a Carry On?*, was heard to complain: 'I know what's going on. Peter Rogers is making another *Carry On* film, and this time he's not paying us anything!'

The debate over money had been going on for years, but the problem really came to a head in the early 1980s when Peter and Gerald embarked on a couple of compilation programmes – *Carry On Laughing* for ITV and *What a Carry On* for the BBC.

These programmes plundered rich *Carry On* archives and presented re-edited highlights of past glories, and morally the *Carry On* stars should have received some form of payment. In the event, owing to filmic rights and contracts, they received nothing. Speaking in 1991, Barbara Windsor complained that the compilations stopped her from getting work: 'People see me in films I made 20 years ago and don't consider me for anything else. I was going to auditions and being told, "Oh, we can't use Barbara Windsor – she's never off the box!"'

She may never have been off the box, but her many appearances were not making her any money. Barbara was convinced that 'if Sid were alive, we would have got something. He loved money – and there's nothing wrong with that. He would have found a way round the contract!'

Actors such as Kenneth Connor were more philosophical, gladly acknowledging that their long-running roles in situation comedies such as *Allo, Allo!* and *Hi-De-Hi!* were thanks to their association with the *Carry On*s.

Almost as a safety mechanism, Peter claimed that, in the very early days, shortly after the huge success of *Carry On Nurse*, he had gathered together a small band of actors who would become the official *Carry On* team. These included actors who did, indeed, go on to become long-standing *Carry On* players (Kenneth Williams, Joan Sims, Charles Hawtrey, Kenneth Connor, Hattie Jacques), and those who would, eventually, fall by the wayside (Bill Owen, Terence Longdon, Leslie Phillips).

Peter insists that 'after the second film was so popular, I decided to cut all the actors in on the deal. The idea was to give them a severe cut in initial salary and make up the difference with a percentage of the film's take. To a man, all the agents immediately said "no!", but I did make the offer.'

Leslie Phillips remembers it differently: 'There was never any talk of a royalty – not to me anyway.'

'Perhaps,' replies Peter, 'his agent didn't tell him!'

Recalling the glorious days at Pinewood Studios, during an interview to promote *Carry On Emmannuelle* in 1978, the late Kenneth Williams – the star who appeared in more *Carry On* films than any other – commented: 'You might not have seen them [the *Carry On* team] for a few months, so it has all the excitement of a new experience – a family reunion. I also like the economic independence engendered by belonging to the *Carry On* team. This means I don't have to accept a play I think is going to be very hard work and not very rewarding simply because I need the money.

'I shall always be grateful to Peter Rogers for letting me conduct my career without being rushed into anything. That's why I get angry when I hear people say that the *Carry On* cast should have some share in the vast profits from the films. I say, "Why the hell should they?" The man who makes the initial investment in a film and takes that kind of risk deserves everything he makes. The actors still get paid if it makes nothing.

'It is also an excellent thing for an actor who works in radio and television to be constantly in circulation in a series like the *Carry On*s. A lot of people call Peter Rogers dictatorial, but then he is certainly a most benign dictator – fatherly, I would say. And he looks after his group of regulars extremely well, especially when they are in a state of stress or in trouble.'

Naturally, at the time, no one realized that some 40 years after the films were made, people would still be queuing up to buy the merchandising rights to re-release the *Carry On*s on video, compact disc and even DVD, and to arrange major retrospectives and gala celebrations.

Peter has always been of a somewhat nervous disposition: 'People frighten me. I used to give my brother sixpence to go into a shop and ask for what I wanted. But I'd think nothing of going to Rank and saying, "I want to make this picture, how about it?" If they didn't play I'd walk out of the room. I never negotiated – that's the way to lose control.'

There is, certainly, a moral – if not legal – question over the cast of the *Carry On*s being manipulated and recycled without them having any control over what is produced. When *Carry On ... Up the Khyber* was voted into the top 100 British films ever made in a millennium poll, survivor Joan Sims complained, 'People think I'm rich and retired, but I'm still trying to scrape a living!'

Indeed, Joan Sims and Barbara Windsor had a right to complain. In the first place, the actresses had been paid only half the wage of actors Sidney James and Kenneth Williams. The men were on a regular fee of £5,000, the women received £2,500. One can hardly blame them, albeit 30 years later, feeling slightly hard done by in the payment department.

One major *Carry On* star commented, 'What's he [Peter] going to do with all that money anyway – be buried in a gold coffin, I suppose!', and there is a sense that the cast have been treated with little respect and consideration. Legally, however, Peter Rogers is completely confident that he owned the rights to the *Carry On* series and that any representation of the series or its stars in a *Carry On* context only needed his blessing to proceed.

Of course, perhaps foolishly as far as his actors are concerned, Peter remains adamant that the *Carry On* title is the star of the series: that even the much-missed, departed core team members were dispensable, that Gerald Thomas was dispensable, that he, himself, is dispensable.

And even now *Carry On* is the benchmark by which every other comic cult is judged, and Peter believes that a new addition to the series cannot be entirely ruled out. The rest of the country nods along in agreement, while secretly facing the truth that the *Carry On* series, as an ongoing working entity, is very much part of a distant era.

Carlton Television screened its much-watched and much-admired documentary, *What's a Carry On?*, during Christmas 1998 with in-front-of-camera and behind-the-scenes contributions from Morris Bright and Robert Ross. *Cleo, Camping, Emmanuelle* (sic) *and Dick*, Terry Johnson's look 'behind the scenes' of *Carry On* productions, took the National Theatre by storm, won the Laurence Olivier Award for Best Comedy, and enjoyed an extensive tour across the nation before being filmed for television with the emphasis firmly on the private lives of Sid James and Barbara Windsor under the title *Cor Blimey!*, broadcast on ITV over Easter 2000.

The ultimate cinematic goal, however, was achieved just before the end of 1998, when the Museum of the Moving Image on the South Bank unveiled its special exhibition, *Ooh! What a Carry On*, celebrating 40 years of Great British Comedy. Robert Ross was signed up as exhibition consultant, and swallowing his pride and a few beers, presented a tasty probe into male sexuality within the films in a lecture entitled 'Screaming Queens, Wannabe Heroes and the Shroud of Innuendo'.

More was to follow: the National Film Theatre screened a selective season of the *Carry On*s' greatest hits in February 1999; Lledo issued a set of six die-cast vehicles celebrating the series; the Variety Club of Great Britain marked Peter's 'marvellous, humorous films' with a set of stamps; and, finally, in May of that year, Bright 'n' Ross Productions presented the World's First Official *Carry On* Convention at – where else? – Pinewood Studios.

After a breakneck tour of the local locations – from Pinewood Green via Maidenhead and Slough – pioneers Shirley Eaton and Norman Hudis were interviewed, while seventies' screen lovers Richard O'Callaghan and Jacki Piper, Valerie Leon and Marc Sinden foregathered with the fans. Peter Rogers – 'Mr Carry On' himself – was greeted like the second coming as the crowd rose as one man in a standing ovation.

The *Carry On*s had finally become an all-conquering, nationally important institution, and even the ill-fated, mistimed disasters of *Carry On England* and *Carry On Columbus* were taken to the hearts of the general public. Reflecting on the golden days of the 1960s, Peter recalls: 'I remember saying at the time that as long as we weren't adopted by the critics as an "institution" we were safe.'

Well, the series is now an institution, and is as safe as Lloyds Bank.

With more *Carry On* days at Pinewood well and truly 'in the can', the authors of this book, Morris Bright and Robert Ross, are proud to have been dubbed 'the Peter Rogers and Gerald Thomas for the new millennium', and prouder still to consider Peter Rogers a close friend.

Today, with everything from *Carry On* toby jugs to *Carry On* calendars filling the market, the *Carry On* series successfully being released on DVD, and the *Carry On* cult at an all-time peak, Peter Rogers is still to be found at Pinewood Studios. After the sad death of his wife, the pioneering producer Betty E Box, in January 1999, Pinewood and the *Carry On* legend have come to mean even more to Peter. Now in his late eighties, but still looking like a man in his mid sixties, Peter relishes his working week at Pinewood, and revels in his elder-statesman position.

Here, then, is the man behind the *Carry On* series: Peter Rogers, 'Mr Carry On', a unique man with a unique career that has been, for many years, shrouded in uncertainty, rumour and secretive misunderstandings. Until now, that is.

Chapter One
A Producer Is Born

Peter Edward Rogers' earliest memory, as a four-year-old boy at the end of the First World War, reads like a scene from *Carry On Sergeant*: enter a group of demobbed soldiers strolling in a park. They bump into an attractive nanny taking her employer's offspring on his daily constitutional. The men feign interest in the child but, in reality, they are only doing what most newly demobbed soldiers, who have spent so much time away from the 'comforts' of home, like to do ... they are ogling the pretty young thing pushing him along.

This witnessing of soldiers out for a bit of ... fresh air might also have been Peter's first encounter with the *double entendre* – the sort of sexual games that would prove the hysterical underpinning for so much of his future work.

'I was born in bed next to my mother on 20 February 1914.' It's a funny line – and one which Peter is proud to repeat. It establishes the closeness that existed between him and his mother, Alice Rogers, until her untimely death from cancer in 1944.

But on that winter's day when Peter was born, he and his mother were far from alone. As well as the doctor, nurse and midwife in the bedroom – and an older brother, Franklin, and father, Claude, pacing the floor in the living-room downstairs – another addition, Peter's twin brother, arrived shortly afterwards. The brother was named Paul – yes, Peter and Paul, after the two little dicky-birds sitting on the wall of the fabled nursery rhyme. The idea, which came from the boys' nanny, appealed to Alice and Claude, and the boys were duly named.

The family lived in Bleak House, Rainham Road, Gillingham, Kent. Their home was situated at the edge of the town, with open country stretching out beyond, and many were the times that the infant twins watched as people made their weekly trip to the windmills to pick up their flour. Their home was also on the main road to Dover and Folkestone. The echoes of the marching of seemingly endless lines of soldiers' feet are still a vivid memory:

'The troops were destined for France and would prepare for their posting at Darland Camp, just a mile from our home. The line of troops was so long that three bands were provided to play along the way and keep up the morale of the men. I don't know the regulations regarding the distance of bands to troops, but presumably the sound of the first band had to be inaudible to the second band, and so on to the third. As you can imagine, it represented a hell of a lot of men and God alone knows just how many came back.'

When Peter was two, his family moved to a house just a short distance away in Rochester High Street, where his father had offices and where they could hear the bells of Rochester Cathedral. The music of pealing bells has remained with Peter throughout his life and, to this day, the sound of church bells ringing brings him a sense of peace.

Indeed, some years later, when Peter was driving home from Pinewood Studios, he passed through the nearby town of Fulmer, Buckinghamshire, and heard the sound of bells ringing. Having asked his chauffeur to stop the car, he got out and sat on a nearby bench to listen to the campanologists doing their business. For some time after this, Peter would organize his journeys home to coincide with the bell-ringers' practice. But then, following complaints from young mothers that the noise was keeping their babies awake, the practice time was changed.

Referring to his own babyhood, Peter says: 'I was told I wouldn't have anything to do with my mother in the milk stakes, which was surprising considering my natural attachment to her. Instead – and, believe it or not, on doctor's orders – I was given an oyster to suck on. That's probably why I eat so many of the damn things today. In those days, of course, oysters were cheap and poor people often depended on them.'

Peter's upbringing was not impoverished, something for which he often seems apologetic. Unlike his future wife, Betty Box, whose life was literally a rags to riches story, Peter's early life – whatever it may have lacked emotionally – was never short of money, clothes or food. His father, Claude, was a successful professional man with whom Peter was destined to have violent quarrels over the choice of his future career. Compromises were reached, but the frustrations and bitterness lingered, and Peter's relationship with his father was never easy at best, and at worst broke down completely.

Claude Rogers was a specialist in valuing licensed property, such as pubs and hotels. Respected in his field of work, he was held in deep admiration by the prestigious Business Society:

'I can remember seeing a thick book on his desk called *Pattinson's Licensing Act 1910*. It was full of interesting information. For instance, did you know that it was illegal for pub windows to be made of clear glass? They had to be obscured up to a certain height so that children could not look in and see their fathers drinking.

'Did you know that a man couldn't hold a pub licence if he had committed even the smallest of offences? I remember, in one instance, a man who had been charged with swearing on top of a bus was refused a licence a decade later. The poor people who were moving out of the pub had to have all their furniture moved back in again. Publicans had to be whiter than white and purer than a parson. They were not allowed to be divorced or unmarried. And did you know that all pub transactions had to be paid for in cash, no matter how much?'

Peter's penchant for reading started early and, while *Pattinson's Licensing Act 1910* may not have been the chosen literature for many young children, the desire for knowledge and the love of books shaped his plans and ambitions for the future.

While at Rochester, the Rogers family experienced Zeppelin raids and spent many nights in a cellar. For a three-year-old, with little ability to understand the damage which the First World War was inflicting on men, women and children, it was very exciting. The sense of excitement, however, came to an abrupt halt one night:

'I remember the bombing of the Royal Naval Hospital at Chatham, which adjoined Rochester. It was a long glass building and a lot of patients were killed. I also remember seeing the survivors of the Zeebrugge raid arriving at Chatham station – and what a pathetic-looking lot they were.'

When the bombing had stopped and life had returned to as normal as possible following the devastating air attacks and the constant passage of troops through the town, life for Peter was stable if not always happy.

The Rogers household consisted of Mother and Father, Peter, his twin brother Paul, older brother Franklin, two maids – one of whom acted as a nursemaid – and a dog. Peter's love of canine beasts started as soon as he learned to walk and, to this day, he has never been without one.

The High Street where they lived was crammed with tall buildings, which, prestigious as they looked, did not have one bathroom or indoor toilet among them. Come rain or snow, sun or moon, the trips to the

outside convenience proved to be anything but convenient. The bedrooms of the houses were on the upper floors and hot water had to be
carried up several flights of stairs every morning for the daily ablutions.
In Peter's house, as with most in the area, this task was performed by
the maids. The Rogers family treated their servants well and all the
maids stayed on until they left to get married. One even hid her
'courting' for 10 years.

Peter liked the maids. He enjoyed the company of women and spent
as much time as he could with them:

'They had a habit of taking me home to meet their families. I don't
know why they picked on me and not my twin brother. I suppose it's
because I always got on so well with them. Whenever we had what used
to be called "company" at home, when aunts, uncles and cousins came
to sit-down tea, they invariably asked, "Where's Peter?" and my mother
would say, quite matter of factly, "He's in the kitchen helping the maids
to clean the silver." My mother would have let me continue in this, but
my father usually hauled me out to meet the "company".'

Life at Rochester was interesting for Peter. Borstal boys used to
march through the town on their way to work on an allotment or
garden. The Borstal Prison was not far away, and the trusted youths
were allowed out to undertake menial tasks. They were easily recognizable in their blue uniforms (the difficult ones wore khaki and weren't
allowed out in public). Most people just looked on in sympathy. There
was never any jeering or name-calling.

A much looked forward to event was when the Royal Engineers,
who were stationed at the barracks in Chatham, marched through the
High Street to the church parade at Rochester Cathedral. For Peter, it
was only a short walk to the Royal Marine Barracks at Chatham to listen
to the band and watch the church parade. He particularly remembers
one marine drum major who would thrill the crowd, on the return to
the barracks, by throwing his drumstick over the entrance and catching
it the other side.

All of this was great entertainment for Peter, who already had an
inbuilt love of music, and the pomp and theatrics appealed to the seed
of showmanship that was beginning to grow somewhere within his sub-
conscious:

'One Christmas Eve, the choir of Rochester Cathedral walked through
the High Street carrying lanterns and singing carols. The carols were
conducted by the Cathedral organist, who walked backwards as he

conducted … it would have been interesting if he'd fallen over in his white surplice because there was a lot of horse-drawn traffic in the High Street at the time. In fact, there was a horse trough right outside our house and I used to like stroking their soft noses as they sucked up the water.'

Peter watched as the world around him unfolded. There were street singers in those days, and people would open their windows to throw coppers down to them. There was also an odd little man who pushed a pram with a gramophone on it and played records. His day to appear was Saturday, and the town folk knew him as 'Old Nothin'. On Tuesdays, a man used to sing with a finger in one ear. Eighty years on, most of the words of the song escape Peter, but part of it went: 'Beetles up the wall they climb/Oh, mother, mother, mother, we'll have a lovely time …'

There were the customary street fights at pub closing time, usually between the Marines and the Engineers. Off would come the heavy buckled belts and they would attack each other. It usually resulted in the sailors stepping in to restore order. To the locals, sailors were almost like policemen. When there was a sailor around, everyone felt safe. Certainly young Peter did:

'As the fights increased, the Marines and Engineers were forbidden to wear their belts outside the barracks. Naval patrols started to walk the streets after dark. These were made up of four ratings and a petty officer. They wore belts and side arms and – much to the chagrin of the man if he happened to be with a girl – they'd pull up any sailor who was not properly dressed. I believe the girls used the title 'petty officer' in an altogether different context.'

Peter was a delicate child, who fell victim to any illness or epidemic that happened to be doing the rounds. A kindly, quiet, attractive child, his aunts and uncles were always declaring that he should have been a girl: 'I don't know what it was,' Peter says, 'but something in my appearance gave them the idea that I had a dominant feminine streak. I dare say that was why I ended up fighting off advances from the homosexual fraternity some years later, in the theatre and at the BBC.'

Peter was difficult about food. His mother, knowing that the likely reason behind so many of his malaises could be attributed to lack of nourishment, did not know what to do with him. Then it was discovered, purely by accident, that if his nursemaid sang or hummed a tune, Peter would scoff up grub with greater ferocity than a vacuum cleaner.

It was all part of his early love of music, which could have presaged the musical career that he would have loved to pursue. But that, along with many other passions, would be scuppered.

Claude Rogers was a good pianist and, late into the night, Peter would lie in bed listening to Beethoven sonatas or Schubert impromptus as they filtered through the house. As soon as he was capable of walking – and while he was barely as high as the keyboard – he would join his father at the piano. Soon after – too young to read a score – he would wait for a nod as his father got near to the end of a page and then turn it over.

As time went on, Peter began to associate the precise movement of his father's fingers with the dots on the music sheets and was able to turn the pages without waiting for the nod. It was a skill that he was proud of, until, on one occasion, a momentary lapse of concentration left him embarrassed and his father annoyed:

'We were on our summer holiday in Cornwall, and the weather was so atrocious that all the residents in our hotel were confined to the lounge where there was a piano but no music. So, my father went into Looe, the nearest town, and bought some. He put it on the stand and I stood ready to turn the pages. Being a brand new copy, some of the pages were stuck together, which I didn't anticipate and, consequently, I turned over two pages at once. My father's moment of glory was ruined, and if looks could have killed, I would have dropped down dead there and then.'

Many years later, Peter was invited to appear on Roy Plomley's *Desert Island Discs* programme. On the day of the recording, Roy took Peter to lunch at the Saville Club and asked him if his interest in classical music had coincided with the success of the *Carry On* films. Peter, annoyed at the implication that sudden wealth was the reason for his interest in music, told Roy Plomley the story about turning over the pages of music for his father, but Roy still seemed to have some doubts. How could the producer of the *Carry On*s know anything about classical music? Peter had his doubts, too, about Roy Plomley:

'I heard the broadcast and noticed that he'd played the wrong side of one of the records. When I told him about it, he said it was only the second time it had happened in the history of the programme.'

One of Peter's choices of music for the programme was Gluck's 'Dance of the Blessed Spirits'. Plomley wanted to play a clarinet version because this instrument was played by the son of an orchestra conductor whom he knew. Peter, however, wanted the piano version. Plomley said there wasn't one. Peter said he regularly played one at home – a version by a Mr Sqambati. Plomley looked blank, but his assistant hurried out of the room and soon came back with the version that Peter had requested:

'I think that answered Mr Plomley's lunchtime question; and he did have the grace to admit in his autobiography that he had more requests for the music played in my programme than in any other.'

Roy Plomley was not the only person to question Peter's musical integrity. On one occasion, Peter wrote to Michael Berkeley, who was presenting a programme on BBC Radio 3. Michael had played one of W S Gilbert's ballads, and, having missed the title, Peter asked him what it was called. Although Michael wrote back promptly, he could not resist a little sarcasm: 'Look who listens to Radio 3,' he said. Peter was offended: 'He probably thought I was some uneducated yob who was only interested in barrel organ music.

'On another occasion, I was waxing enthusiastic about the broadcast of Beethoven's Ninth at a dinner party when a lady at the table leaned over and said, "I had no idea you were cultivated, Peter." Cultivated! Did she think I was brought up on an allotment? Personally, I would have preferred the word "cultured". And that's not all. I had to make a speech shortly afterwards and one of the lady guests came up to me at the end and said she expected me to speak with a cockney accent.'

Peter's personal musical ambitions were thwarted early on by his father. He desperately wanted to be allowed to learn to play the piano at school, but when his father discovered that the music teacher was a gentleman named C Hylton Stewart, the Rochester Cathedral organist, he forbade the lessons. It was not until some time afterwards that Peter discovered the reason for his father's intransigence. Both Mr Rogers and Mr Stewart had, it seems, fallen out over who should conduct the march that Peter's father had composed for the National Savings Company during the First World War, a march which was to be performed by the Rochester City Silver Band in the bandstand at the Castle Gardens.

Evidently, Hylton Stewart won the argument and, as a result, Peter lost the opportunity for a musical career. After he was 21, he taught himself, but it was a long and laborious process: 'First of all, I taught myself to read music by marking the keys with a pencil, one, two, three, and so on, according to the piece of music. I am afraid the usual exercises suffered, though, because my fingers did not have the flexibility and suppleness of a child's, and the world lost a possible virtuoso.

'Later I taught myself the organ and the balalaika, one of my favourite instruments. I gave up the balalaika because it hurt my fingers. After an hour's practice they lost all feeling, which prevented my playing the piano until the feeling had returned. The balalaika strings are made of wire, not gut, you see, and you can't use a plectrum. I imagine the Russians must have concrete digits.'

Chapter Two
The Pen Is Mightier Than the Sordid

When the time came for five-year-old Peter to go to school, he hated and dreaded the idea. It was not so much the unknown mystery of schooling, or the fear of meeting strangers, that bothered him, it was the thought of leaving home. Being taken to a kindergarten for mornings only may not be a great deal for most children, but for Peter it was a day in, day out, tearful experience. To this day, 80 years later, homesickness still fills Peter with dread.

And his fear of leaving home was not something that disappeared with the passage of time. In later years, when Peter made trips to London, visits to pubs would turn into an emotional experience if he happened to hear any music that he usually listened to at home on the radio. Even in his thirties, when Peter had literally been thrown out of his home, he would pay regular visits to Victoria or Charing Cross Stations and study the noticeboards for trains going to Kent. Hovering nearby, he would watch the people gathering on the platform and only when the train started on its way would he return to his attic room.

Many years later, when Peter was happily married to Betty Box, and had established his name within the film industry, trips to some of the most prestigious places in the world were regularly open to him. But even with the trappings of success embracing him, home still beckoned whenever he was away:

'I remember sitting in the back of my chauffeur-driven Rolls-Royce, crawling along in the traffic around Bruton Street, Mayfair, just at the time when office workers were hurrying to the tube station on their way home. It was nearly Christmas, and Betty and I were flying to the Palace Hotel, St Moritz, where we found ourselves in the company of people such as Herbert von Karajan, Rubirosa, Charles Aznavour, Princess Ira Furstenburg, Count this, Count that and Count the other.

'As usual, of course, I hated the thought of leaving home and my Alsatian dog, even though we had live-in staff to look after her. I sat in the back of the car watching the people and thought: You lucky buggers, you don't have to go to St Moritz for Christmas – which wasn't very kind to my wife, who was eagerly looking forward to the trip. Betty loved to travel. If it wasn't for her, I don't think I would have gone anywhere. People used to say, "It's not her, it's him," meaning that I was the skeleton at the feast, the fly in the ointment, socially.'

Peter's trip to St Moritz was not uneventful. The Palace Hotel was run by the Badrutt family, who had owned the prestigious establishment for many years. Young Mr Badrutt, every inch a gentleman – though, according to Peter, quite an amateur one – was very particular about dress. When it was discovered that Peter and Betty's luggage had been inadvertently dispatched to Moscow by mistake, he came to their suite to inform Peter that, as he was without a dinner jacket, the couple would have to dine in the Grill Room instead of the restaurant. Peter was not at all upset. He preferred the Grill Room, which was far less overpowering than the restaurant with its 500 covers and its floral decorations on the table that guests had to pay for.

Badrutt was, Peter remembers, a bit cheeky himself on the dress code front: 'I noticed that during the time we stayed at the Palace, be it day or night, he never appeared in anything other than a well-worn blue blazer and grey flannel trousers that were anything but immaculate. I wondered why the dress code didn't apply to him – he was, after all, always buzzing about the place, table-hopping and mixing with the guests. He could have been excused a black tie, but at least he could have worn a lounge suit in the evenings.'

As a child, Peter's propensity for absorbing knowledge was not great. It wasn't that he was stupid, he just had little interest in cramming his head full of information that seemed to him useless. Instead, his attention focused on his love of music and, as young as kindergarten age, an interest in girls.

One pleasant memory which, 80 years later, remains with him, is of a pretty girl singing a song at the end-of-term concert. His crush on her soon waned, but for years he couldn't get the song out of his head. Many years later, he heard it broadcast by the BBC during the 1945 general election campaign (the one that Winston Churchill spectacularly lost, and the first of the two huge landslide defeats suffered by the Tories in the postwar era). Peter was in a car, stuck in a traffic jam in Finchley, when the music came across the airwaves. Unfortunately, he couldn't make out a single word of it, and the title of the song still remains a mystery.

In his early years, Peter only had one fear greater than leaving home, and that was a peculiar and inexplicable fear of cattle – a fear that was not made any easier for a lad who was growing up in a predominantly farming community in Kent, 'the garden of England'. To this day, he is haunted by a particularly unpleasant memory of an encounter with a cow.

At Rochester a cattle market was held every Tuesday, and the farmers from outlying districts would drive their beasts along the narrow lanes and roads to where the sales took place. One Tuesday, when Peter was leaving school, he came face to face with a herd of cows stomping towards him. One cow would have been bad enough, but a whole herd! Scared witless, Peter took refuge behind a hoarding beside the school gate and waited anxiously for the animals to pass.

As the deafening sound of hooves began to subside and the smell of the cows started to disperse, Peter relaxed. Something, however, must have frightened the herd – perhaps a passing tram or bus – because suddenly from nowhere a big black and white number appeared behind the hoarding where Peter had taken refuge.

Frozen with fear and panic, Peter flattened his small frame against the hoarding and closed his eyes. The cow ran past him, went out the other side of the gate, and into the road again. It didn't even look at him: 'I suppose I should have been offended!' he jokes now. 'But actually, I thanked God for a lucky escape. I often used to call on God – when my dog was ill, for instance.'

Given that terrifying close encounter, Peter could hardly have imagined at that moment that, some years later, during his teens, he would choose to holiday on a farm at Ratcliffe, near Bolton, Lancashire; and that, during this break, he would not only milk and feed the cattle, but make a fuss of the family's Hereford (called Peggy Whitethroat) as if it were his favourite pet. Indeed, in years to come, Peter's fear of cattle disappeared and he was able to keep some very large ones as special pets on his Buckinghamshire estate.

When he was six years old, Peter was moved from his kindergarten to a larger, privately run, mixed sex school that catered for all ages. On his first day there, he was kept in after school for failing to raise his cap to the lady who owned the school when he passed her in the High Street:

'She wasn't a teacher – she simply owned the school. I had never even met or seen her before. I suppose, looking back, she enjoyed walking down the High Street as the pupils were arriving, so she could enjoy the thrill of all the nippers raising their caps to her. If I'd known then what I know now, I'd have raised two fingers. As far as I'm concerned, schoolteachers and clergymen are so far removed from reality they live in a teapot and peep through the spout. When it comes to education, it seems to me you either leave school knowing nothing and understanding everything, or knowing everything and understanding nothing.'

At the age of seven, Peter was enrolled as a pupil at the local public school, King's School, Rochester. The school was founded by Bishop Justus, whose first stop in this country, after his arrival from Rome, was at Canterbury – making it the oldest public school in the country. The bishop ended up being burnt at the stake: 'That probably accounts for the school's strange smell,' Peter quips.

At the beginning of his 11-year stay, Peter liked the school, but claims that it changed from a humane establishment to a sadistic institution. Whether the school changed, or the fears of a young anti-school pupil increased, it is hard to say, but Peter has little time for teachers and accuses them all of sadism. He also insists that the school prefects were worse – enjoying their new-found authority to the hilt. They were even allowed to punish their fellow students with the cane. But it wasn't all pain and horror. He enjoyed his time at the Junior School, where the pupils wore caps and played football, and he attended services at Rochester Cathedral every morning, with an extra visit for Evensong on Sundays:

'Actually, my first day at the school coincided with the centenary celebration of that unfortunate chap, Bishop Justus, and we had to spend the whole day in the cathedral with just a short break for lunch. During the afternoon session, I wanted to spend a penny badly, but couldn't leave. So this small seven-year-old boy had to pee where he stood. The cathedral was packed and I don't think anyone noticed. I could show you the spot to this day, but I can't for the life of me remember the name on the engraved stone slab I desecrated. Just as well, really … I felt guilty enough as it was.'

Peter may not have liked education, but he proved to be a pupil who had the ability to rake in scholastic achievement with the minimum of effort. As a result, he soon found himself moving up to the Senior School – and that's when his troubles really began. The Senior School played rugby football every Wednesday and Saturday afternoon, and in the evenings after school at four o'clock. The ill health which Peter had suffered early on in his life meant he was not a particularly big or strong chap. In fact, he was small for his age. But that didn't stop him from being thrown – quite literally – headfirst into the game. He claims that he did not feel much bigger than the ball itself and that the scrums were as frightening as his early experience of having a herd of cows rushing towards him:

'I didn't enjoy the cold winter evenings. It wasn't very pleasant standing about the field waiting for the ball, and seemingly being ignored by all the other players, who looked like giants to me. There was a games master at the school, but he never taught us anything. In all the 11 years I was there, I never saw him teach or guide a boy in any game whatever. He simply arranged fixtures with other schools, drew up teams from the talent at his disposal, and acted as referee. He seemed to presume that you knew how to play the game, otherwise you wouldn't be standing on the grass in your boots. I was certainly never told what to do on the field. I was just put down as a wing three-quarter – obviously because of my size. I would have been less than useless in a forward pack.'

On the bitterly cold nights when Peter found himself standing on the field doing very little, he took to wearing a vest under his rugger shirt. This was considered a sin on the scale of the stake-burning punishment of the late Bishop Justus. After only one game his keep-warm ruse was discovered by a keen-eyed prefect, who couldn't wait to bring out his long cane and give him a thrashing.

Nevertheless, Peter persisted with the game, using his light weight and quick step to move with great agility around the pitch. Eventually, he came to enjoy it and became something of a mean wing three-quarter – until, that is, he managed to break a collarbone:

'I had scored a try and I'm sure the opponents were trying to get their own back. I was underneath a pile of players and one of the bastards put his knee in. I didn't feel anything at the time, but I'm damn sure it was one of them. My arm was in a sling for some time and I never played quite as well ever again.'

Rochester School had its own Officers' Training Corps (OTC). At 14, Peter wanted to join. His father, however, did not want him to. Mr Rogers Senior was against such things. He had no time for the Scouts Movement either. He said they spent all their time carrying chairs around for the vicar. His father's negative attitude towards the OTC was a double punishment for Peter. Firstly, he was deprived of taking part in something that really appealed to him – the only thing at school that interested him. Secondly, any pupil not taking part in the OTC had to spend the afternoon when manoeuvres took place in detention, taking dictation from a master who walked up and down the room reading quite fast, without pauses, from a history book.

The master hardly seemed to care if the boys got it all down or not, as long as they sat, head down, writing as fast as their hands could move and without let-up. And that is how it was. Somewhere in the school the OTC was performing its duties while Peter and a handful of other 'non-combatants' wrote and wrote. At the end of each detention, the boys handed in their papers to the master, who promptly threw them into the wastepaper basket. Peter was infuriated:

'It always struck me as an odd form of imposition. It was obviously designed to force you into the Officers' Training Corps, which I actually wanted to be a member of anyway. This enforcement to join couldn't have had any effect on one of the prefects, a friend of mine, who had both his withered legs in irons. He could hardly walk, let alone play soldiers in the OTC, but he was still subjected to the miserable detention week after week.'

Peter's father finally relented and let him sign up. Peter was considered a smart, efficient soldier, and was promoted to corporal on two occasions. He had lost his stripes the first time when he fired on an umpire during a field day. He nearly lost them a second time when he refused to attend the Officers' Training Corps Camp at Tidworth Plain, Salisbury, where all the public school OTCs gathered during the school holidays: 'I had attended one and that was enough for me. It was a sweaty Hooray-Henry jamboree where you were shown around by toffee-nosed Sandhurst cadets on horses.'

This was a defining moment for Peter's later-in-life pinstripe rebellion. Besides, he far preferred to spend his holidays on a walking tour with his dog.

He managed to keep his stripes – just – in spite of the commanding officer's attitude of: 'We've got a right one here!' Fans of the first *Carry On* film can appreciate the young Peter's attitude by studying the on-screen antics of Kenneth Williams' upper-class snobbish character, James Bailey, playing opposite William Hartnell as the ultimate barking sergeant. Kenneth, as a supercilious know-all, who finds the whole army discipline that goes with conscription such a terrible bore, rings many bells with Peter's experiences. It is hardly surprising, then, that Kenneth and Peter were to become such good friends. But that was 30 years away from his OTC days.

During his 11 years on campus at King's School, Peter saw all the masters, except the headmaster, Canon Parker, come and go. The Canon, Peter insists to this day, only stayed because he needed the money.

As already mentioned, Peter was a good-looking boy and his early fresh-faced, attractive looks developed throughout his teens – not into a rugged, hard handsomeness, but a continued slightly feminine prettiness. He did not feel he was – nor felt inclined to be – homosexual, but his looks and manner often seemed to give off the wrong signals.

In the future he would have to battle off the advances of gay men in the film industry, but his first homosexual experience which, subsequently, influenced his attitude – not towards gays *per se*, but the practices they often indulged in – occurred when he was just 14.

One afternoon, the pupils of King's School had been to the cathedral for a service dedicated to a pupil who had just died. Once the memorial service was over, the boys were given the rest of the afternoon off. As there were to be no lessons that day, Peter decided to go walking in the countryside – far enough away to give him the sense of freedom he craved.

Peter was walking through a quiet field, not far from his parents' home, when he was approached by a tall, gruff, swarthy-looking man in his mid to late thirties. Without a word, the man grabbed hold of him and dragged him into the bushes. The man then undid his own trousers and masturbated all over the scared youth's garments: 'He had the grace to wipe it all off, but I was petrified. After he had run away, I just sat there thinking the world had come to an end. I was that innocent.'

Some days later, Peter was travelling on top of the bus when he looked down and saw his attacker walking through the High Street. Bemused and confused, believing that God would have struck the man down for his appalling act of deviancy, he was surprised to see that he was still alive. Peter never told anyone about what had happened. He could have told his parents, but knew they would have called the police. Peter's main worry was that people would somehow think it was his fault for allowing it to happen, and that, he felt, would have been worse than the incident itself. He wanted to put the whole thing out of his head:

'It was an experience that 'buggers' description. I was always very backward sexually – if you can understand my meaning! When I was confirmed by the Bishop of Rochester, for some reason that seemed better understood by my parents than by me, I resisted the lecture on the facts of life by saying I knew all about them. In fact, my knowledge of sexual intercourse was so abysmal that, for quite some time, I thought a man inserted his penis into a girl's navel.'

Peter may have felt sexually inadequate as a teenager, but he certainly wasn't backward in coming forward when he finally fell in love for the first time. King's School was positioned close to a rather posh girls' school, which many of the boys' sisters attended. Although there was technically no contact between the two schools, except for the occasional public event, which usually took place in the cathedral, both the boys and the girls were aware of each other through walking in the High Street or travelling on the buses.

Satchel-swinging liaisons were definitely prohibited, so it became the habit for the girls to send messages to the boys via a brother. If a girl fancied a certain boy, she would send him what was referred to as a GP, which stood not for general practitioner but for grand passion.

The attractive Peter received several of these hotly sought-after GPs from one young girl in particular. Having turned them down with some show of distaste, he promptly made an enemy of the girl's much larger brother for the rest of his school days. When the boy later became a prefect, Peter's life was made even harder.

The reason that Peter turned the girl down was not that she was unattractive or that he didn't find her appealing, it was because his eyes and heart were keenly focused on someone else. He had a crush on a girl in another school – a council school, not the snooty private grammar. She was very pretty with a lovely figure. Her name was Dorothy Johnson, and Peter was literally dotty about her. They fell in love almost immediately and, from that moment, his only desires in life were to become a writer and to be with Dorothy.

Peter's writing output was prodigious, even if the quality of the material was not much to write home about. Writing became the bane of his existence, a bugbear in the family, and the petard on which he was finally to be hoisted. He hadn't started by writing poetry or anything like that; he didn't write for the school magazine; didn't write short stories or any of the things that writers usually begin with. No, Peter wrote plays. He wrote them at school, hiding them under the lid of his desk. And his fear of them being discovered was based on their quality, which Peter admitted to himself was not high:

'I found dialogue easy to write, and I can distinctly remember an essay in which I wrote a dialogue between a table and the leg of a chair. The approbation of the English master led me to continue writing in dialogue form, and I churned out romances and dramas like a sausage machine. When the hero or heroine were called upon to kiss, I put a cross in brackets, thus (X). It all sounds rather pathetic, and I suppose it was.'

The strange thing was that Peter was never a keen theatregoer. He liked the cinema and would make a weekly outing, usually by himself or in his teenage years with Dorothy, to see the latest film – particularly Laurel and Hardy and the magic of the new sound motion pictures at the end of the 1920s and beginning of the 1930s. He had never even seen a straight play; his only experience of the stage was when his family went to the local theatre to see the Macdonald and Young tour of the latest musical comedy. Yet, such was the desire to write, and such was the ease which he found in putting dialogue on to paper, that plays was the way he decided to go – at least, for the foreseeable future.

Friends encouraged him to write in his spare time, so that he could take up his father's offer and work during the days in his business. Peter tried this, but it didn't work. The long days at the office meant that he was too tired to write at night. And when he did scribe into the early hours, he was too tired to work the next day. He was always neglecting one or the other.

And something precious was also being neglected too. Dorothy would sit silently with him in the evenings while he tried ceaselessly to write the hit he so desperately yearned for. They rarely went out, and his neglect was beginning to make her nervous about her own future, especially as all her friends had left school and were now getting married. Both Peter's brothers had also left school, joined their father's business and were married. They suggested to Mr Rogers Senior that, for all the good Peter was in the company, he might as well keep him at home and pay him a small allowance to write, 'because you'll never stop him', they said.

Whether Franklin and Paul were genuinely trying to help, or whether this was just a ploy to block any opposition to their own ambitions, Peter never discovered. He has, though, always had his suspicions. Nevertheless, his father acceded to their idea and, whatever his brothers' motives, Peter was happy with the outcome. He was now to stay at home, receive a meagre pocket-money allowance of a few shillings a week, just enough, perhaps, for an occasional glass of beer and a trip to the cinema, and write plays.

Peter sent play, after play, after play, to agents and managers, their addresses gleaned from the *Writers' & Artists' Year Book* – and they all came back. Every one of them. One morning, the postman delivered seven manuscripts by the same post and Peter's mother burst into tears. 'Never mind,' he whispered reassuringly, 'I'll write another one.' And he did: 'I used to write late into the night, into the early morning. My goodness, I tried'.

His romance with Dorothy now seemed to be doomed. They both wanted to get married, but when Dorothy's parents heard that Peter did not want to go into his father's successful business and intended instead to be a writer, she was persuaded that their future would be a disaster – that he would not be able to support her or a family. She ended up in the arms of another man whom she later married – a man who had a regular job in the government, with the promise of a pension and all that went with it. It broke Peter's heart:

'She wrote me a letter saying that when poverty comes in the door, love flies out of the window. When I reminded her of these words many years later, she couldn't remember writing them. I don't think she meant to be cruel – she wasn't like that. It just happened to be an appropriate quotation at the time, I suppose. You see, that is what young people did in those days – they obeyed their parents. I didn't, but Dorothy did. We kept in touch for several years afterwards.'

Chapter Three
His Finest Hour?

Cocooned in his room, beavering away with pen and paper to absolutely no effect, and having lost Dorothy, his first love, Peter's life was not exactly going well. Such misery did, however, result in a rare gesture of sympathy from his father. Claude Rogers had never made any bones about his distaste for his son's passion for the arts, and had never encouraged him to write. He agreed to Peter staying at home with a small allowance only because he realized there was little Peter could do to help the family business.

But his son's constant failure, and the effect this was having on his wife, forced Claude into action. In an effort to help, he introduced Peter to a friend of his, Sir Charles Igglesden, who owned a county news-paper, the *Kentish Express*. And, as a favour to his old chum, Sir Charles agreed to take on Peter as a reporter. It meant Peter living away from home, albeit just 30 miles, in nearby Ashford – a move which had Peter pining for his mother and his home the moment he left.

Taking lodgings at a pub called the Kent Arms, Peter began life as a county newspaper reporter. Sadly, though, he fell out almost immedi-ately with his news editor – a devout member of the Temperance League – who objected to Peter living above a pub. Unable to afford another move just to satisfy his colleague's scruples, Peter had to stay put and suffer the disapproval which the news editor made abundantly clear on every possible occasion: 'I'm sure that if he had had his way I would have been fired on my first day,' Peter says.

In the event, Peter gave the editor good cause to fire him. His first reporting job was to travel to the famous seaside resort of Margate, on the Kent coast, to report on an agricultural show. Getting there was no problem; it was the return journey which caused all the difficulties. Arriving back at Margate station with his pen and pad in hand, Peter asked the nearest porter to direct him to the platform for the Ashford train. The porter pointed to a platform, but failed to mention that the train currently standing in the sidings was not due to leave for several hours. Peter sat in one of the carriages, and sat, and sat, and sat. Three hours later the train moved off.

Back at the office, all hell had broken loose. There had been no contact from their new reporter for several hours, no one had seen him, and everybody was worried because the trip from Margate to Ashford took only 30 minutes. Even the police had been requested to try to trace him. When Peter finally arrived back at the office looking fit and well, everyone jumped to the conclusion that he had stayed on at the seaside to have a good time.

The editor was not best pleased and no one believed Peter's three-hour wait story because they knew that at least two trains an hour departed from Margate to Ashford. True – but not from the platform the porter had pointed out. Why had Peter waited so long in the carriage without checking the porter's information? It was just another occasion when the shyness that was to blight Peter throughout his formative years held him in check. He was literally too embarrassed to go back and ask the porter again, preferring instead to wait until the train he had boarded was ready to leave.

Peter admits that his career at the paper did not look as if it would last long: 'I didn't actually enjoy being a reporter. I never had enough push for that. I didn't mind creeping about the church pews collecting names at a wedding, but I dreaded doing this at funerals. I recall being sent to a remote farmhouse on Romney Marsh to interview a farmer whose wife had just died. I was instructed to obtain a photograph of her. The farmer answered the door and, when I voiced my request, he reached behind him and pulled out a shotgun. "Bugger orf", he growled. So, I buggered off. My news editor said I should have persisted – that I'd never make a reporter if I was put off by little things like that.'

Peter's next *faux pas* was when he was writing about a local flower show – and he soon realized that the fury of a widowed farmer is as nothing compared to the anger of a wronged horticulturist:

'I had stated that a certain gentleman had been highly commended in the cauliflower section. The next morning the gentleman came storming into the newspaper office complaining vociferously that he had *not* been highly commended, he had come third. Not being an expert in the field, I would have preferred to be highly commended than be nominated third. Third sounded such a failure. They made me write a piece apologizing to the irate gentleman. Perhaps that's why, to this day, I hate cauliflower!'

During his time on the newspaper Peter had a second-hand car that had cost him only £50.00 and was always breaking down. One of his fellow journalists, however, took a shine to the car and continually pestered Peter to lend it to him. There was, apparently, sufficient room in the back for the journalist to make love to his many girlfriends. Peter politely refused. He needed the car to go home on his evenings off. The homesickness had not subsided and he longed to be back in Rochester, if only for a few hours.

So, a journalist by day, Peter now had to do his playwriting at every other available opportunity. The problem was that he was groping about in the dark. He didn't know anybody in the theatre – and lived a con-siderable distance from anybody who might be able to help him. His sole ambition was to succeed and he decided he might have a chance if he could only get to meet people in the business. Then, one day, there was a breakthrough: Peter read in his own paper, the *Kentish Express*, that the American woman producer, Auriol Lee, had arrived in London to produce a play by John Van Druten at St Martin's Theatre, off the Strand.

The play, called *Gertie Maud*, was not destined to enjoy a lengthy run, but no one knew that at the time. Peter wrote to Auriol Lee enclos-ing one of his plays, *Green Apples*, a family comedy of adolescence set in adjoining back gardens: 'I remember the occasion very well,' Peter says, 'because as I sat at my desk writing to her, the launch of the *Queen Mary* was being broadcast on the radio.'

Auriol replied promptly to Peter's letter, saying she regretted there was little she could do about his play at the moment because she was committed to the production at the St Martin's Theatre. She was then going back to America, but, on her return, would consider doing the play. For Peter this was wonderful news – and the beginning of a long correspondence in which Auriol referred to him as a 'splurger' because his letters were so lengthy.

On her return to England, Auriol wrote to Peter on a letter headed A D Peters and Auriol Lee. A D Peters was a well-known play agent. For a moment Peter thought his big chance had come, but Auriol was only writing to apologize that, once again, she was unable to undertake his work because she was committed to producing another play by John Van Druten. Peter's only consolation was Auriol's invitation for him to attend rehearsals to meet people and learn something of theatre-craft.

'I later learnt that Auriol Lee and John Van Druten were what, today, is called 'an item'. I attended the rehearsals and met a few people who Auriol thought might help and encourage me, but I was taken aback to discover that one of the performers was either being bitchy about his friends, or indulging in homosexuality, or both. I found the snide remarks about Auriol particularly disconcerting, especially as she had recommended him to me as one of her friends. The homosexuality was particularly worrying, first of all because I seemed to be the one in demand; secondly, because I wasn't interested and was consequently accused of playing 'hard to get'. I was certainly prepared to start at the bottom in the theatre, but not literally!'

After the John Van Druten play, Auriol Lee took Peter on as a dogs-body assistant for her production of J B Priestley's *People at Sea*. Now paid a small salary, Peter was able to move into bed and breakfast accommodation, albeit seedy, and return home at weekends when Auriol very kindly lent him her car for this purpose. His digs may not have been up to much, but the life that came with them more than compensated for the dry rot and smell of mould all around his room.

He made many visits to the house in Smith Square which Auriol had taken for the duration of her visit. Her sojourn could not have been more different from his. The house boasted a uniformed butler and full staff.

On Peter's first visit, Auriol was confined to her bed with flu. Admitted to the house by the butler, he followed the young man up the long winding staircase to Auriol's room, where he was announced as though he was a visiting ambassador.

Auriol was lying in bed surrounded by tissues. She went through the Priestley play with Peter and told him she intended to cast Jean Muir, an American leading lady of 1930s' cinema, as the fading film star, which she most definitely was not. The story goes that Priestley had first met Jean Muir when she undoubtedly looked the part – when she was tired and worn out after a hard day's shooting.

During rehearsals for the play, John Van Druten came to visit Peter at the far end of the gallery where Auriol had sent him to check if the artistes could be heard that far away. Van Druten stayed for a few minutes then vanished, but Peter was disturbed by the questions the playwright had asked him – questions which had nothing whatsoever to do with the play:

'He asked me rather personal questions – where did I live? Did my home have a tennis court? Where did I go to school? What did my father do? What were my hobbies? And so on. After that meeting, I noticed a certain falling off in Auriol's interest in my writing and in me. Was it jealousy? Was Van Druten's relationship with her an echo of his first play, *Young Woodlay*, in which a schoolboy had an affair with the headmaster's wife? Suddenly it seemed to be assumed that I did not fit in theatrically. I had always got on well with Auriol herself, but Van Druten's influence always prevailed, and I was practically eased out of the coterie. There is no doubt that John Van Druten would always fall on someone else's feet. And, no doubt, he was kind enough to his inferiors – if he could ever find any.'

Peter's stay in London was not wasted, however. He had made some good contacts,which resulted in two of his plays being produced before he had even reached the age of 21. The director of his first play invited Peter to meet him to discuss its contents. It was a story about an unconsummated marriage, called *Human Straws*.

The director, whose name was Cunningham, lived in a bedsit in the Seven Dials area of London, near St Martin's Lane. Peter arrived at the tall Georgian house and began to ascend the five floors to Cunningham's flat. He was about to ring the bell when he heard Cunningham talking to someone on the telephone: 'This isn't a play,' the man was saying, 'it's a load of rubbish. But I'll do it because I need the money.'

Peter stood on the landing pondering his next move. His first instinct was to about-turn and leave, but he knew that if he returned home without positive news, parental disputes would erupt. The quarrels with his father had become more regular recently, and he would certainly use this occasion to accuse Peter of being content as long as he had his feet placed comfortably under the parental table.

With this in mind, he knew he had to press on. He pushed the bell and, when the director answered the door and invited him in, asked matter-of-factly: 'Was that my play you were talking about on the telephone?' 'No, it wasn't,' came the reply. Peter did not believe him, but Cunningham went on to direct the play, which had its limited run during the hottest August days in living memory.

Critics who attended the opening suggested that it was hardly the sort of material one would take a maiden aunt to see. In particular, Peter recalls the comments of W A Darlington of the *Daily Telegraph*, who said that his time would have been better employed punting a boat up the river: 'Why punting? What's the matter with rowing? After his comments, I wouldn't have been at all upset if he'd fallen in.'

Peter's second play was a comedy called *Mr Mercury*. Its plot was based on an Australian inheriting a snobbish English family's title, home and possessions. It was full of pomposity-pricking gags and caused the critic of the *Evening Standard* to write: 'We have a new comedy writer in our midst.'

Peter's first play ran for seven days, the second for ten. Taking the longer run as a yardstick, Peter consoled himself with the thought that, perhaps, he should stick to writing comedy. But he was not unrealistic, and was only too aware that both plays were flops. He returned home with his tail between his legs. His father reduced his already meagre allowance and declared, more than once, that the whole operation had been a waste of time and money. Even Peter had to admit to himself that he hadn't really enjoyed it much. He felt as if he was drifting out of control.

The following few years were an agony of inactivity. He continued to write plays that nobody wanted, and continued to take his beautiful Alsatian dog on long walks through the countryside, wondering what was wrong with his little universe. The agents he approached insisted that his work was excellent on dialogue, but weak on plot. Much later, Oscar-winning film producer Sydney Box told him that he was good on plot, but weak on dialogue:

'I must say, though, that when Sydney wanted the dialogue of a film script brightened up, he always called on me to do it. And before Sydney became a film producer, he was famous as a writer of one-act plays. I believe he wrote hundreds for performance by amateurs all over the country. So, who are you to believe? Yourself, of course. If you are honest with yourself, you are your best critic. I like to think that I was honest with myself. If you know your craft, you can't help being honest about it. No self-respecting bricklayer purposely builds a wall with a bulge in it, does he? So why would a playwright intentionally write a flop?'

While Peter bemoaned his fate as a writer, much was going on around him and he was conscious that writing plays that nobody wanted was insignificant compared to the death of King George V, the abdication of Edward VIII, Munich and the declaration of the Second World War.

The war, which was a turning point in the lives of almost everyone in the country, turned out to be the same for Peter. But not in a way that anyone could have expected. His brothers were called up for service in the armed forces and, shortly afterwards, in the spring of 1941, Peter's papers arrived.

But, on the day he was preparing to report to the local Employment Exchange for call-up, he was whisked away from home in an ambulance. He had been suffering from blinding headaches for several days, but nothing could have prepared him or his family for the doctor's diagnosis. Peter had an extreme bout of cerebral spinal meningitis, an appallingly painful and, in those days, almost untreatable bacterial infection of the brain. As the ambulancemen placed him in their vehicle, they turned and told the family's maids that they would never see him again.

He was just 26.

Nobody told Peter or his mother exactly what was wrong with him, but his father was informed and appeared to take it in his stride. Unaware of the severity of his illness, Peter expected to be released within a few days. But the days in the hospital at Sittingbourne became weeks, and the weeks became months. He was placed in an isolation ward and not even his family were able to visit him. He repeatedly asked the nurses what was wrong with him, but they turned away as if incredulous that he didn't know what he was suffering from. The pain Peter endured was colossal. Unable to ingest pills, he had to rely on pain-killing injections every two hours. The memories of his suffering are still vivid:

'I suppose I was lucky to be treated at all. As I was carried into the hospital on my first day, the doctor was just leaving. There was quite an epidemic of meningitis at that time and the poor man was exhausted. He'd done so many lumbar punctures that morning that I heard him say he couldn't do any more. Then he looked down at me and said, "All right, I'll do just one more." Thank goodness he did. He was a German doctor and a few months later I heard that he'd committed suicide.'

The hospital ward was full when Peter was admitted, but as the months passed more and more of the patients who were suffering from meningitis died. He began to think that his own chances of survival would actually have been higher on the field of battle. He lay awake night after night trying to work out how he had become ill, and slowly it began to dawn on him how he had become infected.

During the war, it had been his habit to take artistes from the local theatre to lonely ack-ack sites in the country around the Medway towns. The Theatre Royal at Chatham was owned by the Barnard family and Peter had been at school with the son, nicknamed 'Bushy' Barnard. The theatre ran first-class musical comedy and variety shows. Over the proscenium arch was written the inscription: *Let the evening's enjoyment bear the morning's reflection.*

ENSA, the Government's entertainment department, infamously

dubbed 'Every Night Something Awful' by the long-suffering troops they entertained, neglected the many anti-aircraft sights around the town, with its important naval dockyard at Chatham, and Royal Marine and Royal Engineer barracks close by.

Throughout the war, at dusk, the whole area was enclosed by hundreds of paraffin machines, mounted on lorries parked together. Their purpose was to cover the town in a thick smokescreen. The smell was terrible. Peter would gather a fleet of taxis together, assemble the boys and girls (particularly the girls) from the theatre, and transport them to the lonely ack-ack sites. Of course, the officers fell over themselves trying to entertain the young ladies and there was a great deal of drinking and larking about in the officers' mess:

'I noticed that the poor buggers who fired the guns didn't get a look-in. They sat in the hall when the show was on, but that was all. They weren't allowed to touch the girls. By the time the visit came to an end, it would be about four o'clock in the morning before we finally drove the artistes back to the Medway towns. It was at one of these sessions that I believe I contracted my meningitis. I probably drank out of an unwashed glass.'

Cerebral spinal meningitis inflames the brain and, if you are lucky enough to survive the illness, the lasting after-effects can be devastating. Depending on which direction the brain flops when it ceases to be influenced by the illness, either your hearing or sight is affected. Peter's brain flopped forward and he has had trouble with his eyes ever since:

'My sight would fade whenever I got nervous or frightened, usually among crowds. I saw some truly awful things during my stay in hospital. I remember one patient who bit a nurse's arm in his agony, and she had to have several stitches. Another was carried in on one of those canvas stretchers with thick rope binding. He was in such pain that when he was flipped into the bed, he grabbed the canvas contraption and tore it to shreds. The pain had given him that much strength. He died the next day. Then there was the man who sat up in bed, looking straight ahead. Even when a nurse crept up to him and shouted in his ear, he didn't hear a thing. Obviously his brain had slipped sideways. He didn't last the week.'

One day his mother's home-help, Mrs Morgan, arrived at the hospital to deliver some letters from the family and a daffodil in a pot. Peter had the daffodil placed next to his bedside and looked at it for hours on end. He felt that life had been brought into a ward which was full of death.

Every morning when Peter awoke, his first thought was to see if the daffodil was still standing proud and strong. He thought that if a daffodil could live against all odds, away from its natural surroundings, natural light, fresh air and moist soil, then he too could survive against the odds. He clung on to that thought until he and the daffodil were the only living things left in the ward.

Peter stayed in hospital for almost a year. The only contact he had with his family was via letters, which, with the war now in full swing, were delivered only intermittently. It was a long and harrowing experience, but Peter, who was not a religious man, blessed whoever had looked down on him and saved him. He was determined more than ever now to make a success of his life. It wasn't going to be easy. He was weak both physically and mentally from his enforced bed rest, and it would be many months before he felt able to pick up his favoured pen once again.

When he did, he tried to continue writing plays, but found that he couldn't concentrate. He certainly could not produce a three-act play – which he says must have been a great relief to theatregoers – and any concept of theatre or stage eluded him:

'After I left hospital, I seemed to go a bit doolally. According to the doctors I was emotionally and mentally unstable. I panicked in crowds, even small crowds, and my eyesight would play tricks. One minute I could see quite well; the next, everything would go misty. It depended on my nerves, evidently. Even if I was enjoying a drink or a meal in a pub, I would immediately walk out of the establishment if it began to fill up with people.'

As far as National Service was concerned, Peter was exempt. He was registered NFA (meaning No Further Action), and he carried that card with him at all times. It was his passport and immunity from white feathers and accusations of cowardice. He did the usual fire-watching duty during air raids, while it was still a voluntary activity, but, ironically, when it became compulsory, he was no longer allowed to help due to government compensation laws.

As the war progressed, new hazards overtook old ones. The doodle-bug bomb – a pilotless plane – arrived. When the engine cut out, everyone dived for cover. But in Peter's home town, like the rest of the country, everyone came to take such things in their stride. Families still walked through the parks on balmy summer evenings; boys still walked up and down looking for girls, and girls still walked up and down looking for boys.

During these walks, it was not unusual to witness a doodlebug flying quite low over the local golf course and a counter-attack Spitfire hastily arriving on the scene. The plane would tip the bomb with its wing, so that the doodlebug swerved and fell harmlessly into the estuary. By now, everyone had become so accustomed to the country being bombed that they only gave such events a passing glance.

When his father's chauffeur was killed during an air raid, Peter stepped in to drive his father around. His work took him to Dover on several occasions and, as Dover was being shelled from the other side of the Channel, a sort of official passport was required before anyone was allowed to enter the town. With the exception of a handful of people, such as publicans and town officials, who were needed to keep things running, all the residents had been evacuated.

One evening, Peter was standing in one of the pubs having a drink with a lance bombardier. They were talking about the shelling, which was pretty intense at the time and, while they chatted, they heard a large thump. In a very matter-of-fact manner the officer said, 'That's another one leaving the other side. If you count to four, you'll know where it's landed.'

Peter didn't have a chance to count to four. The shell had landed on a row of cottages, just a few feet away from where he was standing. It wasn't the first time he had been so close to an explosion. There had been another occasion when he was walking his dog in the country near his home. When he reached the hop fields, he noticed that trenches had been dug around the perimeter of the fields. Apparently, the Nazis thought that if they bombed the hop-pickers they would interrupt the flow of beer and thus demoralize the country.

During Peter's walk, a German plane flew so low over the field that, to this day, Peter insists he could see the face of the pilot looking down at him. All the pickers dived into the trenches, and as Peter looked up he saw a bomb come out of the plane. He flattened himself on the grass. In the event, the bomb landed harmlessly, but it made such a noise that Peter's dog ran away in fright. Nazi or no Nazi, Peter was up on his feet and running after her. The plane flew away, Peter rescued the dog, and the hop-pickers continued their work.

As the war continued into its third year, everyone realized that things would not be over as quickly as was originally hoped, and that there was no chance of life returning speedily to normal. For Peter, though, life was beginning to find a new sense of purpose. He had started to write again, but not stage plays this time. Now it was radio plays. He was writing with his ears rather than his eyes, and almost immediately found success. Several of his radio productions, including *The Man Who Bounced*, *Cards on the Table* and *Mr South Starts a War*, were broadcast by the BBC.

On the strength of these plays, Peter visited London once a week to make what are euphemistically called 'contacts', which consisted of frequenting bars and clubs until he met someone who might be of use to his career. Even Peter's father appeared to be coming round to the idea of his son's writing abilities. After years of declaring that Peter would get nowhere with his writing, he was now witnessed asking his professional colleagues: 'Did you hear my son's play last night?'

Unfortunately, radio did not prove to be a sufficiently regular source of work or income. Peter was told by a BBC producer that he was writing too many plays and that it was not BBC policy to transmit one person's creations too frequently. Peter was angry and frustrated: 'There appeared to be no appreciation that one person might prove to be popular, or that one person's works might be looked forward to. So, bang went any idea of making a living out of radio plays.'

One good thing, however, came out of Peter's radio work. He was invited by J Arthur Rank's religious film company to join them as a scriptwriter. J Arthur Rank was a Yorkshireman and a member of the famous flour-milling family. He looked after his family's business interests in the City of London and amassed a sizable fortune for himself. He was also an extremely religious man, a devout Methodist.

During the 1920s, wanting to spread the Word, he had bought the *Methodist Times*. He also saw the film industry as a means to disseminate his religious ideas to a wider audience. His religious film company was particularly struck by Peter's talent with dialogue. At the same time, Peter was invited by Warner Brothers to go to Hollywood as a dialogue writer. Peter turned that invitation down. His fear of being too far from home – and his love of his beloved Alsatian dog – didn't allow for a moment's doubt.

J Arthur Rank thought Peter would be usefully employed on *Thought for the Week*, a religious slot slipped into the cinema schedules on Sunday evenings. As Rank owned the cinemas that these films were screened in, he had every right to include them. The short productions were made either at Norwood Studios or at a small studio, called the Carlton, in a block of flats in Maida Vale.

The standard scene-set was a farm gateway, where a character named Doctor Goodfellow would lean over the gate and talk to the cinema audience. Peter's job was to translate J Arthur's religious tracts into everyday language. The artist who played Doctor Goodfellow was an ex-silent film star named Stewart Rome, who, in the early days of film, used to co-star in productions with Chrissie White. They were the Laurence Olivier and Vivien Leigh of the 1920s.

The scenes were directed by another grandee of the silent film days, known as Captain Norman Walker. Walker loved the work. He had, after all, become involved in films to help spread the Word of God. He and Rank got on like a house on fire.

After years spent making small religion-based productions, Rank decided it was time to enter the film-making world with a full-length production called *The Great Mr Handel*. Released in 1942, the film was directed by Captain Walker and was based on a play by L Du Garde Peach about how Handel, the eighteenth-century composer, came to write *The Messiah*. The cast included Wilfrid Lawson and British leading lady Elizabeth Allan.

Although some publications received the film well – *Kine Weekly*, for example, proclaimed that it was 'A graceful addition to the ranks of prestige pictures' – the film was not a success. Rank summoned the most experienced characters in the business to a meeting at Norwood Studios to find out why. As a member of the production committee, Peter also attended. Among those present was John Davis, who later became head of the Rank Organisation, and Earl St John, a tall, slow-talking Texan, who was the executive producer of Pinewood Studios.

Nobody around the table could really explain the failure of *The Great Mr Handel*, except Earl St John, who summed it up in just four words: 'Not enough Rita Hayworth.' At that time, Rita Hayworth was attracting customers in droves to the cinema, for films such as *The Strawberry Blonde* with James Cagney, and Cole Porter's Broadway musical, *You'll Never Get Rich*, starring Fred Astaire.

Among those also trying to come up with answers for J Arthur's film failure were Norman Walker, Canon Benjamin Gregory and Colonel Hake, who was J Arthur's bailiff cum steward of his estate. These three subsequently went on to form the production company GHN (coined from their initials) which, like Rank, started out making religious films. Many years later, Peter bought it for its tax-loss situation and made his *Carry On* films through it.

One of Peter's chores while working with Rank's religious film company was to follow in the footsteps of Jacob Vagar, a Russian Bible student, who had come over to Britain in 1910, and lodged with a mining family in the Rhondda Valley, Wales. In order to research a script, Peter travelled to Cardiff and then boarded a train which seemed to take forever as it slowly climbed through the winding hills on its precarious track.

When the train eventually arrived at its destination, Peter got out and walked to the village. He forgets the name now, but still embedded in his memory are the cottages with front doors that opened on to the street. They were grey – and there were rows and rows of them trailing off into the distance. Where the houses ended, the mine began and, on the horizon, the great wheel of the mine shaft could be seen.

Peter knocked on the door of one of the cottages and, after explaining the purpose of his visit, was welcomed in. There were five members of the family living in the confines of their small home – a mother and father, son, daughter and grandfather. After a cup of tea, Peter mentioned the upright piano squeezed into a small space of the front room, and asked who played it. He was told that both the grandfather and the daughter played, and Peter then asked if the daughter would mind singing to him. The grandfather asked him what he would like her to sing, and he said, 'I Know That My Redeemer Liveth' from Handel's *Messiah*. Peter can still hear her voice: 'She sang like an angel.'

Then, of course, the grandfather had to show what he could do. The poor man was completely without teeth, but when he began to belt out 'Fling Wide the Gates' by Stainer, he proved to have a magnificent baritone voice. Later, the son decided that Peter should take a walk with him to see something of the Rhondda Valley:

'It was a wonderful walk,' Peter says. 'I had never before passed among such beautiful rhododendrons. After a while, I noticed that the son was tiring. I, though, was used to walking anything up to 10 miles a day with my dog. After that walk, his attitude changed towards me, and he invited me to join him at the Working Men's Club, where I was introduced to his pals. We all had a thoroughly good time.

'I did my script for Rank, but, during my research, discovered that when Jacob Vagar returned to Russia, he was shot. J Arthur didn't want to get involved in anything political and decided to abandon the project.'

Bearing in mind the postwar antipathy towards religion in general, and J Arthur's rather archaic methods of portraying his religious messages, it is not surprising that the Religious Films Unit closed down. The last straw came one Sunday evening at Edgware, when the utterings of Doctor Goodfellow were just too much for the audience, who began to pelt the screen with anything they could lay their hands on.

It is easy now to scoff at the religious fanaticism of J Arthur Rank, but as his biographer, Alan Wood, correctly identified in 1952: 'Methodist principles may seem a curious guide to the promotion of motion pictures, but at least they gave J Arthur Rank a considerable start over other film producers who had no principles at all.'

J Arthur, who was knighted for his work, was heard to exclaim: 'If I could recall to you some of the various adventures and experiences in the film world, it would I think be as plain to you as it is to me that I was being led by God.'

J Arthur Rank, the man who was responsible for founding Pinewood Film Studios, the largest studios in Europe, died in 1972, aged 84. As Peter Rogers recalls: 'People were quick to dismiss him on occasions, but, believe me, there was Methodism in his madness! I will always have the utmost respect for that man's memory, and I thank him for giving me my first break in the film industry.'

Following the closure of the Rank Religious Films Unit, J Arthur Rank suggested to Peter that he should contact Pat Wallace at the Scenario Institute, in Berkeley Street. This was another organization J Arthur Rank had set up to encourage screenwriters. Pat Wallace was the daughter of prolific British crime story writer, Edgar Wallace, who had most of his works turned into a series of memorable second-feature film thrillers. These were made at Merton Park in the 1960s, under the title *Edgar Wallace Presents*.

Pat gave Peter a book to adapt into a screenplay – a gentle story of family life. Peter spent several weeks working on the project before presenting it to her. She told him that Pinewood's executive producer, Earl St John, was the adjudicator of its worth. On the day that the young wannabe scriptwriter was to be interviewed by him, Peter saw him in a club in Grosvenor Square and became a little worried:

'I was there for lunch when I caught sight of Earl. He was at the bar and looked as though he might have been there for some time. I thought to myself, I hope he's not like that when I see him at three o'clock. The interview was due to take place in the Odeon offices opposite the Dorchester Hotel. When I left the club after lunch, he was still there. I arrived at his office at three o'clock, as agreed. He wasn't there, but his secretary said that he was expected any moment. I wasn't so sure. Nevertheless, I sat and waited. Then I saw him come in. He was a large Texan and strode in like John Wayne.

'When I was asked to enter his office, he was smoking a large cigar. I sat opposite him at his desk and could see a screenplay in front of him, from which he was reading a report. But the screenplay wasn't mine. Should I risk telling him, and make a fool of myself and an enemy of him?

'I suffered the interview in silence, and with an increasing degree of angst as he imparted to me that the screenplay was part good, part bad. I couldn't read the name of the actual writer of the screenplay, and that was that. I had no more contact from Pat Wallace. I always thought: what if I had told her that Earl St John had read the wrong script? She would, no doubt, have spoken to him, which would have implicated me in 'spying' on him, so I wouldn't have stood a chance anyway.'

Peter's film-scripting days appeared to be over before they had begun, and it was back to his study, and his dog. Even though he had been commuting to London or Norwood, there was no doubt he was back to square one.

Life at home was also bringing its own sadness. Peter's mother had become ill and the diagnosis was cancer. He stayed at home and nursed her, while all the time she was worrying about what would happen to him if anything happened to her. Peter was now 30, but their bond was as close as ever and he was still her favourite. From her sickbed she made his father promise that he would continue the meagre allowance and let Peter pursue his writing career. The promise was duly made, but very soon broken when Alice Rogers died in 1944, aged just 57.

Peter was heartbroken.

Chapter Five
Action: Cinema Calls

One day, just a few months after his mother died, Peter's father walked into his study and told him that he was going to marry again, and that the new lady had two sons of her own. Peter was shocked. His mother had meant the world to him and now his father was preparing to replace her with another woman. That was not all. The other woman's sons needed space and the only available room was Peter's treasured study. The room would have to be converted into a bedroom:

'Actually, there was plenty of room for all of us, but my father obviously wanted to clear the decks, wash his hands of me and save himself my allowance. I didn't ask him where he thought I was going to live or how. There was no welfare state in those days ... perhaps he thought I would cadge lodgings with my married brothers, but they made it clear they had no room.

'So, my small allowance was over and I was out on my ear. About time too, some might say. On the other hand, nobody forced him to keep me and, when there was a glimmer of hope in my writing career, he was the first to boast about it. What caused me the greatest sadness was that he broke his promise to my mother.'

The last time Peter and his father were close to each other was one night near the end of the war, when they were both undertaking firewatching duty outside the house. As a doodlebug landed a few doors away, both men fell into the gutter. Now it was time for Peter to find a way to stay out of the gutter.

The first thing Peter had to do was to cobble together some money. Wherever he was going to stay it was going to cost something, and the fear of having nowhere to live was only superseded by the fear of not having anything to live off. He started by selling the few possessions he owned. The local library bought his collection of non-fiction publications, which included volumes of Jung, Adler, Havelock-Ellis, biographies, books on medical jurisprudence and so on. Next to go was Peter's valuable collection of classic gramophone records.

Then, with some cash in his pocket and a few clothes thrown together in a suitcase, Peter boarded a train to London. He was on his own:

'I had no idea where I was going or what I was going to do. It wasn't exactly a day of jubilation for me. I couldn't help feeling sorry for myself. Thank God I didn't have my dog to worry about as well. My dear Alsatian had died just after my mother. They both had cancer. So, at long last I was free, although it wasn't the kind of freedom that I had anticipated or wished for. The first thing I had to do was find some-where to live and then look for a job. The war was still on so that might not to be too difficult. I never considered finding lodgings and looking for a job locally. Intuitively I knew I must gravitate towards London.'

Peter returned to the Thermionic Club, which had been a useful venue for him in his radio play days. The club was named after a piece of equipment called the 'thermionic valve', without which a radio would not work. It seemed an apt name for a club situated just a few yards from BBC Broadcasting House, Portland Place:

'It was there that I met people like Tommy Watkin, managing direc-tor of Broadwood pianos, whose office was not far away in Hanover Street. He was always anxious to replace Steinways with Broadwood pianos throughout the BBC, but he wasn't very successful in that. Then there was Dr Bodman, a young specialist, whose consulting rooms were in Portland Place. They were both puzzled to see me stagger in with my suitcase. "Where are you off to?" they asked, amused. When I told them what had happened, avoiding a good many details that would have made it sound as if I had a persecution complex, the young doctor immediately suggested that I should use his flat in Kensington Close as he wasn't using it himself. He had a house in the country, away from the bombing. It was a stroke of generosity I had not expected and, for the immediate future, I had a roof over my head.'

The next thing Peter had to do was find a job. One of the club members suggested that he should apply to the BBC to become an announcer. Peter was aghast. He had never envisaged himself reading the news, but that was not what his friend had in mind. He was thinking that Peter could introduce variety programmes and suchlike.

Peter still dismissed the idea, but the gentleman persisted and even arranged for him to see John Snagge, who was head of the spoken word department at the Beeb.

Peter duly presented himself to the famous Mr Snagge, whose

slightly adenoidal diction was associated throughout the country with the commentary for the annual Oxford versus Cambridge Boat Race. Peter did not try to disguise his own voice, speaking in the only way he knew how. All John Snagge wanted to know was which public school Peter had attended and whether he had been in the first XV or the first XI. Peter did not get the job – and he was never sure if it was his voice or background that let him down.

Club friend Tommy Watkin then came to Peter's aid. He knew someone, who knew someone, who knew Tom Hopkinson, the owner of *Picture Post*. Peter was duly introduced to the news editor, Ted Castle. Their mutual dislike was instantaneous. Ted was from the old school of journalism. He had a big office, a big desk and a big secretary with a big desk to match. Peter was a friend of the boss. He wore an overcoat and paisley scarf, and sat with legs crossed – every inch the 'gentleman' reporter:

'He looked so bitter, I got the impression he must have been weaned on a gherkin. If arseholes could fly, then his office would have been an airport. He hated me on sight, which was something I could take in my stride. I could guess what was going through his mind while I sat there: "Thought you'd get in through some social contact with Tom, did you? A privileged prick, I suppose."'

It wasn't until some years later that Peter learned of Ted Castle's socialist political leanings and realized that he must have represented everything that was an anathema to the man – appearance, accent, clothes, and so on.

Peter wasn't offered a permanent job on *Picture Post*, but rather a series of assignments. One of these was a visit to Worcester College for the Blind. Because of the blackout laws and the situation of most of the scholars, none of the corridors was lit, and Peter found himself groping his way in the darkness with the aid of a small torch:

'It was a fascinating experience. I seemed to rely so much on my ability to see, and could hardly move without fear of walking into something and hurting myself, yet the boys were hurtling past me like bats in a cave on their way to their rooms or the bathroom. The darkness meant nothing to them. Another fascinating aspect of life at the college was that the boys played rugby on the outdoor field by using a ball with a bell in it. In this way they were able to chase after the ball without actually seeing it very clearly, and didn't seem in the least bit worried about the rough and tumble of the chase.'

After the Worcester College assignment, there was a long gap before the next one – a very long gap indeed. Ted Castle had finally got his way and Peter had been fired: 'I asked him when I was going to get another assignment and he said "never", and that was that.'

Tom Hopkinson kindly introduced Peter to a New Zealander named Arthur Heyway, who was the managing editor of one of Clarence Hatry's journals called *World Press News*. This much-respected publication acted as the trade journal of the press itself. Hatry was prepared to take Peter on. Peter didn't consider trade journalism a comedown, wasn't proud and, anyway, wasn't in a position to be so. He convinced himself that at least the publication was dealing with journalists and the problems they faced, which was a different angle on things.

There was a snag to the job, though. As the end of the war approached, a new law stated that employers were duty-bound to take back on to their staff any previous employee who had been demobbed from the services. Peter knew what this law meant for him, but hoped that he would so impress the people who mattered that, in the fullness of time, they would offer him full-time employment. But, once again, he had news editor trouble: 'He wasn't a very nice little man. He wanted to take me down a peg or two, and started by beating my wages down to well below the union minimum.'

Peter had no choice but to take what was on offer. He was now living in half an attic in Notting Hill Gate. Peter refers to it as 'half an attic' because his portion of the room consisted of a bed, a table and a chair under a sloping roof. The rest was jammed with packing cases and furniture and was screened off by a heavy curtain. It wasn't exactly home, but had to serve as such for the foreseeable future.

Peter was expected to be at the office by eight o'clock in the morning, which, given he was working for a weekly trade paper, sounded rather early to him. But so anxious was he not to lose this job that, on his first day, he got up early and walked quickly through the eerily quiet streets of Notting Hill to the tube. He had no idea what time it was because he had pawned his wristwatch the week before when he faced the grim prospect of going without food. The tube station was closed.

It was, he discovered, only 5.30. He made his weary way back to his attic room, climbed the many stairs of the building, which housed the local branch of the Midland Bank, and lay down again on his bed.

The next time he set off he was in luck. The streets were waking up and the tube station was just opening. He was the first customer on the train that morning. When he arrived at the office in Tudor Street, on the stroke of eight o'clock, the offices were still shut. Puzzled, he went to a café round the corner and had breakfast. At nine o'clock he returned to the office just as it was opening up. He was confused:

'When I met the news editor I told him I had turned up at eight o'clock. "Whatever for?" he asked. "You told me to," I replied. "Did I?" he said in a slightly taunting fashion. He said no more and neither did I.'

Later Peter discovered that it was just one of the news editor's 'little jokes'. He was not amused.

Peter's first assignment on *World Press News* was to count the number of pubs in Fleet Street. Evidently, the managing editor had had a bet with another managing editor, in the nearby Coluna Club, about the number of drinking houses that were open to journalists through-out the heart of newspaper land. To count them all, Peter had to walk down one end of the long street and then up the other. It was early in the morning and all the licensed houses were closed. Back in the office, Peter hit on the idea of writing the piece in stages, starting off in a sober manner and progressing in a more drunken style as he figuratively vis-ited all the hostelries. The news editor was impressed; so was the man-aging editor when he won his bet.

Relations between Peter and the news editor warmed, and an invi-tation was extended for drinks one evening. This soon became a regu-lar practice and the habit continued for the remainder of the editor's stay with the paper. This time the editor was dismissed before Peter left. But the drinks continued.

Just before the news editor was dismissed from *World Press News*, he was assigned to go to Europe to report on press facilities and conditions among the press corps. For this job he was fitted out in the uniform of a war correspondent, and Peter remembers that the man fancied him-self in the outfit: 'When I arrived at his flat one evening, he produced a revolver, which was the largest I had ever seen … it was empty, of course, but that didn't stop him from waving it about like Dick Turpin.'

During the evening's drinking session the news editor's wife, Jessica, pulled Peter on to her lap, spilling his drink, and gave him a drunken hug. Meanwhile, 'Dick Turpin' was still brandishing his gun around in the air, and Peter had even more reason to be relieved that the weapon was empty. The incident, though, had repercussions. Many years later during the making of a *Carry On* film, director Gerald Thomas asked Peter if he knew a woman called Jessica: 'I said the only Jessica I ever met was my former news editor's wife. It then transpired that my production manager was a friend of hers, and had told Gerald a story about me trying to seduce Jessica, forcing her husband to fend me off with a revolver!'

One of Peter's more enjoyable assignments for *World Press News* was to attend a conference in London for what was referred to as the 'Negro' press. At that time, the use of the word 'Negro' was both allowed and encouraged. Peter was introduced to several of their editors, and the article he wrote was subsequently syndicated throughout the 750 such newspapers then in publication in America. The only criticism he received came from an editor who said that he should have spelled the word 'negro' with a capital 'N'.

Because Peter had been the last to join the newspaper, he was last in the queue when it came to the handing out of holiday entitlement. He ended up with two weeks in September and being a sucker for nostalgia, he decided to return to his native Kent, where he spent the first week over the Royal Star pub in Maidstone. Although he relished many happy hours walking along the bank of the River Medway to places such as Teston, East Farleigh and Barming, the holiday also brought back a rush of memories of family day trips out and picnics in the fields while his father Claude was fishing. The nostalgia did not, however, prompt Peter to visit his father, who lived just a few miles away. Following the pain of his mother's death and his subsequent eviction from his home of 30 years, it was too soon to return to play-act at happy families.

For the second week of the holiday, Peter moved to another nostalgic location at Bodiam in Sussex, staying at the Castle pub. This was situated opposite Bodiam Castle, where, once again, he had picnicked as a child while his father fished in the castle moat and the adjoining River Rother.

It wasn't the most exciting vacation that Peter remembers – and his memories of it are tinged with sadness. His two brothers also lived nearby, yet he did not visit them. When Claude kicked him out, they had made it clear they couldn't accommodate him, and there had been no contact with them since that fateful day. Peter wasn't really sorry when his fortnight's holiday was over and he could return to work and, above all, the company of his colleagues.

Ironically, Peter's first encounter with a censor wasn't, as one might imagine, as a result of Barbara Windsor's bra flying off during the infamous exercise scene in *Carry On Camping*. That potential confrontation was still a quarter of a century away. He first met a censor, Admiral Thompson, during his time at *World Press News*.

Peter had to visit the admiral regularly to be kept up to date with any new reporting restrictions that affected the press during the war. At that time, the ills of censorship were regarded as a necessary price to pay to avoid the enemy finding out what was happening in the country. The public, therefore – if they were told a story at all – were often told only half of it. Facts had to be withheld or amended to paint a brighter picture than was actually the case. One story, which still causes Peter to laugh out loud, was an incident concerning the Great Thaw. All the papers ran stories about a thaw which followed a prolonged stay of freezing heavy snow. The irony was that because it was vitally important to the war effort that Germany remained unaware of the crippling weather conditions facing Britain, the papers had not been allowed to report the heavy snowfall in the first place!

Peter is proud of his days at *World Press News*. It brought him into contact with many fascinating people and provided him with some wonderful journalistic pieces which he looks back on with considerable pride. He interviewed the famous American commentator Quentin Reynolds as he luxuriated in his bath at Claridges. He was the man who always referred to Adolf Hitler by his family name of Schicklgruber.

There was also a meeting with the cartoonist Sollon, who told Peter how he saw his subjects – each with their prominent features, be it nose, eyes, ears or hair. He did an immediate caricature of Peter, which, to this day, Peter regrets not keeping.

And there was the American lady who ran the Black Star picture agency in London, who summed up the difference in approach between British and Americans to pin-ups by insisting that the British weren't aware that girls had tits or bums. When Peter wrote that story, he mentioned that she had a voice you wanted to touch. It was an expression which caught on.

Peter's happiest time reporting – and the change of direction which was to shape the rest of his career – came out of the blue when the managing editor of the paper decided to include a film section within the publication. Naturally, as Peter had some experience in the film industry, he was put in charge of it. From then on, Peter was virtually his own boss. He was relieved of day-to-day reporting assignments, including the one which news editors loved but reporters loathed: go out and find some news. It also meant that, after attending film previews in the evenings, he was no longer expected at the office so early in the mornings.

His first evening assignment was at the Savoy Hotel, where husband-and-wife, director-and-actress team, Herbert Wilcox and Anna Neagle, were launching their latest production, *I Live in Grosvenor Square*. Peter was sitting at the press table with the other film correspondents, including respected critic Peter Noble, who became a very helpful friend and took Peter under his wing. If he saw Peter diffidently holding back instead of tackling a visiting star outright (echoes of his dislike for confrontation), Peter Noble would manoeuvre the star in his direction: 'He was a very kind man – especially for a critic. He would often give me information for my stories, and was a brilliant journalist in his own right.'

Peter Noble married Marianne Stone, an attractive young actress who probably featured in more small parts in British films than any other actress. She appeared briefly in nine of Peter's *Carry On* films, from *Carry On Nurse* in 1959 until *Carry On Behind* in 1975. She would have made it the round 10 appearances if her role in *Carry On Matron* hadn't been edited out before the film's release, but she chalked up assignments in other Peter Rogers' productions, including *You Know What Sailors Are!* and *Bless This House*.

She also appeared in literally hundreds of other productions, notably the Hammer science fiction double, *The Quatermass Experiment* and *Quatermass II*, and the Peter Sellers' comedy *The Wrong Arm of the Law*, popping up here and there, often for just a single line or two. In recent years the Nobles' daughter, Kara Noble, became infamous as the radio journalist who sold the topless photograph of Prince Edward's then fiancée, Sophie Rhys-Jones, to the *Sun* newspaper.

Many years after the Savoy evening, when Peter was an established and successful film producer, Peter Noble came to interview him in the Dorchester Hotel. Entering the lounge in his somewhat flamboyant fashion, he called out, 'Where's that famous film producer Peter Rogers?' Thankfully, Peter remembers, the lounge was empty of residents and visitors:

'The waiters knew it was a joke, but that was the kind of embarrassment Peter Noble could cause with his extreme kindness. He was carrying a copy of the *Evening Standard* and, during lunch, I noticed that he was slipping a piece of his fillet steak between the pages of the paper at the side of his plate. I asked if there was something wrong with the food. He said no, he was taking it home to Marianne. I called the head waiter and asked him to wrap up half a dozen slices of fillet of beef for Mr Noble to take away. The head waiter's name was McCresny, a delightful man, and he made up a package for Peter Noble to take home.'

One of Peter's chores as the film editor of *World Press News* was to interview the managing director of J Arthur Rank's optical equipment establishment. The MD himself had requested the interview and Peter's managing editor had agreed to it. So off Peter went by public transport from Fleet Street to the Slough trading estate, a few miles short of Maidenhead. If Peter had made the proper inquiries, he would have discovered that he could get a train to Maidenhead and a bus straight to the factory. As it was, with his shyness still in full throttle, he tried to find his own way there, going via Uxbridge, Slough and Langley. It took him nearly the whole morning to get there.

In one of his rare daring advances, Peter managed to get an interview with Filippo del Giudice, the famous producer and controller of Denham Studios, Buckinghamshire. Much to the chagrin of the studios' press officer, who only found out about the incident afterwards, Peter just walked into del Giudice's office and asked to see him:

'I was with him for several hours and he never stopped talking – much of it off the record. He was particularly vitriolic about the critics. I did a two-page spread about him which was, perhaps, flattering. So much so that my editor wanted me to find someone who would say unflattering things about him. I refused. It was a typical ploy of news editors: if someone said kind things about someone, then they wanted someone else to say bad things.'

One advantage which Peter found in having a press pass was that it allowed him to attend Promenade Concerts at the Albert Hall during their summer season. Because of his love of music he was there every night, film launches permitting.

Many film functions were held in private rooms at the Savoy Hotel because of its close proximity to Fleet Street. It was there that Peter was to meet his future wife, Betty Evelyn Box, who was destined to be as unique a lady in the film industry as he was as a producer. Subsequently, they were to form the most prodigious film-making couple in British cinema history. They never became a film-making partnership, but with their respective directors they were responsible for over a hundred productions, most of them made at their 'second home', Pinewood Studios. When Peter saw Betty, literally across a crowded room, he did not know that she was already a big player in the industry.

Sydney Box, Betty's older brother by 11 years, was holding a press reception in the River Room at the Savoy. *World Press News* was among the invitees, and Peter was present as their film representative. Sydney Box had scored an enormous success with the film *The Seventh Veil*. The story revolved around a concert pianist who is torn romantically between her psychiatrist, her guardian and two others. The cast included James Mason, Ann Todd and Herbert Lom, and was duly rewarded with an Oscar for the script, written by Sydney and his wife, Muriel Box. On the strength of such prestigious recognition, J Arthur Rank had asked Sydney to take over the running of Gainsborough Studios, which operated out of Shepherd's Bush and Islington. He was, therefore, an obvious candidate for an interview:

'He was a balding, benign, smiling gentleman who walked with a limp because, I discovered, he had dislocated a hip as a child. When I asked him for an interview, he said, "You write it and I'll sign it!" He went on to tell me that he was planning a film called *Holiday Camp* and asked if, as a writer, I had any ideas. I hadn't, but promised to send him some.

'That night, I was introduced to his sister, Betty. She was a producer in her own right and was accompanied by her own publicist, Betty Callaghan. Both were attractive ladies – Betty Box a blonde and Betty Callaghan a brunette. They immediately struck one as great friends. I was instantly attracted to Betty, but our conversation on this occasion was brief and formal – not personal, just professional.'

And that was Betty, a female producer at a time in the industry when such a thing was considered literally unthinkable. Indeed, Betty went on to become one of the most successful woman producers Britain has ever known, making, among other films, the long-running *Doctor* ... comedy series from the books by Richard Gordon. These hugely popular films made household names of Dirk Bogarde and Kenneth More. She was awarded the OBE in 1958.

Chapter Six
'I Do', Then Back to Work

Peter returned to his desk at the office and, whenever a spare moment arose, jotted down ideas for *Holiday Camp*. Wooing Betty, though, was never far from his thoughts:

'I couldn't get her out of my mind and started writing to her. I discovered that, although she had an apartment in Nell Gwynne House, Sloane Street, she spent most of her time with her brother and his wife, Muriel, at his apartment at Maitland Court, Bayswater. As my half-attic was only down the road at Notting Hill, I would visit Maitland Court in the evenings and leave my letters with the porter in the hope that she would receive them.'

Things started looking up for Peter when Sydney Box, on seeing his ideas for *Holiday Camp*, invited Peter to join a team of screenwriters that also included Sydney himself, his wife, Muriel, Ted Willis and Mabel and Denis Constanduros. The film evolves around a summer holiday camp, where a murderer, who is hiding out from the police, affects the lives of families and guests in different ways. The wonderful assembly of British character actors and actresses included Jack Warner, Kathleen Harrison, Flora Robson, Jimmy Hanley and Dennis Price.

Peter wanted to jump at the opportunity to join the team, but how could he give up a permanent job on the strength of co-writing a screenplay for just one film? Sydney Box immediately offered him a full-time contract as a scriptwriter at Gainsborough Studios: 'It seemed too good to be true, but, as I was to discover, that was what Sydney was like. The list of people he gave a first break to is endless – and I am proud to have been one of them.'

Peter's managing editor was not best pleased when Peter announced that he was leaving to become a scriptwriter. Others in the news room reacted, as Peter had expected, with snide remarks and innuendos about him being rewarded for making up to Sydney Box's daughter. He kept pointing out, but to no avail, that Betty was Sydney's sister: 'I didn't mind being insulted, but I would have preferred them to get their facts right. After all, they were supposed to be journalists'.

Shortly afterwards, Peter was installed at Gainsborough Studios as a salaried scriptwriter.

Things were looking up on the romance front too. He now found himself regularly meeting Betty for dinner at the Number Three Club in Grosvenor Square. The club was next to the old American Embassy building before it was moved to the other side of the square. The romance blossomed and very soon Peter found himself a co-opted member of the Box family, enjoying regular Sunday lunches at Maitland Court.

It wasn't long before Betty offered Peter her flat on the ninth floor in Nell Gwynne House, which she told him she never used. After half an attic, this was sheer luxury, and Peter was exceptionally happy with his new digs until the night the lift started playing up and then literally plummeted from the ninth to the ground floor. It didn't exactly fall like the proverbial stone, but it was fairly close: 'Something had happened to put the lift out of skew, and it dropped out of control between each floor, with a small corner of the cage resting briefly on the lift shaft before it continued its descent.'

Peter flattened himself against the wall of the lift, his arms spread out to balance himself as it fell between each floor, and finally came to a crash-landing at the bottom. The doors opened and, feeling thoroughly shaken, he walked out into the hall. He was met by an angry doorman who demanded to know what Peter had done to his lift! 'It's what your lift has done to me!' Peter exclaimed, walking away.

The Boxes were horrified: Betty beside herself with concern that Peter might have been hurt. It was probably the first time she realized she had fallen in love with him.

The threesome, it seemed, had become a foursome – Peter, Sydney, Muriel and Betty. They were always together, at work and in restaurants in the evenings. Peter was invited because of his courtship of Betty and, although the word wasn't used, he was regarded as the 'boyfriend'. They all had one love in common – film – the element that cemented their relationship. They were always talking scripts and writing them. Peter shared screenplay credits with Sydney and Muriel and, occasionally, they allowed him to write solo. This was a convenient arrangement. Muriel had been wanting to move away from a scriptwriting position at Gainsborough to pursue her love of directing.

Peter's love of Betty remained unabated and his feelings were now reciprocated:

'My relationship with Betty was not of the passionate, whirlwind courtship variety. We had a calm and somewhat undemonstrative relationship. We didn't walk hand in hand or anything like that. I had great respect for her, and we were as one in our thoughts and affection. We were able to sit and read together without talking – happy just to be in each other's company. In a way, I suppose we took each other for granted as if we'd always been like that. I was writing scripts and Betty was producing them – among others, of course. She was in charge of the Islington Studios branch of Gainsborough Pictures, while Sydney looked after the main studios at Lime Grove. I was known to the press as Mr Betty Box. I didn't mind. I told them that while other men tended to hide their light under a bushel, I hid my light under a box!'

Betty helped to bring Peter out of himself, and sometimes he wasn't sure just how far out he was coming. During his time at Gainsborough, Michael Redgrave, the great British actor and head of an impressive acting dynasty, gave a fancy dress party at his home in Chiswick. Betty suggested that Peter should go as a ballet dancer, and the studio's wardrobe mistress fitted him out with a tutu skirt and bra. Betty went as herself and Peter soon began to wish he had. The couple set out in the car. As they neared Chiswick, Peter lost his way. Drawing up alongside a bus, he got out to ask directions. The bus driver politely pointed the way, but, recoiling from the tutu and bra, couldn't get back into his cab quickly enough.

Gainsborough, like all film studios before and since, went through difficult patches. Like Pinewood, its Islington base had all but closed for the duration of the war. Bar the occasional production and army training film assignment, all remained quiet on their stages. But it wasn't the Nazis who were the problem, it was Columbus. Gainsborough had been producing good-quality films since hostilities had come to an end. The success of *Holiday Camp* had led to the first postwar film series, *The Huggetts*, with Jack Warner and Kathleen Harrison as the parents of a seemingly average family with above average problems. There were to be three more incredibly popular spin-offs from their first cinematic appearance: *Here Come the Huggetts*, *Vote for Huggett* and *The Huggetts Abroad*.

The problems for the studios arose during the 1949 production of *Christopher Columbus*, starring Frederic March. The film told the story of Columbus seeking the patronage of the Spanish court following his successful voyages. It was not well received and was generally regarded as interesting but not stimulating. *Time* magazine observed: 'Even 10-year-olds will find it about as thrilling as an afternoon spent looking at Christmas cards.'

The film was one of the first at Gainsborough to be made in colour, and the sizes of the stages had proved to be a problem. They were not big enough for the scale of the production and, because of the number of lamps in use, the doors had to be opened every two hours to let the heat out. J Arthur Rank decided to inspect the studios for himself, and Peter was detailed to give him a tour of the place. By now Rank was over 60, but he climbed the iron ladders and fire escapes like a 30-something.

The result of this inspection was the closure of both the Lime Grove and the Islington Studios. It wasn't just down to the production of *Christopher Columbus*: the Rank Organisation itself was on the brink of collapse. And the closing of these two studios, with everyone moving to its flagship studios, Pinewood, was considered to be the only sensible option if Rank was to stay afloat.

Four decades later, Peter had his own problems with Christopher Columbus when the *Carry On* team was trying to revive its cinematic successes of the sixties and seventies with the 1992 film *Carry On Columbus*, starring Jim Dale. That too was a failure. As famed comedy actress June Whitfield is oft quoted: 'They should have called it *Carry Off Columbus!*'

Amidst the moving of studios and other changes going on around them, Peter and Betty decided to tie the knot. For some time they had been living in the same flat in St John's Wood, which was convenient both for the Lime Grove and Islington Studios. Living together was not exactly the done thing in those days, and the couple hadn't made a song and dance about it. They weren't embarrassed, either. Nevertheless, Peter and Betty found it easier to pretend to their Hungarian maid, Mrs Juliusburger, that they were cousins.

Mrs Juliusburger was an aristocratic refugee whose family had been stripped of both title and possessions by the Russians during the war. She spoke impeccable English and, seeing that both Betty and Peter had separate rooms, had no reason to question the arrangement. The Hungarians were used to family members, of all ages, sharing accommodation.

Peter and Betty got married at 9.30 a.m. on Christmas Eve, 1948, at Marylebone Register Office. It was a quiet affair, just the wedded couple, and two work associates, Tony Darnborough and Vivian Cox, who were present as witnesses. Peter hadn't told his family. The first they – and indeed, the world of show business – knew about the marriage, was in the 'read-all-about-it' of that day's edition of the *Evening News*, where a picture of the two of them had made it to the front page.

As soon as the wedding was over, they returned to business. Betty was working on two films at the time, *Marry Me!* and *Don't Ever Leave Me*. It must have been an omen – Peter and Betty remained solidly together for the next 50 years. Returning to their flat, after spending Christmas with her family, there was a note from Mrs Juliusburger on the doormat. It read: *Dear madam, I congratulate you on your marriage to your cousin. I wish you both every happiness. Mrs E Juliusburger.*

Working from Pinewood took a bit of getting used to. Betty immediately went into production, but the team ship had altered. Whereas at Gainsborough, Sydney Box was boss and could appoint or dismiss personnel as he saw fit, the situation at Pinewood was different. The Gainsborough contingent, of which there were only four main players, were regarded as the interlopers.

Sydney Box decided to take a year's sabbatical and went off to tour America in a caravan. Peter decided to cut back on his scriptwriting contract and concentrate on writing and producing for himself:

'I had learnt a good deal from Betty. She virtually taught me my job as a producer. But now it was time to move on. We had offices next door to each other at Pinewood, but we started to see less of each other during the day as we both went our separate ways as producers. We drove to and from work in separate cars, and never discussed a production we were involved in. Make no mistake, we weren't rivals in the business – we could never have been that – but we were producing films for rival distributors. Rank didn't seem to want me as a producer, so I made my films for Associated British Cinemas (ABC). There was some dissension on the Rank board over Betty's appointment. Michael Balcon, of Ealing Studios, had never liked the idea of a woman producer and said so. Thankfully he was out-voted, but he certainly vetoed any idea of Betty and me working together.'

The early 1950s was a time of great change at Pinewood Studios, Peter's new workplace. The managing director, John Davis, imposed limits of £150,000 on all productions. Many old-timers – long-standing executives – faced with pay cuts of 10 per cent, departed the studios, not always voluntarily but always with a decent handshake. Davis had one aim, and that was to streamline the studio's operation and fill cinemas with popular films which people would want to go and see. This, he believed, was the only way to save the Rank Organisation and Pinewood Studios.

Like all the other established producers, Betty Box took her new orders on the chin. They knew they were in for a difficult time, but felt that their love of film would win through. Betty took on a new director, Ralph Thomas. They had first met at a showing of her film *Miranda* in 1947, but he had ended up, at that time, working for her brother, Sydney, as a director.

The teaming of the two at Pinewood was a direct result of the Rank Board deciding to match producers and directors to work on projects together. It mixed and matched people until it came up with what were good working teams. The teams then went to the Pinewood story department for ideas to produce and direct. A team, therefore, was only ever as good as the material it was handed. Several teams were put together, but only Betty and Ralph survived. This feat was achieved primarily because Betty found her own subjects to make into films, and didn't depend on the Pinewood story department which was often deemed inefficient and lacking in good ideas.

Betty and Ralph's first venture under the new rules was a film entitled *The Clouded Yellow*, starring Trevor Howard as a sacked secret service agent who finds himself embroiled in a murder plot while tending a butterfly collection. The implausible storyline gave way to good production values and an excellent cast, which included Jean Simmons, a young Kenneth More and Peter's old friend Marianne Stone.

The film was a big success and Betty's place at Pinewood was assured. Her new working relationship with Ralph Thomas was to last for 30 years and over 30 films. Away from work, Peter, Betty and Ralph, and Ralph's wife, Joy, became inseparable friends. They worked together and holidayed together. That friendship continues to this day with Ralph and Joy's son – famed film producer Jeremy Thomas – who is also one of Peter and Betty's godchildren.

Peter didn't find the early fifties quite as easy as Betty. He worked on various small productions before buying the film rights to Edward Hyams' book *Sylvester*. He wrote 14 versions of the script before Earl St John, Pinewood's executive producer, who had to approve all productions in the studio and justify his decision to the Board in London, eventually accepted it.

It was a naval comedy and Peter wanted Kenneth More for the lead.

Since Betty had made *The Clouded Yellow*, they had become friends of Kenneth and his wife, Billy. For some reason Earl St John didn't want Kenneth. Peter wanted to know why, but the question was avoided. Eventually he discovered that, contrary to Earl's wishes, Kenneth More had been cast in the film comedy *Genevieve*. In fact, the whole cast had not been up to Earl's liking. It was made quite clear to Dinah Sheridan, Kay Kendall and John Gregson that the executive producer was not happy with either them or their performances.

As far as Kenneth More was concerned, the Rank Board felt he had not enough experience, and that he was known only for one or two minor roles in films which had been shown mainly in the southeast of England. The Board would have preferred Dirk Bogarde and Claire Bloom to have taken up at least two of the roles.

Genevieve was made in the autumn of 1952, with the freezing weather only slightly colder than the atmosphere at Pinewood. And such was Earl St John's faith in the film, it was then put on the shelf for 18 months. The rest, of course, is history. *Genevieve* is now regarded as one of the best and certainly the most quintessential of British film comedies; and Kenneth More was to become the number one British box office star of the fifties.

However, at the stage when Peter wanted him in his film, *You Know What Sailors Are!*, Earl had refused. Peter spoke to Kenneth, who was prepared to take the second lead in the film. Again Earl said no. Even when Kenneth said he was prepared to take on the third lead, the casting was vetoed. Peter had no choice but to look elsewhere and decided on a new, fresh-faced, budding film star, Donald Sinden.

The film was directed by Ken Annakin, with whom Peter had worked on *Holiday Camp* and the *Huggett* series a few years before. Even with a new star and a director on board, Peter's problems were not over:

'What I didn't know was that a Pinewood contract producer named Julian Wintle hadn't made a film for over a year. Without any warning to me or knowledge of my plans for the production, Earl St John had agreed with Annakin that my film should go through Wintle's company as 'A Julian Wintle Production'. I knew nothing of this until after the first day's shooting, by which time there was nothing I could do about it. I decided not to work with Ken Annakin again.'

Peter's time on the production of *To Dorothy a Son* was a far happier – if a trifle odd – affair. The film, starring Shelley Winters, was

scripted from a stage play which Peter had bought and adapted for the
screen. The plot revolved around a second-rate American singer who is
destined to come into a fortune if she can prove that her former husband has not got any children from any new marriage. The man – an
out of luck composer for documentary music, played by actor John
Gregson – does indeed have a wife, played by actress Peggy Cummins,
who is about to drop their first child. Things get even more complicated
when the man discovers that the divorce from his first wife, performed
in Bolivia, is not legal and that he now has two wives!

Shelley, delighted with the script, complimented Peter profusely
and was constantly hugging him. If anything she liked the script too
much, insisting that not one word be changed or she wouldn't do the
film. Then, to Peter's amazement, she ordered that the script be
deposited at the Bank of England, to stop anyone changing a word of
dialogue.

Peter thought she was a wonderful actress, but wasn't sure how long
he could go along with her funny ways. Before she had even arrived in
England, she insisted that the production company find her a home to
live in as she couldn't possibly stay in a hotel because she had a small
child with her. Peter remembers:

'Small child? It was hardly weaned. I found her a very nice house in
South Street, Mayfair. She moved in, but next morning said she couldn't
stay there because it was too damp for the child. As the child was always
damp anyway, I didn't think that mattered very much. Anyway, the
house wasn't damp – London was damp. She decided that she'd rather
live in a hotel.'

Peter obliged and booked her a suite at the Savoy, on the Strand.
Shelley was delighted with the hotel. The hotel, though, was not delighted
with her. Guests kept complaining that a noisy baby was continually
running up and down the corridor. The hotel people telephoned Peter
and asked him to take her out of the hotel.

Peter remembered a very nice apartment in a block called 55 Park
Lane. It was occupied by a single lady who had been introduced to him
at a party. Peter persuaded the lady to take a six-week holiday in the
south of France while Shelley occupied the apartment: 'At last we had
found her somewhere everyone was happy with. She stayed there
throughout the shooting of the film.'

Although, like Betty, some of the Gainsborough refugees had
settled down at Pinewood, the Box family felt, since their enforced

move from Islington, that they had lost some of the special atmosphere of working together. Rumours that Sydney Box had not taken a sabbatical, but had been ordered by the Rank Board to stay away for a year, while changes were made in the early 1950s, didn't help the feeling that the Boxes were not quite at home at Pinewood.

When the small Beaconsfield studios came up for sale in the mid 1950s, the Box family bought it. After the war, Beaconsfield had undergone an extensive refurbishment, courtesy of the government, which had spent £146,000 equipping the site for the Crown Film Unit. The unit produced 75 information films a year for the Central Office of Information. It was disbanded in 1951 and taken over by Group 3, a subsidiary of the National Film Finance Corporation (NFFC), whose aim was to encourage and promote new film talent.

Productions at the time included *Miss Robin Hood*, with Margaret Rutherford, James Robertson Justice and a relatively unknown comedy actor by the name of Sidney James. *The Love Match*, a film based on the highly successful stage comedy, starring Arthur Askey, Thora Hird and future pioneering *Carry On* leading lady, Shirley Eaton, was also in production. But, by the mid 1950s, the NFFC felt that having its own studios was an unjustifiable expense. That's when the Box family moved in. If there was any feeling of satisfaction that they had taken it over from Michael Balcon, who had given Betty Box such a difficult time, no one was prepared to gloat or, indeed, even mention the fact.

The idea was that, eventually, Peter, Betty, Sydney and Muriel would all work there together to make films. As it turned out, Peter was the only one to work there. Betty's successes at Pinewood were now coming in thick and fast. In 1954, her production of Richard Gordon's *Doctor in the House* became the highest grossing film in the country, a record she repeated with *Doctor At Large* in 1957, and again three years later, with *Doctor in Love*.

There was no way that Rank wanted her to leave Pinewood. It was thanks to productions such as hers that it continued to stay afloat. Peter was happy to take charge at Beaconsfield and is proud of his success: 'We kept the studios for only two years and in that time we only had one day empty. But, in order to keep the studios ticking over, I had to take in all kinds of films, a good deal of them second features. The only major production I had there was a TV series of *Ivanhoe*, starring Roger Moore.'

While at Beaconsfield, Peter decided it was time that he, like Betty, took on a dedicated director with whom he could work on future projects. He saw how Betty's partnership with Ralph Thomas was working and realized that this was the way forward for him. His attention had been drawn to a young man who had been editing Betty and Ralph's films. These films were exceptionally popular and this was, in no small part, due to the exceptional editor. Any decent producer looking for a director knows that you look for someone with editing experience. They are the ones who can see a film come together in their head as they are filming it, literally shot by shot.

Peter approached Betty and asked if he could have her editor as his director. The name of the editor was Gerald Thomas. He was the younger brother of Betty's director, Ralph Thomas, who, as if proving the point, had himself started out in the business as a film editor. Peter had already met Gerald socially. Betty and Ralph were away for considerable periods of time on location and, as the younger unmarried brother, Gerald was designated to look after Ralph's wife, Joy, by taking her out to dinner and so on. Since Peter was on his own, he went along too. The two men got on well together. Peter's request, therefore, was neither unexpected nor unwelcome. Betty and Ralph agreed.

Gerald Thomas was born in Hull, Yorkshire, and his early ambition had been to become a doctor. His studies were interrupted by the Second World War, where he served as an officer in the Royal Sussex Regiment in a variety of countries, including Germany, France and the Middle East. Because of the war, he had fallen behind with his medical studies and, rather than start again, he decided to pursue a career in films. He got a job in the cutting rooms of Two Cities Films at Denham Studios, nearby to Pinewood.

He was assistant editor on films such as the 1948 version of *Hamlet*, directed by its star, Laurence Oliver, and *The October Man*, starring John Mills. These proved fruitful films to cut his teeth on, before becoming a first-time editor, in 1949, on the historical melodrama *Madness of the Heart*, starring Margaret Lockwood. He edited the hugely popular *Doctor in the House*, and enjoyed a big break in 1955 when he went to Hollywood to edit Disney's *The Sword and the Rose* before returning to edit his brother Ralph's production of *Above Us the Waves* at Pinewood. By then, Gerald Thomas was regarded as one of the top editors in the country.

But he wasn't known as a director and almost immediately Peter found that he was faced with a problem: 'It wasn't as easy as I thought it would be. I couldn't persuade the distributor to accept Gerald as a director, so, as he was under contract, I used him on a second feature at Beaconsfield and wrote one or two scripts for the Children's Film Foundation – like *Circus Friends* in 1957 – to keep us going.'

Gerald recognized there was a problem and was prepared to listen to Peter and ride it out. Their big break came later that year, when Peter wrote a script based on Arthur Hailey's story *Time Lock*. The 73-minute film was a tense thriller, centred around a small boy who is accidentally trapped inside a bank vault by his father – played by Robert Beatty – as it is being locked for the weekend.

The film was shot at a breakneck, three-week schedule speed, at a cost of just £30,000 (equivalent to less than £425,000 today). Peter pulled all sorts of strings to make the film look more expensive than it was. He cadged the use of a British Overseas Airline Corporation (BOAC) helicopter for two days and, because the film was supposed to be set in Canada, persuaded the authorities to divert the traffic on the main thoroughfare to Slough on to the opposite side of the road to make it appear that the traffic was driving on the right.

Gerald Thomas directed the film, which was an instant hit. The distributor now agreed to allow Gerald to direct Peter's next film, *The Vicious Circle*, a thriller, written by Francis Durbridge – with John Mills as a doctor on the run after a dead woman is found in his flat. It was another success and it looked like the Rogers/Thomas partnership was finally up and running in the eyes of the industry.

All he needed now was a full-time contract screenplay writer and his film-making team would be complete. Enter Norman Hudis: 'I first met Peter Rogers when I was a publicist at Islington Studios. He was associate producer there, and I wrote his biography for publicity purposes. I've come full circle now, because, once again in a very personal sense, *that* is what I am doing now, by talking with you all these eventful years later.'

And eventful years they were – particularly between 1957 and 1963. Like Peter, Norman had always wanted to be a writer and had kicked off in journalism. After the war, there was a need for quick-thinking, fluent, presentable writers to work under pressure to produce publicity material to help sell films. He started his publicity career working on Betty Box's early films for Rank. He then went on to write a play about newspaper life in a country under dictatorship. This was produced in rep and received fair reviews. Earl St John spotted a budding writing talent and immediately put Norman under contract as a screenwriter – more to learn the job at that stage than to fulfil any early potential. Peter, though, recognized Norman's potential immediately and, in 1957, signed him up for a seven-year contract.

Norman remembers his first project for his new boss: 'Peter approached me and said he wanted me to write *The Tommy Steele Story*. I said, "Who's he?" And I have maintained that same with-it interest in rock 'n' roll from that day to this. In my defence, let it be said that Tommy had only been noticeable for about three weeks. However, I met with him, wrote the script very quickly and it was knocked off in – I think – three weeks, complete with umpteen songs by Lionel Bart and Mike Pratt. It went out as a second feature, but it was clearly an attraction and became the first feature on the posters – unprecedented, I think. It took what is known as a fortune.'

Peter made two films with Tommy Steele – or, to be factually correct, only one. The first, *The Tommy Steele Story*, was actually set up and produced by film veteran Herbert Smith, who, for many years, was studio manager at Denham. Peter's only involvement on the film was the overall supervision of the production and he was given the title of executive producer. Then, when Tommy's partner, lyricist and composer, Lionel Bart, approached Peter with a script called *The Duke Wore Jeans*, he jumped at the chance to make a film with Tommy, who had proved such a huge success earlier.

Peter says he lived to regret that decision: 'I liked and admired Lionel Bart, but Tommy! I said to Gerald, "Never again". I found him vain, conceited, bad-mannered and, the biggest crime of all, unprofessional. The cameraman I was using at that time was Otto Heller, one of the most highly paid in the business. We called a full lighting rehearsal for a Sunday morning. The unions were quite happy and, from 8.30 a.m. they were all there – cast, crew, everybody – but no Tommy.

'We rang his mother, who said he'd left hours ago. He was still in bed. He turned up at 12.30 p.m. without a word of apology, and too late to rehearse for lighting. We had dismissed the crew at the appointed time of midday.'

Lionel Bart came to Peter again with a script of *Oliver Twist* in which he visualized Tommy Steele starring. Peter made it quite clear that, even if Tommy was available and able to play a lead role in the proposed production, he was not prepared to work with him again. Peter claims that he suggested that Lionel should turn the script into a stage musical, and to include a ballet in Fagin's kitchen, which is what happened with great success.

Ironically, Lionel Bart's first choice of actor for Fagin, for the stage show of *Oliver!* in 1960, was none other than Sid James. Sid declined the role, thus stepping aside to allow Ron Moody to enjoy the biggest success of his career. Some 35 years later, the role of Fagin was taken up by Jim Dale, a *Carry On* favourite and close friend of Sid James. But the *Carry On* coincidence didn't end there. Although a great composer, Lionel Bart could not actually write music. To help him with *Oliver!* he turned to Eric Rogers, singing every word of the new musical and having his friend write down the notes for him. Eric went on to compose the music for 23 *Carry On* films.

Whatever the personal relationship between Peter Rogers and Tommy Steele, there was no doubting that the audiences loved both of Tommy's films. Peter was delighted with their reaction. He appeared to have got the mixture just right. His second features were hitting well above their weight at the cinema, and the box-office returns were impressing the industry. Just how he was going to keep up this impressive early record was anyone's guess.

Then, one day in late 1957, an unwanted script arrived on his desk. Starting life under the title *The Bull Boys*, it was soon to become *Carry On Sergeant*. The rest, as they say, is history.

The Bull Boys, a romantic drama by R F Delderfield, dealt with the effect of army conscription on a couple of ballet dancers. The rights to this story originally belonged to Peter Rogers' brother-in-law Sydney Box, who had no luck in finding backers or a distributor for the project. Even the promise of film star Leslie Caron did nothing to push it further. One of the script's main problems was its length. At just under a whopping 200 pages, it was twice the length of a normal 90-minute feature film. Even more important, although it had several interesting comic moments, the script was frowned on for being too heavy-handed in its critical look at the Army and the 'bull' that goes with the institution.

Peter took the script and tried to persuade various well-established comedy writers to have a crack at turning the story round. Among them were Ray Galton, Alan Simpson, Eric Sykes and Spike Milligan. All the writers refused. Indeed, Peter's initial experience with most of them was frosty or just plain bizarre:

'I had long admired the work of Eric Sykes – particularly his radio scripts for Frankie Howerd. In fact, Eric was my first choice to rework *The Bull Boys*. Sadly, I must have caught him on a very bad day. He had just gone through a nasty experience with a film producer who had taken a script he had written and failed to pay him for the privilege. He had vowed never to work with a film producer ever again and, in no uncertain terms, told me exactly what I could do with my script!'

Mind you, that was as nothing compared to the response that awaited him when he approached Spike Milligan. Spike, having suffered a nervous breakdown due to the exhausting timetable for writing his groundbreaking radio series, *The Goon Show*, was in less than cheerful spirits:

'I knocked on the door of his office, entered, and was confronted by Spike waving a loaded revolver around his head. He bellowed at me to get out at once and shouted that he was very busy at the moment. His actual words were, "I can't see anybody just now. I'm just about to kill myself!" With this, I hastily left. I didn't think he would be in a very fit state to work on my screenplay after the pressing business that was obviously at hand!'

Conveniently, all these great comedy writers were housed in the same place: 'a Dr Barnardo's – or, more to the point, Bedlam for comedy scriptwriters – run by the sympathetic agent Beryl Vertue.'

Despite his nerve-racking encounters, the day was not completely wasted. John Antrobus, another one of Vertue's skilled pen-pushers, who would later write *The Bed Sitting Room* with Spike Milligan, was assigned to Peter's film: 'He was a charming fellow and a very good writer. But he was at his best with sketch ideas and comedy of the absurd. Although he wrote several very funny scenes, which survived in the final script of *Carry On Sergeant*, his overall screenplay lacked logic. Rightly or wrongly, I have always felt that audiences like to believe in their comedy.'

Finally, like a fool, Peter suddenly realized that he had the perfect writer for the job already under contract – Norman Hudis. Without further delay, he handed the amended script – with the ideas of John Antrobus intact – to Norman. There was just one 'simple' instruction: Norman was to make the tired Delderfield plot work and turn it into a fully-fledged comedy. This was to be Norman Hudis's big break and if he had any nerves about Peter's request, he certainly didn't show them – not in public at least.

Meetings were held between Peter, Gerald and Norman to see how the original storyline could be altered to make it funnier and more interesting. During one of these early sessions, Norman suggested a whole new theme, one which was to become the familiar pattern for the next few movies: take a bunch of incompetents – unwilling and over-eager – allow them to make a hash of their army service, and then, for sentimental reasons, come up trumps in the end, under the shadow of an ogre (in the case of *Carry On Sergeant*, William Hartnell's character), who turns out not to be so fearsome after all.

Peter liked it and Norman set about working on the script. Indeed, the only part of Delderfield's story that remains in the final version is the very first scene where a national serviceman is called up on the day of his wedding.

Because Beaconsfield Studios were full up with the *Ivanhoe* TV series, Peter decided to make the film at Pinewood. The distributors were horrified. Pinewood was acknowledged as being the most expensive studio in the country. They suggested he take the film to the ABC Studios at Elstree. After all, they argued, Anglo Amalgamated films were released through ABC cinemas.

Peter had never worked at Elstree, but he had worked at Pinewood, where he knew and respected the efficient workforce. He held meetings with the studio heads to work out a method of operation to keep the costs down: 'The secret was to restrict the number of bodies allocated to the film. It had become the habit of such studios, including Elstree, to load the film with idle-for-the-moment salaried staff if there was insufficient production in the studio to meet the overheads.'

Peter managed to persuade the management at Pinewood to restrict the workforce to a certain number. Persuading the works committee was slightly harder, but Peter found the ultimate bargaining tool – the end of picture party. These parties had become something of a tradition in the industry. The cast and everybody who worked on a film – carpenters, electricians, riggers, the lot – would gather on the last evening of shooting for drinks and snacks. The Rank Organisation had put an end to such affairs because of J Arthur's religious beliefs about the evils of drink. However, as an independent producer, Peter was not subject to such restrictions and happily agreed that he would reintroduce the event on all of his films. The works committee was delighted and agreed to Peter's workforce terms.

Peter may have had the workers on his side, but across the industry – particularly at Pinewood – his decision to make a film for under £80,000 was treated with derision. It couldn't be done, people claimed, and, if it could, Pinewood with its reputation for high-quality productions certainly wasn't the place for it. Even Betty Box's films had come in on budgets of £125,000, and that had been for *Doctor in the House* some five years earlier. Peter ignored the brickbats and, perhaps with an apocryphal nod to the title of the fifth entry in the *Carry On* series, decided to carry on regardless.

The filming of *Carry On Sergeant* began on 24 March 1958, with a cast which included Kenneth Williams, Kenneth Connor, Hattie Jacques, Bob Monkhouse – and three of the stars of the hugely successful television situation comedy *The Army Game*, William Hartnell, Charles Hawtrey and Norman Rossington.

If the film was to have an Achilles' heel to spoil its success, there were those who thought that *The Army Game* could have been it. This show was based around the exploits of a group of conscripts who are determined to serve their time by doing as little as possible, and avoiding anything that resembled work. When the series began on 19 June 1957, National Service was still compulsory, so the public could easily identify with the characters and the situation the characters found themselves in. By the time *Carry On Sergeant* would be released in cinemas, 39 episodes would already have been broadcast on ITV, and there was a concern that the show might dent any potential popularity for the film.

Norman Hudis remembers: 'I recall many saying, while it was shooting, "Who'll pay to see a khaki comedy with *The Army Game* free on TV?" Believe me, I'm not crowing over those who were wrong. I've been superbly wrong myself – most recently, when I declared, "No one will want to see the eighth remake of *Titanic*."'

Although Peter remains cagey about the suggestion, he does not deny that the success of *Carry On Sergeant* may well have been partially attributable to the fact that three of the major cast members from *The Army Game* appear in the film. It certainly didn't do any harm, of that everyone agrees. And it certainly didn't harm the late actor Norman Rossington who, when interviewed in 1998, recalled:

'I had been appearing in *The Army Game* on television when, out of the blue, I received a letter on 29 January 1958, which said that from mid March they wouldn't be renewing my contract. I don't know if Gerald, Peter and Norman Hudis created *Carry On Sergeant* with *The Army Game* in mind, but when they heard I was sacked they asked me to play Herbert Brown. We started filming on 24 March 1958 at the Queen's Barracks in Guildford. While I was filming, Granada had loads of mail complaining that I had been taken out of *The Army Game*, and I was reinstated. After the success of *Carry On Sergeant*, I got £50.00 an episode – up from £33.00 a fortnight.'

During the making of *Carry On Sergeant*, Peter sent copies of the day's filming – 'rushes' – up to London to Nat Cohen and Stuart Levy, the bosses of Anglo Amalgamated. After they had viewed them, Peter received frantic calls from Nat Cohen demanding to know what the devil Peter thought he was doing – that there was nothing funny in what they had watched. Peter remained calm: 'I realized they had never seen rushes before. Later, I discovered that they'd never seen a "fine cut" either, that is the finished film before the music or sound-effects track have been added.'

Peter stopped sending the rushes to London and told them to wait for the finished film. They either trusted him or didn't, but they didn't bother him again.

There may have been little laughter up in London, but at Pinewood and on location at Guildford Barracks, in nearby Surrey, the behind-the-scenes camaraderie, which was to become an intrinsic part of the success of the *Carry On*s, was in place almost from the word go. There was an occasional exception: the actor Patrick Newell (who went on to play 'Mother' in the cult television series *The Avengers*) was supposed to appear as one of the recruits in the *Carry On* film, but as Peter recollects:

'He was quite a posh chap. He turned up for the first morning of filming at Guildford Barracks in his Rolls-Royce, and caught sight of the sergeant who was going to drill the actors to make them look convincing on screen. Unfortunately, it turned out to be the same sergeant Patrick had suffered under when he was serving in the army. "There's no way I'm going to be drilled by him again," he said, and he promptly got back in his car and drove off. He never did appear in the film.'

Following Gerald Thomas's call of 'cut', after filming the infamous scene where the incompetent recruits have to make their way round the army assault course, Bob Monkhouse became the first of the stars to suffer the practical jokes played on actors by other cast members. In the film, the national servicemen had just swung across a muddy ditch on a rope. The punchline was Charles Hawtrey swinging across, but not getting to the other side. He hangs over the mudbath and, eventually, lands right in it. Bob wasn't required to make the jump, but, when the cameras stopped rolling, decided to give it a try. Peter recalls the fun:

'He grabbed hold of the rope and off he went. Immediately he started to slide down it. He frantically tried to hold on, but couldn't get a grip. The harder he tried, the further down he seemed to slide. He ended up plunging into the mud. The crew were laughing so hard that, unfortunately, no one thought of leaving the film to run and capture the scene. That would certainly have been one for the archives. It transpired afterwards that while Charlie Hawtrey was being carefully helped out of the ditch, Kenneth Williams had smeared butter on the rope. After that, he spent the entire film calling Bob Monkhouse, Mr Bob Mudhouse.' The recruits in the film may have appeared incompetent, but the cast most definitely were not. Peter's original plan for the climactic sequence, which shows the cast confidently marching round the drilling square, was to use a real squad with close-up shots of the actors' faces to imply that it was them on parade. He did not, it seems, have confidence in the skills of the regimental sergeant major, who, believe it or not, was named Tommy Atkins. According to Peter he was the shortest soldier anyone had ever seen, but he took the actors aside and drilled them one to one. Peter admits:

'After an hour or so, you wouldn't have known them from regulars – except, of course, for Charles Hawtrey. He never really mastered the arms drill, but he did it in such a way that you didn't noticed the difference. Whether he did it for comedy effect, I don't know. Being an actor, and wanting to upstage others, it is possible that he tried to make himself noticeable, but it didn't work. The other actors certainly outshone some of the real squaddies.'

All did not run completely smoothly, though. For the actual passing-out parade there was no military band available on the day of filming. Peter thought quickly and brought in a women's band: 'We had one of the ATS bands – and very good they were too.'

The weather in April 1958 was also unseasonably warm. As the final scenes for the film of the recruits' passing-out parade were being set up, some of the extras did literally that. It had become so hot by midday that a few army band members, bedecked in their glorious uniforms and brandishing their heavy instruments, couldn't stand on the spot any longer waiting for the word 'action', and collapsed. Peter claims that if you watch the film carefully you can see one or two tottering about, ready to keel over.

The extra uniforms appearing each day also caused some confusion among the officers and troops stationed at Queen's Barracks. Unsure of who was 'real' and who were actors, and unprepared to take the risk and incur the wrath of a 'real' officer, there were many occasions when actors like Eric Barker, who played Captain Potts, or William Hartnell, who played Sergeant Grimshaw, found themselves receiving salutes from those of a lower rank. They politely returned the salutes without saying a word.

When the film was finished, Peter ran it for the staff and management of Pinewood Studios, including many of the people who had worked on it. The private view cinema was packed, with some people standing. The interest was less in the film than everybody wondering whether a 'cheapy' really could be made in a 'Rolls-Royce' studio.

To Peter, the film wasn't cheap. It was made on a modest budget, which finally came in at £74,000 – £1 million today – but to Peter it looked as expensive as any other film costing four times as much. He was, however, a little apprehensive about other people's reactions:

'I didn't know what they were going to think or if they were going to condemn and criticize us just for the sake of it. But, during the film, they never stopped laughing – and that was good enough for me. I sent the film up to London to Nat Cohen and Stuart Levy. The same thing happened at their offices. The film ended up among the top three box-office successes of the year. No one could deny it was a huge hit. Anyone who did, should have attended the Last Night of the Proms that year. The conductor for the evening was Sir Malcolm Sargent, and some wag held up a huge banner on which had been written *Carry On Sargent!*'

The effect of the film spread even to the highbrow charity première of Laurence Olivier's melodramatic film *The Devil's Disciple*. In a particularly tense sequence, a redcoat officer turns to his non-commissioned officer and mutters the immortal words, 'Carry on, Sergeant.' 'The whole audience roared with laughter!' Peter recalls with glee.

There are those who argue that the *Carry On* film series actually started with the second film, *Carry On Nurse* After all, when *Carry On Sergeant* was made, it was just a one-off production. It was only due to its huge success that more of the same was called for, and a regular cast gathered to make similar films on similar subjects with the words *Carry On* in the title.

Certainly, following the success of *Carry On Sergeant*, Peter immediately saw the potential for not just one, but up to six films bearing the *Carry On* prefix. He had the writer, the director, the cast – and now the grudging respect of the industry. He certainly had the respect of Nat Cohen and Stuart Levy at Anglo Amalgamated. But with success comes envy, and Peter found himself fending off an attack from the makers of a film entitled *Carry On Admiral*, made the previous year.

Also a comedy, this film revolved around a drunk MP changing clothes with a naval officer and trying to carry off the act while on board a navy frigate. The film starred David Tomlinson and Peggy Cummins and, coincidentally, future *Carry On* star, Joan Sims. It was written and directed by Val Guest, who started his career writing screenplays for Will Hay in the 1930s, and was still making films almost 50 years later. Having been a fan of *Carry On Admiral*, but especially of Val Guest, Peter had actually approached him to direct *Carry On Sergeant*. Guest, however, wanted too much money, so Peter opted for Gerald Thomas, who was already under contract to him.

There was mooted criticism that Peter had pinched the *Carry On* name from the *Admiral* film, an accusation which Peter says is nonsense: 'The phrase "carry on" was a normal, well-established instruction, barked out by officers up and down the army ranks. We just "borrowed" it. It was actually the late Stuart Levy's idea, although following the success of *Carry On Sergeant*, Nat Cohen insisted it was he who decided that we should use it. Whoever it was, it certainly wasn't taken from the title of *Carry On Admiral*.'

In an attempt to cash in on *Carry On Sergeant*'s success, the makers of *Carry On Admiral* had their film re-released in 1959. It took just £11,000 countrywide: 'People knew it wasn't the real thing,' Peter says with a wry smile. 'Audiences aren't stupid, you know. At least mine certainly aren't.'

Following the success of *Carry On Sergeant*, Peter met up with Nat Cohen and Stuart Levy, who wanted to know what he was going to make next for them. He tried to interest them in a dramatic subject, but they didn't want to know. He then told them that he owned the film rights to a play, *Ring for Catty*, co-written by comedy actor Patrick Cargill (of *Father, Dear Father* fame) and Jack Beale. This play was based on life and death in a sanatorium for patients who were suffering from tuberculosis. It wasn't supposed to be an outright comedy, but it had humour interwoven in the patients' life stories:

'I actually remember going to Anglo and declaring that my next film would be a comedy set in a hospital. I can recall seeing Stuart's beaming smile disappearing immediately, as he moaned, "No, no, no – not that bloody *Ring for Catty* script you've had hanging around. Give us another *Carry On*, and give us one fast."'

Without hesitation, Peter took the idea of *Ring for Catty* and turned it into *Carry On Nurse* – although, by the time it had been under Norman Hudis's surgical knife, nothing remained from the original plot. Shortly afterwards, Peter, sensing the story had not been used properly, turned it into another comedy called *Twice Round the Daffodils*. The writers had no complaints. As Peter remembers:

'Being a writer myself, I always appreciated the work that goes into scripting a story and it became my habit to give writers a percentage of the profits. In this particular instance, because I based two films on one story, Patrick Cargill enjoyed a cut from both productions. He also appeared briefly in two future *Carry On*s as well.'

So, having been given the storyline, Norman Hudis started work on the script for *Carry On Nurse*. His life was made that much easier by having a wife who was a nurse. Rita Hudis was able to give him all sorts of ideas and stories to work on. Rita's experience was called upon once again in the early 1980s, when she became medical consultant on the long-running, hit American TV comedy drama series *M*A*S*H*.

Peter soon became aware that Norman was not finding the writing of *Carry On Nurse* as easy as he had found the writing of *Carry On Sergeant*. When working on the first film, Norman had had six years of army experience to call upon. Now there was another institution due for a mocking, but, even with Rita's help, Norman just didn't have the intimate know-how of the subject. Then, suddenly, as if by auto-suggestion, he was rushed into hospital with acute appendicitis. Here was the opportunity he had needed to witness first-hand the regimentation of our beloved National Health Service, with its stiff rules and even stiffer nurses' hats. Perhaps, most importantly, there was the friendly earthy humour of the men's ward.

When Norman left hospital, he wrote the first draft of the film script for *Carry On Nurse* in super quick time – just over a week. He handed it in on 25 June 1958. Norman Hudis's experiences were dramatized as those of Ted York, played by actor Terence Longdon. York played a journalist who was using his stay in hospital for an appendix operation, making notes for his editor for a series on hospital life.

Peter was more than happy with the results, but wanted some reworking. Norman remembers their early script meetings as being something of an oddity. Both describe these as brief at the outset: 'Let's do one about nurses or teachers,' Peter would say. 'We'll use the same team of actors, of course. You can write anything, Norman, so why bugger about with long conferences. Go away and write it.'

Norman Hudis takes up the story: 'So that's what I did. I wrote it, sent it in, was called to Pinewood, and was almost invariably received with "We're very disappointed." Then came the broad headings of the disappointment. Two phrases stick in my mind to this day: "It's not what we expected," and, from Gerry, "I agree with whatever Peter thinks!" This last line became a joke between us.'

Peter admits he can be exacting. He knows what he wants and how he wants it done. He says that he has a gut instinct for what is funny and what is not. That, added to his natural shyness, is one of the reasons why he has never been able to watch any of his films at a première.

While Norman wrote, Peter was casting for the film. He wanted as many of the same stars as possible from *Carry On Sergeant* – that is, the ones whom he deemed had been the funniest on screen. Naturally, back came Kenneth Connor, Kenneth Williams, Bill Owen, Charles Hawtrey and Hattie Jacques. Norman Rossington, who was now busy again churning out countless episodes of *The Army Game* for Granada Television, returned for a brief cameo. Shirley Eaton was back as the love interest, although this time there was no Bob Monkhouse for her to fall in love with. His place was taken by Terence Longdon, who had also appeared in the first film.

One person Peter could not get was Dora Bryan, who had played Nora, the besotted NAAFI girl, in *Carry On Sergeant*. Dora's stage career was blossoming and she was unavailable. Peter decided to replace her with a young, pretty, comedy character actress whom he had long admired, and who had already starred in several of Betty's films, particularly the *Doctor ...* series, which by now was preparing to shoot its fourth title in six years. The actress's name was Joan Sims, who, ironically, throughout her career has been mistaken for Dora Bryan. As the accident-prone Nurse Dawson, Joan was to make an instant hit and go on to star in 23 of the 29 *Carry On* films that followed.

There were to be two other stars in *Carry On Nurse*, both of whom were to bring to the film some memorable comic moments, with one scene in particular taking pride of place in the annals of British film comedy highlights. The actors were Leslie Phillips as Jack Bell (delivering such immortal lines as 'Ding-dong, you're not wrong', with typical caddish fruitiness) and Wilfrid Hyde-White, whose face turned decidedly red when he heard what Peter Rogers was planning to do with a daffodil. But, by then, it was far too late!

Carry On Nurse began filming at Pinewood Studios on 3 November 1958. For most of the cast it meant spending five weeks in bed. As Leslie Phillips recalls: 'It was an extraordinary experience. I would get out of bed in the morning, put on my clothes, go to the studios, take off my clothes, and get straight back into bed again. When the day was over, I would put my clothes back on, go home, have some dinner and, because of the early starts, go to bed. This went on for over a month. We all had a wonderful time, though. There was so much laughter. It wasn't like a hospital at all. Dear Kenny Williams had me in stitches –

if you know what I mean – he was such a dear funny person. We became quite good friends.'

In his autobiography, published in 1985, Kenneth Williams speaks glowingly of his time working on *Carry On Nurse*, which:

... entailed my first screen love-scene, and since tender and emotional acting was never my forte I was relieved on seeing the rushes that I had carried it off all right. The success was really ensured by my partner, Jill Ireland: she played the role with such vulnerable attractiveness that we couldn't fail. Even so I was particularly gratified when Peter Rogers congratulated me afterwards. Gerald was always encouraging but Peter seldom gave unqualified praise. When he wasn't enthusiastic about a scene he could be disconcertingly frank. Once when an actor complained, "I should have more funny lines – I'm a comedian," he retorted, "Your secret is safe with me," and exited amid a gaggle of giggles.

The early *Carry On* films – or at least those *Carry On* films written by Norman Hudis – relied far less on the use of jokes with a rude double meaning, and an increasing number of shots of scantily clad ladies. The Norman Hudis technique was to put the emphasis more on gags about people in difficult situations, with liberal doses of slapstick thrown in for good measure. Nevertheless, Peter was learning, even at this stage, that the British Board of Film Censors would want changes if it was to pass his films in the lowest 'U' category – suitable for all to see. Peter's battle stretched back to the very first film:

'They had suggested some cuts to *Carry On Sergeant* and, after removing the offending items, Stuart Levy at Anglo just told me to put them back without telling anyone. Can you imagine what would have happened if I had taken his advice? I would never have worked again. Stuart's idea of negotiation was to woo the censor with long liquid lunches and drag him around the local striptease establishments. That probably worked when Anglo were bringing across the more risqué foreign films they liked so much, but I didn't relish that ploy with my films. I may have built the *Carry On*s on innuendo, but they were family entertainment all the way. I wanted our business ideals to reflect that.'

Peter's tactics were clever: 'We would slip in a couple of jokes that we knew would distress the censor. Part of the game was to visit him in his Soho office, feign annoyance at his suggested cuts – nine times out of ten he picked the planted, more obviously saucy gags – and we would then bargain with him. The censor's yardstick was, in fact, quite absurd. He was terrified that if a father watching the film laughed at a naughty joke, his kids would ask him what was so funny and force him into explaining the sexy connotations.

'I remember once that, instead of putting up shots from our film at the trade showing, we simply set up a display of Donald McGill seaside postcards. That was our sort of humour. But it was all part of the fun. The only time the censor really got my goat was when he insisted on a line being removed from a *Carry On* when we knew that a similar joke had been passed in another film two months earlier. The censor's explanation was infuriating – "Oh, but Peter, that was an American film and it cost a lot more money than your film!"'

Perhaps because of the very nature of the subject – a men's ward in a hospital – there were several bones of contention in *Carry On Nurse*. From bedpans, to men away from the comforts of home for long periods of time, from nurses bathing naked men, to frustrated nursing sisters, there were rich pickings for the censor. And Peter learned early on that he could get most of his lines passed, if he was prepared to compromise:

'I remember in *Nurse*, there was a scene where Kenneth Connor's character was arguing with the nurses who wanted to take off his pyjama bottoms. Eventually they whipped them off and he jumped quickly into bed. One nurse then utters, "Never known anyone make such a fuss about such a little thing!" Kenneth was supposed to smile, then look under the sheets somewhat dismayed. The censor was having none of that, of course. He said we could keep the gag as long as we took out the shot of Kenny looking under the sheets. I gave in. People got the gag anyway. So, we got one laugh when, perhaps, we could have had a pair.'

The biggest laugh in *Carry On Nurse* is undoubtedly the scene at the very end. Throughout the film, the character of the colonel, played by great British character actor, Wilfrid Hyde-White, has had all the nurses and orderlies on the hop, ringing the buzzer in his private room to call them in for all sorts of trivialities. They rebel and decide to play a practical joke on the old codger. Enter Hattie Jacques as Matron to discover that the colonel is lying on his front, having his temperature taken, with, of all things, a daffodil placed up his rectum.

Filming the gag wasn't easy, as Peter recalls: 'Poor Hattie got a fit of the giggles – and when one wag on the set made a noise like a champagne cork popping out of a bottle, as she lifted up the daffodil, she was a complete goner. Gerald tried take after take, but she couldn't keep a straight face. We had to abandon the shoot for the day.'

One person who wasn't laughing was Wilfrid Hyde-White. The daffodil-up-the-arse gag was not fully described in the original script, and the actor was not prepared for it. He was not present when Hattie's line and actions were being shot and, therefore, had no knowledge of what was to come. He felt that he had been treated badly, and threatened legal action. Peter reassured him that he had not literally become the butt of an embarrassing joke, and that there would be no actual shot of a bum, Wilfrid's or otherwise. The legal action was dropped and the gag stayed in.

Originally, the daffodil gag had been placed about three-quarters of the way through the film, and the actual ending was meant to have been a romantic conclusion to the love story relationship between journalist-patient Ted York (Terence Longdon) and Nurse Dorothy Denton (Shirley Eaton). Indeed, the editing had gone so far down the line before the change was called for that the music had been added to the soundtrack. Peter, however, having recognized immediately that the daffodil gag was a show-stopper, wanted the scene to be moved to the end of the film. Gerald agreed and the editor was recalled.

Anyone who watches the film might well wonder why the music seems to get unduly louder, almost to a climactic crescendo, when Shirley Eaton and Terence Longdon talk and walk through their final scene. Now you know why: 'It was a daring decision to make, re-editing a film at the last minute,' Peter says. 'Remember we are talking about the late fifties when we could not call upon the new gadgetry at the disposal of today's editors. It meant literally cutting a couple of pieces of film and sticking them together differently. But we knew we had to do it. And I'm very glad we did.'

And glad Peter could afford to be. The film did even better than *Carry On Sergeant* at the box office. It was made for less than *Carry On Sergeant* (around £71,000) and, to date, has recouped its cost more than twelve times. The film was the highest grossing film in Britain in 1959, and the cast knew they were on to a winner.

Leslie Phillips recalls the reaction of a friend who went to see the film with him: 'He was actually my doctor and the man rarely found anything very funny. He certainly didn't have much time for show business. Anyway, I took him to see *Carry On Nurse* and, when he came out he said to me, "Do you know something, Leslie, that is the best film I've ever seen." Believe me, that was praise indeed.'

The success of *Carry On Nurse* extended far beyond these shores. America took the film to its collective bosom and turned it into a massive hit on the other side of the Atlantic. The film had originally been rejected by American Distributors, then one independent company, run by David Emanuel, put it on first in California, then across the States. As a gimmick, he had 2.5 million plastic daffodils made and gave one to each person as they left. It helped spread the word and, except for New York, where it had a gala opening, the film was hugely successful.

Gerald Thomas travelled over to the Big Apple with Shirley Eaton in tow. Peter stayed at home: 'I was naturally disappointed that the film was not doing so well in New York, although it was not made for that type of West End audience. I certainly had no intention of going over for the gala opening. I don't go to premières in this country and I wasn't going to travel several thousand miles, simply not to go to one there.

'To this day, I've never been to America and have no wish to. Noel Coward wrote a song for his revue, *Words and Music*, entitled "I'm the Clergyman Who's Never Been to London". Well, I'm the film producer who's never been to America. Betty went several times and enjoyed it. She loved New York, Hollywood, Las Vegas. I think she enjoyed Canada more and I probably would have too. Betty was a great traveller. She always wanted to see new places, which she did, of course, with all her location shooting.'

Some eight years and twelve *Carry On* films later, Talbot Rothwell paid homage to Norman Hudis's scene-stopper in *Carry On Nurse*. During a scene in *Carry On Doctor*, a nurse, carrying a vase of daffodils, played by Valerie Van Ost, enters the room of private patient Frankie Howerd. She puts the vase down on the locker by the bed and pulls out one daffodil to sniff its scent. Frankie Howerd, getting the wrong idea, says: 'Oh, no, you don't. I saw *that* film!'

Now, how's that for barefaced cheek?

Chapter Eight
Laughing All the Way to the Bank

Following *Carry On Nurse*'s success both at home and abroad, Peter once again approached Anglo Amalgamated with a dramatic subject and, once again, Stuart Levy said, 'No, give us another *Carry On*.' It was at this moment that Peter really began to believe that he could make a series of *Carry On* films. However, in order to make a series, he had to be sure that he could keep a repertory company of players together, to say nothing of a repertory company of key technicians. So, Peter took a gamble and, in front of his bosses, said that he wasn't interested in just another *Carry On*:

'I told Stuart and Nat that I wanted a contract for three more films. Off the top of my head, I recited the subjects and Stuart agreed. I came away with a contract for three films and the 'off' to make a series of *Carry On*s.'

Nat Cohen and Stuart Levy were pleased and excited by the prospect of more success and, having secured Peter's services and the *Carry On* name, they began to build on the idea of a new British comedy series. They made Peter a director of Anglo Amalgamated. Anglo, of course, then expected Peter to move the production of the *Carry On*s to Elstree. And this became something of a running joke: every time Peter started a pre-production on a *Carry On*, Elstree was on the phone: 'We were just wondering if you were bringing this one to Elstree, Mr Rogers.'

The third *Carry On* was *Carry On Teacher*, which began shooting in the second week of March 1959, just under a year after filming had started on the 'one-off' film, *Carry On Sergeant*. Once again, Peter had assembled his regulars – or at least those members of the cast that he wanted to become regulars. Back was Kenneth Williams, Hattie Jacques, Kenneth Connor, Leslie Phillips, Charles Hawtrey and Joan Sims. This time round, they were joined by Ted Ray, a new lead for them, but an old hand to British radio and television comedy. Ted was a huge star in his own right and, in a rare mark of respect, had his own title card in the film's credit sequence, instead of being bunched with five or six others as was the customary style of the *Carry On* series. Peter recalls:

'We made a slight exception with Ted. It is certainly true that I have always said that the biggest star of a *Carry On* film is the title itself and no star's name goes above that, but, on occasions, I was happy to give a special credit to one or two stars. Ted Ray, remember, had been a huge star for over 20 years before he came to us. He had made the whole nation laugh during the war with his own radio shows. I admired his work and was delighted when he agreed to be in our film.'

In *Carry On Teacher*, Ted Ray plays William Wakefield, headmaster at an inner city school, who is looking to spend his twilight years in the profession running a new super-school. Much depends on his ability to prove to visiting inspectors that he is in control of his pupils and his teachers. And so the scene is set.

Norman Hudis presented a script which poked fun at another one of our country's great institutions, and there was the usual mixture of underdogs winning through at the end. Whether it was Kenneth Connor's lovelorn teacher winning the hand of Rosalind Knight's school inspector, or Leslie Phillips' child psychiatrist winning the heart and mind of Joan Sims' PT instructor, or, indeed, Ted Ray's headmaster winning back the respect of the school, which he decides to stay with at the end of the film, *Carry On Teacher* presented some memorable moments both on and off screen.

By now Peter's team was getting used to being in each other's company and the camaraderie shone through. Peter is proud of the bonds which formed so early on: 'They all got on so well – particularly with Ted Ray. He was, after all, the new boy, but the actors in the *Carry On*s were pros who knew another pro when they saw one.'

Ted was certainly a professional joker. Peter remembers the time when Ted approached Leslie Phillips and barked, 'You've got my number!' Bemused, Leslie asked what number. 'That number, UMD 412. That's the number I've always wanted.' Leslie realized that Ted was referring to his car registration. The joke continued throughout the making of the film. Every time Ted went past Leslie, he'd bark out again, 'You've still got that number.'

On the last day of filming, Leslie decided to get his own back, and with Peter's permission got the prop-master to make up a set of car registration plates bearing the number UMD 412. They stuck one on to the back of Ted's car, but didn't manage to get the front one in place before Ted returned to his vehicle. That night, when Leslie was at home, he received a phone call from the police saying they had stopped a man who was claiming to be Mr Ted Ray, and who appeared to be driving his car. 'However,' the policeman added, 'the back of the vehicle appears to be Mr Ray's car!'

Of course, it then clicked for Leslie that it was actually Ted on the phone. According to Peter, Ted had arrived home, driven into his garage and, when he came to close the garage doors, caught sight of the UMD 412 plate.

One of the biggest laughs in *Carry On Teacher* comes from the character Alastair Grigg, played by Leslie Phillips, whose infatuation with Joan Sims' character, Sarah Allcock, leads him to over-pronounce her surname at every available opportunity. The censor was not at all happy and Peter had something of a fight on his hands. The censor was Arthur Watkins, who, ironically, went on to write a play in which Leslie Phillips took the lead role. He saw *Carry On Teacher* and said that he didn't mind the actor looking at the girl, and saying 'Miss Allcock', but he didn't want any emphasis on either the first or the second syllable.

Peter spoke to Leslie and asked him if he could flatten out the pronunciation slightly, so that his voice hit the same level for each part of the word. This was considered to be the only way to avoid any suggestive implications. Leslie was delighted to help: 'I carefully flattened it, but the flatter it got, the dirtier it became. It all seemed very daring in those days. Take a look at it now and it's all very modest really.'

The truth is that there was only one actor who could deliver a line so simply, and yet achieve one of the biggest laughs in the whole of *Carry On Teacher*, and that was Leslie Phillips. Peter Rogers knew it, as did Norman Hudis, which is why the line was written for Leslie in the first place. The line got a huge laugh from audiences and really set the film alight. As for Charlie Hawtrey, he was nearly responsible for the studio being literally set alight.

This occurred when Peter and the rest of the cast were taking a tea-break during filming, and listening to Charlie telling them a story about his early days performing in a West End thriller. Charlie was playing two roles in this serious crime piece – a man and a woman. The distinguished thespian Eric Porter was in the house one evening and came backstage to see him. The actor recalls that Eric congratulated him on a wonderful performance and then said that he was desperately keen to meet the young actress who was playing the stunningly attractive girl in the second half of the play. Without missing a beat, Hawtrey cried, 'Darling, *you have!*'

Anyway, while Charlie was recounting this story, his mother, who regularly visited the set, was enjoying a cigarette and listening so intently that she inadvertently dropped the end of her lit cigarette into her open handbag. As the story continued, smoke was seen coming out of the bag. Joan Sims, who was the first to spot what had happened, cried out, 'Charlie, Charlie, your mother's bag is on fire!' Without pausing for breath, Charlie tipped what was left of his tea into the bag, snapped it shut and carried on the conversation as though nothing had happened. It was a definitive sign of his eccentricity.

At the conclusion of filming *Carry On Teacher*, Peter got the cast and crew together for a special thank-you party at a hotel in Harrow. The cast secretly decided to thank Peter and Gerald by presenting them each with a gift. Leslie Phillips was chosen to go and buy some special cufflinks for the guests of honour; and Ted Ray delivered a speech which he had written entirely in verse, and which he presented to them as an illuminated address. When the party came to an end at the hotel, they all decamped to Kenneth Connor's home nearby and continued singing and joking well into the next day.

Carry On Teacher was another huge success, and it looked as though Peter had found his dream team. Unfortunately, Ted Ray had performed so well as the anchor man in *Teacher* that it upset ABC at Elstree to whom he was actually contracted. When ABC discovered that Peter wanted to make Ted a regular *Carry On* cast member, they told Peter to drop him. It was a terrible blow, not just professionally – Ted was an obvious asset to Peter's films – but emotionally. The two men had become firm friends, and it was not the sort of news Peter wanted to break to Ted.

Peter protested, but ABC threatened to discontinue the release of Anglo Amalgamated films if the *Carry On*s starred Ted Ray. Peter later discovered that the fly in the ointment was the casting director at ABC, who, it transpired, was embarrassed because he had had Ted Ray under contract for several years and had never used him. Finally, acceding to ABC's demands, Ted Ray was dropped from the *Carry On*s after just one appearance.

Ironically, both his sons were also to have brief *Carry On* careers – Robin appeared as an assistant shop manager in *Carry On Constable* and Andrew Ray, as well as appearing in Peter's production of *Twice Round the Daffodils*, had a featured role in two of the 1975 *Carry On Laughing* television series.

Ted Ray did, however, take the lead role in Peter's film *Please Turn Over*, made immediately after *Carry On Teacher*. The film was written by Norman Hudis, with the plot revolving around a teenager who writes a sexy best-seller about a dysfunctional family, which the whole town assumes is based upon her own. All the main cast members play two roles – the 'real' family and the family that the daughter has written about.

The film was directed by Gerald Thomas, and among the cast joining Ted Ray were Leslie Phillips, Charles Hawtrey and Joan Sims, who Peter insists literally stole the film with her portrayal of the family charlady:

'Joan was brilliant. She'd stand there as this maid, fag hanging out of her mouth, hair in a bun covered by a scarf or whatever, and trussed up in her faithful pinny. When the family weren't around, she would nick their booze. It was archetypal stuff and Joan played it so well. Of course, she then had to become this sexy French maid when she played the character from the daughter's novel. Well, the change couldn't have been more different. She was convincing as both. More importantly, she was funny as both.'

Please Turn Over was a *Carry On* in all but name. Peter was to make several comedies over the next few years, all of which could have been *Carry Ons* by virtue of the writer, cast, crew and director all being the same, but he decided not to flood the market. As it was, he was already making almost two *Carry Ons* a year. Then Anglo Amalgamated started to have problems with the cinema owners. They wanted to leapfrog the current Peter Rogers' release and wait for the latest *Carry On*, which they knew was being shot at Pinewood. Stuart Levy had to tell them that if they didn't take the current Peter Rogers film, they wouldn't get the new *Carry On*. It was a bluff, of course, because Anglo depended on the exhibitors as much as the exhibitors depended on Anglo, but the bluff worked and Peter's films continued to get showings, *Carry On* or not.

With Ted Ray now out of the running for another *Carry On*, Peter had to find a new lead actor to take his place. His initial thought was to try to widen the national appeal of the *Carry On* series, and to consider Scottish comedian Chic Murray. But he abandoned this idea in favour of one of the nation's favourite comedy character actors, Sid James. It was inspired casting.

Since arriving in Britain from South Africa after the war, Sid had appeared in fairly minor roles in the majority of the 80 or so films he had acted in. But, by the mid 1950s, he had become a huge hit on radio, starring alongside Tony Hancock. It was in *Hancock's Half Hour*, both on radio and television, that he started working with fellow *Carry On* stalwarts, Hattie Jacques and Kenneth Williams. Peter – along with the rest of the nation – could see how well they had all bonded.

Peter also had first-hand experience of Sid's film skills. The actor had worked on Betty Box's and Ralph Thomas's reworking of the Alfred Hitchcock classic, *The 39 Steps*. But, more importantly, Sid had shone in a comedy role as a police constable in Betty Box's *Upstairs and Downstairs*, which had been released earlier in 1959. All in all, he seemed a natural choice for Peter's new film.

Filming for *Carry On Constable* began in the second week of November 1959, in order that actors with pantomime commitments could whip off the six-week filming schedule before dress rehearsals for the pantomimes kicked in. For all its importance in the longevity of *Carry On* comedy, this police film looked, for a while at least, as though it would not get off the drawing board. The *Carry On* formula was to pick an institution, such as army, hospital, school, and so on, and poke a bit of fun at it.

Peter chose the police for this production and Norman Hudis, who was having trouble finding any inspiration, arranged to spend a week with the officers at the police station in Slough. Witnessing serious criminals at work – and some of the aftermath of their handiwork – put Norman off the whole idea. He became convinced that writing a comedy on the police was almost impossible.

Peter advised him to take a break from the idea, work on something else and then come back to it. He did. In fact, *Carry On Constable* was originally to have been made before *Carry On Teacher*. The break did Norman good. As soon as *Carry On Teacher* was out of the way, he sat himself down and watched several episodes of the classic BBC police series *Dixon of Dock Green*, starring the ever-loveable Jack Warner as the friendly bobby on the beat, PC George Dixon.

Then, having found his inspiration, he wrote *Carry On Constable* in just a couple of weeks, with a storyline revolving around the basic plot of a host of incompetent police recruits – played by the usual suspects,

Kenneth Williams, Kenneth Connor and Leslie Phillips – drafted into a station when the local PCs all go down with flu.

For the outdoor scenes of the young constables on duty, Peter chose the streets of Ealing. Always aware of the cost of exterior location filming, and the possibility – especially in November – that the weather might not be kind, Peter liked to make sure that his cast and crew were never more than a couple of miles from Pinewood. Then, if things turned bad, everyone could up sticks and return to the studios where a scene could be filmed at short notice on the sound stages. Peter loathed wasting a day's shooting.

As with *Carry On Sergeant*, the cast were dressed in realistic uniforms. In this, the first *Carry On*, there were many occasions when, as already mentioned, 'acting' officers were saluted by squaddies who were unable to tell the difference between them and the real thing. This time round, it was the general public who were fooled by the policemen's uniforms. Occasionally, it could cause problems. As Peter recalls:

'I remember one day when Kenneth Williams was standing on the corner of a street, waiting for Gerald Thomas to call "action" from some distance away. He was approached by a woman who thought she had recognized him: "Don't I know you?" she asked. Kenneth tried to be polite and replied, "I'm so sorry, but, if you don't mind, I'm being directed." "Why?" asked the woman, "are you lost, dear?"

'Later that day, Kenneth filmed the scene where he took a scatty old lady, played by the wonderful Esma Cannon, across the busy High Street against her will. A real old lady witnessed what he had done and, unaware of the filming, asked if he wouldn't mind helping her across the busy road, which he promptly did.'

On more than one occasion during the filming, the stars almost landed Peter Rogers in trouble with the police. Leslie Phillips and Kenneth Williams enjoyed stepping out into the middle of the busy High Street, lifting their hands and stopping the traffic for no reason. After a few seconds, they would then wave everyone on. No one questioned them. They were, after all, 'policemen'. But Peter, who had to seek permission to film his actors dressed as bobbies on the street, knew they were treading a fine line, and that if they were reported, it would mean the end of filming. He was immensely relieved, therefore, when the cast were back at Pinewood filming the interior sequences.

Carry On Constable was the first of the film series to show any nudity, although, unlike the more permissive entries of the late 1960s, it was just a quick flash of bum from the raw – in more ways than one – coppers, Leslie Phillips, Kenneth Williams, Kenneth Connor and Charles Hawtrey. The scene involved the constables gathering in a shower which, when turned on, shot out a blast of freezing water. They then dash out of the shower, grabbing their towels as they do so, and run towards the cells where, due to lack of police accommodation, they are having to live. They are unaware that a woman drunk, played by Joan Hickson, is in an adjacent cell and, as they approach at great speed, they catch a glimpse of her and Joan Sims as WPC Passworthy. They turn around and dash away. Hence the flash of bum.

According to Peter, the censor gave them fewer problems with this scene than some of the stars and crew: 'Oh, the censor was fine. He just wanted the shot trimmed back slightly so we didn't show too much arse. The problem started with Charles Hawtrey, who wasn't too keen about baring his all. He was concerned about how white he looked and that his bum would flare on camera. I said we'd get make-up to put some powder on all their arses. A few of them moaned a little about it, but no more than the make-up man, George Blackler. He said he had made up some of the finest faces in the business, including Margaret Lockwood's and Jean Kent's, and that he had now really reached the bottom!'

To get the desired effect and stop the flaring, the men were placed face down on tables so that the make-up could be applied evenly. Leslie Phillips didn't know whether to laugh, cry or complain, but suggested they should all make a stand, which lightened the atmosphere and got everyone laughing. Once the filming started, the final take was delayed by Joan Sims, who kept laughing as she made her entrance. The sight of the made-up bums was just too much for her.

Gerald also took longer than usual to set up the shot so that nothing would accidentally appear on screen which shouldn't, and cause the whole scene to be taken out of the film. He told Peter he wanted the extra time, and that it would be worth it as it was one of the funniest scenes in the film. Peter agreed. They were both right. The audiences loved it.

Just as things seemed to be going smoothly, Peter was summoned to Equity, the trade union representing actors and actresses, in St Martin's Lane. He was bemused as to what the union could want with him. He was always fair, and, while he may not have paid over the odds for actors, he certainly never paid less than union rates. He was sensible with the distributor's money, but never stingy. Preparing to deflect any

TOP: The Rogers family in 1921: seven-year-old Peter sitting with his mother, Alice; and father Claude between Peter's two brothers, twin brother Paul (left) and older brother Franklyn (right).

LEFT: A marriage made in cinematic heaven – Peter with his beloved wife Betty E Box in the late 1940s.

FAR LEFT: Peter at the beginning of his film production career in a post-war publicity pose.

LEFT: Betty and Peter relax in her flat in Lancaster Gate in the late 1940s.

BELOW: An informal shot at Peter and Betty's Mill Hill home used for the couple's Christmas card in 1960.

LEFT: Peter and his director Gerald Thomas (left) with their teen-idol star, Tommy Steele, for *The Duke Wore Jeans* publicity in 1958.

TOP: Running a happy ship – the cast and crew for Peter's 1960 naval 'epic' *Watch Your Stern*.

RIGHT: Peter with *Watch Your Stern* star, Kenneth Connor, during a break from filming.

OPPOSITE: Peter celebrates at an after-shoot party with Joan Sims, as Hattie Jacques looks on.

THIS PAGE: The bosses of Anglo Amalgamated visit the sets; Stuart Levy (top), *Carry On Regardless* (1961) and Nat Cohen (right) with Kenneth Williams, *Carry On Jack* (1963).

COME UNTO US ALL YOU WHO ARE HEAVY LADEN

ABOVE: The producer and director with the cast of *Carry On Again Doctor* (1969). Left to right: Sidney James, Joan Sims, Peter Rogers, Gerald Thomas, Barbara Windsor, Charles Hawtrey, Kenneth Williams, Hattie Jacques and Jim Dale.

RIGHT: Phil Silvers celebrates his birthday on Camber Sands with Peter and Gerald during the filming of *Follow That Camel* (1967).

accusations that may be made against him, he worked out exactly what he paid every member of his cast and crew.

His preparation, however, was to count for nought. He could not have been more surprised by their accusations against him. He was told that one or two young ladies were complaining that they had been invited to a private apartment, owned by Peter Rogers, to give an audition for a spanking scene in a *Carry On* film.

Now, although Dilys Laye may have wanted a quick spank from Sid James in *Carry On Cruising*, Peter's films didn't go in for that sort of action. He did not know whether to take their comments seriously or not. He was about to make a joke of it all when he realized the Equity officials were taking it all very seriously. Peter protested that he didn't even have an apartment. He only had a home with his wife, Betty.

It later transpired that there was a television producer with an almost identical name to 'Mr Carry On' himself, and it was this 'gentleman' who was holding the auditions. The only way Peter could combat the complaints before they did serious, irreparable damage to him and his career, was to take out a full-page advertisement in *The Stage*. In this, he pointed out that he was the only person casting for *Carry On* films, and that all his auditions were carried out at Pinewood Studios.

What upset Peter more than anything was the fact that he always took time to look after the ladies in the cast. He preferred the company of women and his good looks made him popular among the female stars and extras alike. Most people were friendly and called him Peter, some even had his home phone number. As Peter recalls: 'One of them rang me up in the middle of the night – about three o'clock in the morning – saying that Nat Cohen had called her and wanted her to go round to his flat. If she didn't, she might not be in any more *Carry On*s. I told the girl to take no notice, that Nat had probably gone home after a successful game of poker, had probably had a drink too many, and that he must have been joking. I knew he wasn't, of course, and promised the girl that she would definitely be in the next *Carry On*.'

The actress had longer to wait than she might have expected. Almost as soon as the custom had been established, the production of two *Carry On*s a year stopped, with the next one not being made for over a year. That had not been Peter's intention. As ever, he continued to come up with ideas for his scriptwriter to work on. While one *Carry On* was being made, Peter always ensured that the next title was ready to be written.

There was talk of two *Carry On*s for Norman Hudis to script. The first was *What a Carry On*, one of the original titles that Peter had mentioned to Nat Cohen and Stuart Levy when he delivered his wish-list for a series of films a year earlier. But this film never got much further than the pre-production development stage. Its basic premise was a series of sketches, with the characters finding themselves in all sorts of troublesome situations. Just what linked the sketches together, to give it a cohesive feel of being a film and not a review show, had not been worked out before the project was put temporarily to one side.

The theme was returned to a year later, when Norman wrote *Carry On Regardless*, about the working lives of a group of out of work misfits who find themselves thrown together at the Helping Hands Agency – a business which sends them all out on individual assignments to help clients in need of a particular service, whether walking a pet chimp, cleaning a house or translating the foreign ranting of an outraged housewife.

Peter then got Norman to work on a script for *Carry On Flying*, to be based on the exploits of the Royal Air Force. Constantly wary of anything that might potentially damage the reputation or the box office of his films, he soon withdrew that idea as well. Peter's major fear was the risky subject matter. He hated the idea that, between the making and showing of the film, there could be a plane crash which would make a comedy appear in very bad taste and force the film to be withdrawn.

For the same reason he did not proceed with an idea by writer Michael Pertwee that year. The potential film was called *Carry On Smoking*, about the lives of firefighters. What if a major tragedy hit the headlines at that time? Again, the film would have to be withdrawn on grounds of respect and decency.

So, although *Carry On Constable* was released early in the year, 1960 remained minus a *Carry On* in the sense of Peter Rogers' production company actually making a film. There were, however, two productions put into action by Peter that year. The first was a naval comedy called *Watch Your Stern*. This film traded on the success of *The Navy Lark*, a BBC radio comedy show, which had initially starred Dennis Price and Jon Pertwee and had started in 1959. The series enjoyed its own popular spin-off film version in 1959, with a cast that included the *Carry Ons*' very own Hattie Jacques.

The script was written by Alan Hackney and Vivian Cox, Peter's long-time friend and witness at his wedding. Peter also cleverly cast one of his popular team of actors, the lovable rogue Leslie Phillips – who had appeared in both the radio and film versions of *The Navy Lark* – alongside his other regular comedy repertory ensemble. Kenneth Connor starred as the accident-prone Seaman Blissworth, with supporting turns from Eric Barker, Hattie Jacques, Joan Sims – and Sid James, sporting the most unconvincing beard in British cinema history:

'Well,' says Peter, 'he could have grown the real thing, but unfortunately it was only needed for about half of the film, at which point the plot demanded he shave it off. Since scenes are rarely shot in the order in which they are finally cut together, we might have filmed one sequence two-thirds of the way through the film near the beginning of the schedule. Try growing a beard that quickly! Anyway, I thought his beard looked just fine.'

The film's plot was another example of a comedy of errors, performed by a group of misfits who pull through in the end. It may not have been a *Carry On*, but Peter was happy to milk the popularity of the films, without directly announcing a connection with the series. The publicity slogan for *Watch Your Stern* read: *The Latest and FUNNIEST of a Great Line of British Comedy Hits!* The publicity material was half right. It was the latest Peter Rogers production, but it wasn't the funniest. As with *Carry On Admiral*, audiences knew the real thing and, somehow, *Watch Your Stern* wasn't it.

Norman Hudis, meanwhile, had been working on another script, which was filmed and released that year under the title *No Kidding*. This now rarely broadcast movie tells the story of a group of wealthy but neglected children, who spend time at an old house which is turned into a holiday home for their visit. Again, Peter cast Leslie Phillips, this time in the lead role.

The film was an agreeable comedy, but didn't capture the people's imagination. In its first week in Plymouth, it only took £8. Norman thought the film was quite good but began to realize later why it had not been a success: 'I was pleased with one line: "Why do people who want to save the world, always start by neglecting their own children?" Years later, when I was at Universal in America, I pitched a storyline of the daughters of 12 millionaires who were kidnapped simultaneously. American director Mervyn Le Roy instantly retorted, "People don't care about the problems of rich kids." I wish we had all realized that at the time – no kidding!'

Ironically, the house which was used in *No Kidding* was soon to become Peter and Betty's own home. The couple had spent much of their early married life together at their first real home in Mill Hill. The house itself had originally belonged to Betty's brother, Sydney. As the couple became busier in their respective careers, the roads did too. It was becoming impossible to get to Pinewood. What started off taking 30 minutes for the 20-mile journey had now doubled and was getting worse.

The couple considered a helicopter. There was some wonderful grassland in northwest London, and Pinewood certainly had enough space to accommodate one. They soon realized, however, that by the time they got clearance to fly each day, it would probably have taken longer than the driving itself. And anyway, Pinewood was not keen on the idea. So Peter and Betty went house-hunting.

Peter remembered the vacant house, just outside Beaconsfield, in which he had filmed *No Kidding,* and wondered if it was still empty. It had originally belonged to a South African couple, who had built it in the 1930s. They had spent so much time working on the house – and it had grown so large – that when it came to actually occupying it they sold up and moved to something smaller. It then became the Princess Marina's Children's Home. When that worthwhile cause moved out, the property was left empty.

The house had eight bedrooms, almost as many bathrooms, and what seemed like miles of corridors. Peter and Betty thought it would be far too big for them. Then they saw the circular drawing-room, the 12 acres of land that went with the property, and the huge paddock and stables which would be ideal for their horses. They fell in love with it. When they came to put an offer in, however, they found that they were too late: actor and close friend Dirk Bogarde had got there first.

Dirk renamed the house Drummer's Yard. There was a tradition in the French theatre that, at the beginning of a play, a boy would come on stage and beat a long stick on the floor three times before the performance began. The boy was known as the Drummer. Dirk, being a fan of the theatre and knowing that the house had previously been a children's home, simply renamed it Drummer's Yard.

Peter and Betty were invited there regularly for meals. Every time they visited, Peter said, 'If you ever want to sell up, Dirk, please tell us first.' Just one year later, Dirk did just that. The house had been in need of some repair, and he and his partner had spent considerable sums of money doing it up. Additionally, the cost of the central heating was horrendously expensive.

Along with Peter and Betty went their animals – the horses, a pit pony and, of course, Peter's beloved dogs. The house and its vast gardens became a haven for all sorts of wildlife, and the couple spent the warm summer evenings on the patio drinking wine, while around them, squirrels and white pigeons fought for their attention and the scraps supplied by their generous hosts.

Peter loved the countryside. It reminded him of his childhood days in Kent. At night, while Betty slept, he would lie awake with the windows open, listening to the sound of birdsong: 'One certainly didn't get that in Mill Hill,' he quips. 'One night I was convinced that I had heard a nightingale. I had always thought them to be magical birds and was so pleased that I woke Betty up. I asked her if she could hear the bird. She said she couldn't and went back to sleep. I woke her up twice more and still she couldn't hear it. I was very frustrated – wanting to share my find with her. My frustration turned to extreme disappointment when I realized that it wasn't a nightingale, but Betty, who was fast asleep and whistling through her nose!'

At weekends, Peter would set about organizing their new home to the couple's liking. The white pigeons had become something of a feature in the garden, so a huge dovecote was erected to accommodate them. Within weeks, the dozen or so creatures had either mated very quickly or called in their friends, because suddenly there were a hundred of them. Worst of all, they had fleas, which when the weather grew hot and the balcony doors and bedroom windows were opened, invaded the house.

At first, Betty blamed Peter for the flea invasion. He had rescued a mongrel bitch, which he had found abandoned in a hedgerow with her pups. But it soon became clear that the pigeons were to blame. Not usually a violent man, Peter volunteered to shoot at them to frighten them off. He took his shotgun and blasted it in their direction from the window of his bedroom. He wasn't actually trying to kill them, just frighten them away, but he hit one of the birds on the lawn. He rushed out to see if it was still alive. The lead shot had damaged the bird's wing and it was trying in vain to fly.

Peter picked it up, dashed back to the house and, placing it in one of Betty's hat boxes, force-fed it some brandy for the shock. He then called out the vet, who looked after the creature at great expense for six weeks. Duly recovered, the bird was reunited with its flea-ridden friends.

Next, Peter tried to do away with the pigeons in a more painless fashion. He picked up some chemicals from the vet and added this to their food. The chemicals drugged them and soon the lawn was littered with semi-comatose birds. Betty and Peter quickly loaded them into laundry baskets and placed them in the car.

They drove over 30 miles away to the far end of Aylesbury. By now the birds were getting restless and were eager to be released from their uncomfortable captivity. They let them go in the woods. Peter was delighted to see the back of them. And that was that ... until they got home: 'Would you believe it, they were all back again. They couldn't have followed us because, with heavy traffic holding us up, they got home before we did!'

Peter's final solution was to close up the entrances to the dovecote and stop feeding the pigeons. Slowly the creatures began to leave. Many ended up in his neighbour's garden: 'We weren't too concerned about that. They had a heron which kept flying into our garden and stealing the fish from our pond, so I guess that made us even.'

The day after New Year's Day, 1961, *Carry On Regardless* went into production at Pinewood Studios. The team were back together again. Well, almost. Leslie Phillips, worried that he would become typecast as a perpetual member of *Carry On* films, suddenly decided to leave the team. He loved the films and he loved working for Peter and to this day, they remain good friends. But in 1961, following three *Carry On* appearances – and several other productions for Peter – he decided it was time to go.

Peter was naturally upset: 'Leslie was a great bonus to the films in the early days. I was so sad that he decided to leave us. I know he went on to work with Betty on several more occasions, and I really wish he had found time to work with us some more. That man remains one of the most professional people in the business.'

Leslie remembers his time on those early productions with great affection: 'They were such fun to make. We always laughed – particularly Kenny Williams. We had a lot of fun together – although he could be difficult. I always like to have a bit of peace before I do a take – time to compose myself, so I can hopefully get it right the first time. But with the *Carry On* crew it was almost impossible to get any peace. One day I had a lot to do in a scene and Kenny was messing about. I shouted at him: "For goodness' sake, will you shut up!" He was dumbfounded. He followed me about for days and kept saying, "You do love me really, don't you? You don't really feel like that, do you?" I smiled and said, "Oh, piss off." I never realized just how sensitive he was. He was wonderful. They all were.'

Chapter Nine
The Title Is the Star!

Leslie Phillips may have gone, but Sid James was back for *Carry On Regardless*, along with Kenneth Connor, Charles Hawtrey, Joan Sims, Kenneth Williams – and, in a supporting role due to poor health, Hattie Jacques. This film was a series of sketches concerning the situations that the characters get themselves into while working for Bert Handy (Sid James) and his Helping Hands Agency.

No situation was too outlandish for scriptwriter Norman Hudis to squeeze a laugh out of – whether it was Charles Hawtrey caught up in a boxing match, or Kenneth Connor, as the bumbling Sam Twist, getting into a state when arriving for an evening's babysitting only to find voluptuous 'mother' (Fenella Fielding) awaiting him. This risqué gag is centred around the fact that the breathy vamp doesn't actually have a child, and wants to use Kenneth as a tool to make her neglectful husband (Ed Devereaux) take some notice of her.

This scene, one of the funniest in the film, was scissored by the British Board of Film Censors. In Norman Hudis's original script, when Fenella, in full sexual flow, is trying to talk Kenneth into helping her, she protests, 'Oh, please, Mr Twist, don't make it hard for me!' Kenneth's response is, 'As a matter of fact, madam, you're making it a little bit hard for me!' This was too much for the censor, so the offending word 'hard' was replaced and the joke was lost.

Carry On Regardless unwinds into a jolly series of loosely connected skits and comic sketches, with the action moving swiftly from one scene to another. Peter gathered an amazing array of British comedy actors and actresses to play even the smallest of roles. The cast included ITMA radio favourite Molly Weir, the gobbledegook-talking Stanley Unwin, Norman Wisdom's stooge Jerry Desmond, the ever-reliable Nicholas Parsons, boxer Freddie Mills and even Patrick Cargill, co-author of *Ring for Catty* – the play which launched a thousand quips in *Carry On Nurse*.

It should also have included veteran actress Eleanor Summerfield, but as Peter remembers: 'Poor Eleanor had this wonderful scene with Charles Hawtrey when he was delegated [by the Helping Hands Agency] to sit in her bedroom while her husband was away and write down everything she said in her sleep. There is a whole comedy of misunderstanding revolving around her trying to get Charlie into her bedroom. It was great fun. But the censor wanted too many cuts and it ruined the whole scene. In the end, we just took the whole sequence out.'

The departure of Leslie Phillips was just one of two major rewriting problems that had to be quickly overcome. Peter and Norman worked together on cutting back the fairly major role that Leslie was meant to have had as the upper-class Montgomery Infield-Hopping in *Carry On Regardless*. Having trimmed back the part as much as possible, Terence Longdon took over. Annoyingly for Leslie, it didn't seem to matter to the press whether he was in a *Carry On* film or not. A Bristol newspaper reviewed *Carry On Regardless* and gave him a roasting for his performance – and he wasn't even in it!

The next problem arose when Hattie Jacques fell ill and was unable to take on the part of Delia King. Again, hasty rewriting was the order of the day, but, this time, the character could not be cut back because, on top of the Leslie Phillips cuts, this would have meant that the film would have run short. Delia King, therefore, was rewritten as a more sexy voluptuous character, and Peter cast Liz Fraser in the role.

Despite being unwell, Hattie still wanted to make an appearance in the film, so a small cameo part was written, with her playing, quite fittingly, a hospital sister to Joan Hickson's matron. This was a complete role reversal for the two ladies who, in the earlier *Carry On Nurse*, had respectively played matron and sister.

Staff illness, just before filming was due to start, was something that Peter could manage with a bit of hasty reworking, but nothing could have prepared him for the injury that Kenneth Williams inflicted on himself while filming *Carry On Regardless*. Kenneth and Joan Sims were in a scene which involved their characters assisting in a department store – Kenneth was demonstrating toys and Joan was showing off negligees. Kenneth was supposed to shoot off the end of a seesaw, when Charles Hawtrey falls off a ladder – from which he has been demonstrating the latest safest way to clean windows – and lands on the other end of it.

While waiting on a high rostrum, securely tied to a rope, and nervously awaiting Gerald Thomas's cry of 'action' (the film could then be reversed to make it look as if he shot off the seesaw rather than jumped on to it as it was filmed), Kenneth tripped and fell. He let out a terrible cry. Peter takes up the story:

'He was clutching his private parts and yelling that he'd grazed his penis. I sent him off to the first-aid department and we carried on filming. After he had been gone for some time, he was needed back on set, so I went to look for him. When I arrived at the first-aid room, there he was lying on his back, with the ugliest nurse I have ever seen slapping liberal quantities of Savlon on his affected part. He didn't seem to be in any pain. In fact, he looked as if he was enjoying the experience. I said, "Come on Kenny, that's quite enough of that." And he rather reluctantly returned to work.'

There was one occasion during the making of *Carry On Regardless* when Peter genuinely feared for Kenneth Williams' safety. It occurred during the scene of Kenneth walking the chimpanzee, when the cast and crew were out filming on the streets of Windsor. For the scene, Kenneth had to escort the animal from the front door of a house, down a flight of stairs and into the street. Simple.

Kenneth stood in the hallway of the Georgian house, holding the chimp's hand, waiting for his cue from director Gerald Thomas. Suddenly the chimp picked up an iron doorstop and started flailing its arms about, smashing pictures on the wall. Kenneth froze to the spot and was spattered with glass. Eventually, having managed to restrain the chimpanzee, Kenneth was able to respond to Gerald shouts of 'action'. Down the stairs he and the chimp came, and up the street they went. 'Cut', called Gerald.

Both he and Peter wanted to know why it had taken Kenneth so long to come out of the house. 'We were convinced he had been larking about,' remembers Peter. 'I was shocked when I heard what had happened. I had to go and see the owners of the house, apologize profusely, and assure them that I would pay for any damage caused. Now you know why we always say in the business that you should never work with children or animals.'

In the same scene, Kenneth has to hail a London cab and ask the driver to take them both to the zoo. The driver, played by former cabbie and bit-part actor, Fred Griffiths, says to Kenneth, 'I'll take you, but not your brother.' For years, Norman Hudis, who was never on set during filming, assumed that Fred had thrown in the ad-lib himself. The line had certainly never appeared in the script. But it was actually

Peter who, seeing the opportunity for an extra off the cuff gag, quickly wrote it down, and got Gerald to include it in the final version of the film.

The tradition of practical jokes that had established itself with the first *Carry On* film, *Carry On Sergeant*, showed no signs of abating during the fifth *Carry On*. In one sketch, Joan Sims, as Lily Duveen, had to attend a wine-tasting session and act as a hostess. The comedy derives from Miss Duveen's over-indulgence and ensuing drunkenness, which results in her belting Nicholas Parsons, stumbling on Michael Nightingale, insulting that distinguished character actor, Howard Marion Crawford, as the wine-tasting organizer – and generally causing a fracas.

Peter admits that Joan became the latest victim of a *Carry On* practical joke: 'Her white wine was supposed to be water, but we switched the water for neat vodka. She didn't say anything. She obviously knew what we had done, but wasn't going to give in. I made Gerald cut a few times, so that she'd have to keep sipping it. I don't know how much she had or how it affected her, but watch the film – she's either very convincing in the part or very drunk!'

Although Peter was quite happy with the film script, Norman Hudis never felt that *Carry On Regardless* was one of his better pieces of work. Some of the actors, too, were not convinced that it was a particularly good film. In his diary entry for Friday, 17 March 1961, Kenneth Williams wrote: 'Saw *Carry On Regardless* which was quite quite terrible. An unmitigated disaster.' Nevertheless, the film did well at the box office, and more of the same was called for.

Peter's next film, which followed the exploits of a group of music students, was called *Raising the Wind*. This proved to be his favourite non-*Carry On* film, and not just because of the wonderful cast, which included James Robertson Justice, Kenneth Williams, Sid James and a return from Leslie Phillips. The film gave Peter an opportunity to indulge in his passion for music.

The screenplay was written by Bruce Montgomery, who had been the music director and composer for all the *Carry On*s thus far. Bruce had been a music student and many of the ideas for the hysterical goings-on in the film were rehashed from his own experiences. He was also an author of detective novels, writing under the pseudonym Edmund Crispin.

Peter, therefore, had no doubts about giving Bruce a crack at writing the screenplay as well as the music, and admits that the film is a blatant rip-off of his wife's *Doctor in the House*, substituting music students for medical students. Even the exterior location for the music academy was University College Hospital in London's Gower Street, the same location used for *Doctor in the House* and *Doctor At Large*.

Peter, who was always somewhere on set during filming, actually made a particular point of watching the filming of *Raising the Wind*. He had insisted that all the actors who were to be seen using musical instruments had to study for a few weeks beforehand to conquer the basic rudiments and give a convincing portrayal of a real-life performance.

He was also rather pleased with a cameo performance by a budding new star by the name of Jim Dale. Listed 39 out of 41 cast members, his character is known only by the instrument he is playing – the bass trombone. But he has a bit of slapstick comedy in the film when he loses his music and disrupts everyone around him. Jim delivered his final line, 'Oh, I've been sitting on it all the time', in a snide way, which was an exact mimic of Kenneth Williams' 'stop messing about' voice, popular from *Hancock's Half Hour*.

Having done this, Jim thought it might be the end of his film career with Peter and Gerald: 'At the end of the scene, Kenneth walked off the set, and seemed to storm over to Peter and Gerald, looking as if he was complaining. He was really flustered – making his usual flamboyant gestures. And I was the chap he was continually – and animatedly – pointing his finger at. I thought, "This is it!"'

What had actually happened was that Kenneth had gone over to Peter and Gerald and said, 'Anyone who has the cheek to impersonate me must be good. Make sure you use him again.' And that's exactly what Peter did. Jim became a mainstay of the *Carry On*s, making ten films in six years between 1963 and 1969. And Jim and Kenneth became very good friends.

Unfortunately, Bruce Montgomery's relationship with Peter Rogers did not fare as well, and was shortly to end on an off-key note. Bruce had complained on more than one occasion that no one – apart from the BBC – was prepared to commission musical works any more. Peter asked him how much it would cost to commission a cello concerto. Bruce named the figure and Peter paid him, but not one note was ever written:

'If I had had the same deal with Malcolm Arnold, who also wrote for me at that time, I'm sure I would have had a wonderful score. The problem was that Bruce Montgomery was a heavy drinker, who used to drive up to the studios each day from his home in Brixham, Devon. One morning, a strange man led him into my office, explaining that he had discovered Bruce quite drunk by the roadside and given him a lift. After copious helpings of black coffee, Bruce was able to view the film and discuss the type of music I wanted.'

Peter could just about cope with Bruce's drinking, but then found out something else which angered him. He discovered that Bruce was not writing most of his music any more, but was farming it out to another composer, called Eric Rogers. Eric was no relation of Peter's, but Peter knew of him – primarily as a composer and conductor who was called in when anyone wanted dance or jazz music in a film: 'He was a round, jolly fellow who was also a brilliant pianist and clarinettist.'

Bruce Montgomery would only work for Peter for a few months more before Eric Rogers became Peter's full-time music man for his films: 'Incidentally, when I started using Eric Rogers, the Rank Organisation sent me a directive asking me not to use any more of my relatives in my films. Even if I had, so what! Gerald Thomas was Ralph Thomas's brother and they had both worked on Betty's films. The unions even encouraged members to sponsor their relatives rather than strangers into the business. The directive was typical, though, of the Civil Service mentality of the Rank Organisation at the time.'

Irrespective of the problems he had with his musical directors, Peter's passion for music remained unabated. During a rare day off, when he was having a look around Harrods' music department, he came upon a magnificent Bösendorfer piano, which was elaborately decorated with gold figures and standing on huge gilt swans. It was the most ornate piano Peter had ever seen. Peter asked Mr Gold, the manager of the department, about the instrument. Mr Gold informed him that it had been a present from Napoleon III to Empress Eugénie, that the asking price was £3,000 (around £30,000 today), and that an American religious group had expressed an interest in it. Peter explains:

'Over my dead body, I thought, and bought it. It took eight men to carry the thing. A friend of mine visited Harrods not long afterwards and was admiring a display of garden furniture in the entrance hall. She said to a shop assistant that she thought it was all terribly expensive and doubted if anyone would buy it. He said, "You'd be surprised. Some idiot bought that grand piano upstairs." I was *that* idiot.'

Hardly. When, some years later, Bösendorfer was holding an exhibition in Vienna, Peter lent them the piano, and received a telephone call from a man offering £11,000 for it. Peter refused, but told Bösendorfer that he couldn't take the piano back because he and Betty were about to move to a smaller house which couldn't accommodate it since he already had three other pianos and two organs. Bösendorfer put the piano on display in the window of its premises in London's Wigmore Street. It carried a label: 'Property of Peter Rogers'.

When Peter finally agreed to sell the piano, Bösendorfer offered him £5,000 which, after the offer from Vienna, Peter was loath to accept. He went to Christie's, the auction house. The managing director examined it and suggested a reserve price of around £15,000. Peter gave Christie's the go-ahead to sell and then forgot about it:

'At teatime one day, I said to Betty, "Isn't this the day of the auction? I wonder what the piano fetched." Betty phoned Christie's. I heard her say what I thought was 16. When she put the phone down, I said, "So, he wasn't far out when he said 15." "15?" queried Betty. "It reached £65,000." They told her that it had been bought by a European royal. So, who knows, perhaps it went back to the Napoleon family after all that time.'

In late 1961, Peter returned to the story that Anglo Amalgamated had rejected in 1958, in favour of further *Carry On*s. In fact, it was the casting of Patrick Cargill, in *Carry On Regardless*, that had prompted Peter into action. He dug the piece out and began working on it. The tragic-comic outline dealt with life on a tuberculosis ward and, obviously, held strong memories of when Peter was ill in the 1940s. Norman Hudis had used one or two strands of the rejected story in *Carry On Nurse*, but they were barely recognizable from the original and Peter asked him to write the film script for *Twice Round the Daffodils*.

While Peter felt that the film wouldn't have them rolling in the aisles – and it wasn't that kind of film anyway – he knew there was humour to be derived from the human drama and how the characters react within themselves and to others when faced with such an illness and a long stay in a hospital away from loved ones. There were also to be serious episodes in the film, and Peter was careful to choose a cast which didn't look as through it was the *Carry On* ensemble trying to squeeze laughs out of a difficult subject. Such was his respect for Kenneth Williams that, even though Kenneth was renowned for playing outrageous comic characters, he was offered a part in the film, alongside Donald Sinden, Ronald Lewis, Joan Sims, Juliet Mills and Nanette Newman.

As Peter remembers, Kenneth was particularly subdued at this time: 'It may have had something to do with him performing in the West End each night. The lights on the set were quite warm and often the cast had to stay on the set even if they weren't saying anything at that moment – if, for example, we were filming a wide shot or concentrating on one character, with the others in the background. Poor Kenny kept falling asleep, although he insisted he never did. One day we stuck a banana in his hand, attached a rude notice to his pyjamas, and took a picture of him. The next time he denied he had fallen asleep, we pulled it out and showed it to him.'

What little spare time Kenneth did have, he put to good use. He was due to appear in a charity show for the Campaign for Nuclear Disarmament (CND) in the middle of December. Appearing with him was comedy actor Lance Percival, who also happened to be in *Twice Round the Daffodils*. Many was the time that Peter found them huddled in a corner of the sound stage, running through their lines.

Although Anglo Amalgamated was never overly happy with the idea of a film about life on a TB ward, it bowed to Peter's judgement. With the kind of success he had been having, the studio could hardly refuse. Peter, the cast and the crew thought they had put together a good film. But as Norman Hudis recalls, the reaction from some quarters wasn't as welcoming as they had hoped: 'We believed that the subject could include comedy moments because we were under the impression that the disease had been virtually eliminated. It turned out that 5,000 people died of tuberculosis that year. The kindest headline we got was "Carry On Coughing!"'

The first day of January 1962 was the beginning of the end of an era in the *Carry On* story. For, while the cast spent the day being fitted out for costumes at Berman's in central London, Norman Hudis was putting the finishing touches to what would be his last *Carry On*. It wasn't a decision which either he or Peter had officially come to at that stage, indeed they were meant to be working together on another production shortly afterwards. But history was soon to show that *Carry On Cruising* would be Norman's last entry for the series.

Based on a story, by comedy actor Eric Barker (who had suggested a *Carry On* centred around the trials and tribulations of a coaching holiday), the film follows the same sentimental bumbling path as the previous five entries. This time, regular headlining star Sid James was playing the captain of a ship where the crew appear to have left and have been replaced by a bunch of well-meaning incompetents. Sid, of course, is trying to win the captaincy of a new cruise liner and needs to impress the guests.

The film should have been a time of great excitement for cast and crew because, for the first time, *Carry On* was to break into glorious colour, and the proposed budget was hitting a new high with £140,000 put aside for the production. But the weeks leading up to the new *Carry On* proved to be a trying time for Peter.

As mentioned before, he had always made it quite clear to actors and press alike that the real star of the *Carry On*s was the title itself. No actor was ever placed above the title and, with the rarest of exceptions, all the regulars' names appeared together on the title sequences. However, just before filming *Carry On Cruising*, Peter was approached by *Carry On* stalwart Charles Hawtrey, who had other ideas.

In reviewing *Carry On Regardless*, a national paper had written that the star of the film was Charles Hawtrey, and the reviewer couldn't believe that a *Carry On* would ever be the same without him in the cast. Charles went to Peter and demanded that he be given top billing and a star on his dressing-room door. At first, Peter thought he was joking, but he wasn't. Charles claimed that he had every right to top billing. He had received this unqualified praise, his film track record went back to 1922, and included work with comedians Will Hay, George Formby and Benny Hill and, more to the point, he had been in every film since *Carry On Sergeant*.

Peter wasn't prepared to accept Charles's ultimatum that if he didn't have top billing and a star on his dressing-room door he would not appear in the film: 'I repeated to him that no one star was indispensable. He didn't believe me. I wasn't prepared to be told what to do – and that is how Lance Percival, at short notice, ended up playing the ship's cook in *Carry On Cruising*. Charles soon came back for the next film and the argument was forgotten.'

Kenneth Williams very nearly joined Charles Hawtrey in this walk-out on *Carry On Cruising*. Salaries for all the stars had remained fairly static over the past few films and Kenneth believed it was time that, as a major player, he received a salary commensurate with his position within the cast. Peter promised that a rise would be forthcoming, but not during *Carry On Cruising*. The budget had been carefully worked out to take into account the costs of colour film and travel.

Like the rest of the cast, Kenneth began to think that with an increased budget, the use of colour, and a subject like cruising, the *Carry On*s would finally leave their Pinewood locations for sunnier climes. After all, Betty Box had been going on location for years with the *Doctor ...* films, so it must now be a case of better late than never.

Kenneth agreed to make *Carry On Cruising* and waited expectantly for news of their impending voyage. It soon became apparent, however, that instead of a cruise around the Mediterranean, a couple of days on a liner in Southampton docks was more likely. And, in the end, the only people who went to Southampton were Peter, Gerald and the film crew to take some shots of the outside of a ship on water. The bulk of the film, like all the other *Carry On*s, was made at Pinewood Studios.

Hattie Jacques was also missing from the film. There really wasn't much of a part for her to play and, following her recent illness, she was still finding her feet. Joan Sims wasn't to make it to the final cast list either. For years, those in the know have stated that the reason Joan was left out of *Cruising* was down to a punishing theatre schedule in *The Lord Chamberlain Regrets!* which had tired her out and required her to take some time off to rest. But she had been appearing in this play with actor Ronnie Stevens, who also appears in *Carry On Cruising*.

The truth, some believe, is somewhat different from what was presented. While making *Carry On Regardless* the previous year, Joan had struck up a friendship with one of the crew – a carpenter on the set. They went out a few times and enjoyed each other's company. It wasn't anything very serious, but it was a fun time and Joan was happy. At the end of filming, Peter called her to his office and asked if it was true that she was dating a carpenter from the production. She admitted that it was, and Peter made it quite clear that he did not approve of one of his artistes going out with one of his crew. Peter did not go as far as ordering her to stop going out with the man; he knew he had no right to do so. But he did impress upon her that he would not be happy for the situation to continue.

In the event, Joan did not appear in *Carry On Cruising*, and Dilys Laye, who had already appeared in several of Betty Box's films as well as Peter's *Please Turn Over*, took on the role of Flo Castle opposite Liz Fraser, who was back for her second *Carry On* appearance.

With all these problems going on, Peter might well have wished he had taken a cruise himself. Not so. 'It's all in a day's work,' he proudly proclaims, 'that's what producers are there for – to sort out problems and ensure we all run a happy ship. If you watch *Carry On Cruising*, I think you'll agree that's exactly what he had. It's a very funny film and all the cast are just wonderful. As far as dear Joanie Sims is concerned, I would *never* have treated her in such a way. Don't forget she made *Twice Round the Daffodils* immediately after *Carry On Regardless*. If I had wanted to kick her out of the series, I wouldn't have employed her for that film, now would I!'

Peter was happy to be filming *Carry On Cruising* in colour, but found that his budgets had to be set much higher. Confident that Peter would continue to be successful, and that colour was the way forward, Anglo Amalgamated didn't complain about the extra cost. Peter also used colour for his next film, *The Iron Maiden*, in 1962. Known as *The Swinging Maiden* in America, the story centred around an aircraft designer who was continually falling foul of his bosses over his love of traction engines. It was a typically English sort of film, all steam engines and cream teas on the village green. The cast was led by Michael Craig, who – following Dirk Bogarde's temporary departure from the series – had just taken over one of the leads in Betty Box's *Doctor in Love*.

In *The Iron Maiden*, Michael was joined by Cecil Parker and Roland Culver, and the real-life traction engine fan, the Duke of Bedford. The film was, of course, directed by Gerald Thomas, and Peter returned to his friend Vivian Cox to co-write the screenplay with Leslie Bricusse, a man – better known for writing lyrics – who would go on to win an Oscar for *Dr Dolittle* some five years later.

Dubbed by some as a feeble attempt to recreate the success of *Genevieve*, the film did not do exceptionally well and Peter quickly moved on to his next project, *Nurse On Wheels*, based on the novel *Nurse is a Neighbour* by Joanna Jones. Back to filming in black and white, Peter was reunited with his favoured scriptwriter, Norman Hudis, and a cast that was remarkably similar to his other *Carry On*s and medically themed films.

The part of Joanna Jones was taken by Juliet Mills, who was joined by new Rank heart-throb Ronald Lewis (both had just appeared in Peter's *Twice Round The Daffodils*). The impressive supporting cast included Noel Purcell, Esma Cannon, Athene Seyler, Norman Rossington and Jim Dale, who was, with every passing Peter Rogers production, climbing up the cast list of importance.

To all intents and purposes, the film was *Carry On District Nurse*, and the original casting for the lead role was Joan Sims. Indeed, Joan was looking forward to moving away from being one of an ensemble cast to becoming a lead in her own right. Furthermore, Peter had instructed Norman Hudis to write the role of the nurse with Joan Sims firmly in mind. Norman recalls:

'I handed in the script saying I hoped she would be pleased with it. Peter, though, looked worried – not at the script, but at the casting. Something was bothering him and he knew he had to act on it. Peter was a strong producer, but he was also an emotional man and knew he had to make a painful decision. I was soon told exactly what that decision was.'

Joan had been putting on weight. It's a problem she has been afflicted with throughout her career. Most of the time it didn't matter. Being the great character actress she is, audiences would watch her performances and not look upon her as a 'decoration' that was added to Peter's films. Unfortunately, though, with *Nurse On Wheels*, one of the underlying plots is the on-off love-affair between Joanna Jones and the good-looking farmer, Henry Edwards. Realistically, Peter felt that he had no choice but to recast:

'It was terribly painful, but I had little option. One of the reasons people enjoy my films is that the characters are always believable. Joan just wasn't suited for that role at that time. I called her into my office and apologized, but said I was recasting. I gave her a copy of the script and told her to choose any other female part in the film. She opted to play the vicar's daughter, who ends up romantically linked with the town's doctor. She took it very well. She was very professional about it.'

Peter also honoured the fee that she was to have been paid in the lead role, even though she now had taken on a far smaller character part.

There was a good atmosphere on the film, helped by the spate of birthdays throughout the production. Peter loves a celebration and was quick to bring out a cake and champagne on every occasion. There was certainly plenty of opportunity:

'First, darling Juliet celebrated her 21st and we really went to town with that cake. A few days later, it was Gerald's birthday. It was a similar cake to Juliet's, except the light from the candles was that much brighter! We then found out that Ronald Lewis was celebrating his 33rd. We were a bit busy filming that day, so he ended up with a canteen bun and a solitary candle.'

When any of the stars were not required in a scene, they would often retire to a local pub in the small Buckinghamshire village where *Nurse On Wheels* was being filmed. Peter would buy the drinks, and many was the occasion that a visitor would walk into the pub and see what looked like a district nurse, sitting with a vicar, drinking gin and tonic or whisky and soda, and reading the racing pages of the morning paper. The locals thought it was hilarious.

Nurse on Wheels set two milestones. One provided an opportunity to say 'Welcome', and another the opportunity to say 'Goodbye'. Because of Bruce Montgomery's drink problems, Peter had finally severed the link with his lyricist and composer and taken on Eric Rogers. *Nurse On Wheels* was their first official collaboration together. More importantly, it was to be the last film which Norman Hudis was to write for Peter.

After some twelve films in six years, the partnership which had taken them both on a whirlwind trip from relative cinematic obscurity to fame and, in the case of Peter, financial success on a big scale, was all but over. What finally sealed the end of the relationship was Norman's failed attempt at a script for Peter's next idea, *Carry On Spying*. James Bond had just made a huge impact on cinema screens across the world in *Dr No*. It had been a phenomenal success and the next Bond, *From Russia With Love*, had gone straight into production at Pinewood.

Peter felt the genre was ripe for a spoofing. But the script Norman presented to him wasn't at all what he was looking for; the plot involved secret agents infiltrating an atomic plant in England by disguising themselves as CND supporters and taking part in a CND demonstration – in the days when such demonstrations consisted of everyone lying down in the road. There was a grizzled First World War security guard on duty, with a chest full of medals which he wore proudly. Suddenly the undoubted patriot exclaimed, 'They're right, this is a filthy weapon.' With that, he left his post and went to lie in the road with the other supporters.

Norman thought it was a point worth making and one that could be quite happily included within the general comedy situation of the film. To this day, he isn't clear why Peter rejected the script: 'Did he feel I was going so far off the main course with such a scene that it was time to part, or – as I now feel – did he realize that if the series was to take on a slightly more fantasy-based comedy then it was time for me to leave? It was a creative decision which I cannot argue with. Of course, it hurt at the time.'

Peter insists that he would have been happy for Norman to continue working for him, but agrees there were differences of creative opinion. In the end, the matter was taken out of their hands. In America, Norman was still known as the man who had written the phenomenally successful *Carry On Nurse*. He even had an American literary agent, who had approached him after witnessing the year-long run of *Carry On Nurse* in Los Angeles. From 1964, Norman started visiting the USA to work and eventually moved there in 1966, where he has lived and written ever since.

Peter says he will always be indebted to Norman and his work: 'We had a good relationship and he was a good writer. No one should forget that he was the man who wrote the first six *Carry On*s. I have said it before, and I will say it again, I regard him as a genius. I am glad to say that, even after he left, we continued to keep in touch. And, over 35 years later, we still speak and write regularly.'

At the time they went their separate ways, Peter's last gesture was to pay Norman for the months outstanding on his contract when it came to its sudden end. Norman repaid this money when he received his first earnings in America.

Chapter Ten
Something New, Something Blue

Following the huge success of the first six *Carry On* films, and various spin-offs and semi-related productions from the Peter Rogers and Gerald Thomas stable, it was more than possible that, with the departure of writer Norman Hudis, Peter's comic reign could come to an end. The rescue package, however, literally arrived on Peter's doorstep:

'Talbot Rothwell came to me by post – or, at least, his script *Up the Armada* did. It is very rare for a scriptwriter to send a script to a producer's private address – the scripts usually come to the studio, either from the writer himself or through an agent. I don't know how Tolly, as Talbot was known, came by my private address, but I'm jolly glad he did. I thought the script was very funny indeed and couldn't wait to meet Tolly, who turned out to be a very charming gentleman.'

Ironically – and with perfect comic timing – Tolly's unsolicited screenplay arrived just as Peter was pondering on where the next *Carry On* film was to come from. It was at the suggestion of his agent, April Young, that Tolly – at the time a 46-year-old comedy writer with an impressive track record – sent some material to the *Carry On* producer. He was an ideal person to take over the mantle of *Carry On* architect Norman Hudis, and develop the risqué side of the comedy for a more permissive Swinging Sixties' audience.

Talbot Nelson Conn Rothwell was born in Bromley, Kent, and seemed destined from a very early age to tickle the nation's funny bone with the corniest of jokes. His earliest memory was arriving home after an unsuccessful day at the local fishpond and bemoaning to his mother that, 'No newts is good newts!' Groaning one-liners would become his stock-in-trade. After leaving school, he worked for three months as a town hall clerk in Brighton – the perfect, kiss-me-quick seaside location which the *Carry On* series utilized twice, in *Carry On At Your Convenience* and *Carry On Girls*.

He served with the Palestine Police and, during the war, joined the Royal Air Force. He was captured by the Germans and, amazingly, spent some time in the infamous Stalag Luft 3 Prisoner of War Camp alongside *Carry On* star Peter Butterworth and *Maigret* actor Rupert Davies. Together they worked on the legendary wooden horse escape plan and, ironically, one of Peter Butterworth's most amusing anecdotes concerned his failing to get a part in the film version of the legendary wartime escapade because he was 'the wrong type'!

It was during his days in the Stalag camp that Rothwell tried his hand at acting in the camp shows, and writing plays and bits of comedy material for his fellow PoWs to perform. As such, Peter Butterworth was the first *Carry On* actor to speak some of his own dialogue.

After the war, Tolly found life hard as a jobbing comedy writer but, eventually, penned several successful West End shows, including material for the legendary Victoria Palace revues of the Crazy Gang. He also wrote radio and television sketches for headline stars such as Ted Ray, Arthur Askey and Terry-Thomas. However, although hardly a newcomer to the profession, he wasn't as well known or as successful as he would have liked to have been – and his agent's suggestion that he should approach Peter Rogers proved to be good, sound advice.

Naturally, the industry was aware that the *Carry On* series was now suddenly without a writer, even though there was still a short period to run on Norman Hudis's seven-year contract. Indeed, with Norman shortly to depart for America, the door was open for somebody else to enter. No film producer in his right mind would drop a series that was as popular and as commercially successful as the *Carry On*s.

Peter Rogers – a producer who never suffered fools gladly and listened to his gut instinct about most things – was instantly impressed by the quality of Tolly's comedy writing. He explains, 'If something doesn't absorb me in the first two pages, then I don't bother with it. This piece of Talbot's, though, interested me all the way through.'

Obviously taking its inspiration from C S Forester's *Captain Hornblower* books – and with a hundred images of Errol Flynn, Burt Lancaster and Douglas Fairbanks swashing their buckles on the high seas – Rothwell's screenplay wasn't written in the traditional *Carry On* style for the simple reason that it wasn't originally intended to be a *Carry On*. The story was planned as just another comedy film and Tolly thought Peter Rogers would be the best producer for the job. He wasn't consciously trying to take over Norman Hudis's mantle as *Carry On* writer. Peter recalls:

'I liked the story very much indeed and invited Talbot to the Dorchester to discuss it. We had tea and I immediately told him that I would like to see a screenplay as soon as possible as I was interested in producing the film. I think I surprised him somewhat – producers are rarely that frank so quickly. He wrote the film script in less than three months, and that was that. My job as producer, as always, was very much a hands-on operation and I liked to comment and suggest elements for the script – although I always insisted I wouldn't get a credit. I was the producer, that was all.

'The script eventually became *Carry On Jack*. I merely made a few comments about characterization, knowing that I very much wanted Kenneth Williams to play the role of the cowardly Captain Fearless. It was a part that would fully reflect Kenneth's great talent as a character actor for the first time.'

Well aware that this film was destined to became part of the *Carry On* series, Peter didn't have to ask Tolly's permission to change his original title, but he did so out of common courtesy. Amazingly, he reasoned that although the writer had little say in the matter, Tolly might not take kindly or might not want to be associated with the *Carry On* series – a collection of films critically dismissed as 'fat-headed farces!' by one less than well-informed reviewer.

Naturally, Tolly was delighted to become the *Carry On* writer and was destined to remain with the series until 1974. Originally, Peter had wanted to call his initial film *Carry On Up the Armada*, but the all-powerful censors – although later allowing *Carry On ... Up the Khyber*, *Up Pompeii*, *Up the Chastity Belt* and *Up the Front* – refused to grant Peter permission to use the title. It was, apparently, just too blatant an innuendo for the sensitive audiences of 1963.

However crucial, given all the effort, work and pre-production saga behind *Carry On Jack*, it wasn't to be the first film written by Tolly, which Peter Rogers would put into production and release. That honour went to the quirky, quickly made, ground-breaking, kitchen-sink comedy *Carry On Cabby*, which started shooting in the spring of 1963.

Based on an original scenario by Morecambe and Wise's Associated Television (ATV) and film scriptwriters, Sid Green and Dick Hills, the plot was a fairly radical slice of feminist clout, with a feuding married couple running two taxi firms in direct competition with each other. The idea was a sound one, but Peter wanted his new golden boy to write the final script. It was a frantic rush job and, amazingly, Tolly wrote the film in just two weeks.

A real quota-quickie, in the old sense of the phrase, this cheap and cheerful, black and white, bittersweet comedy was originally commissioned and filmed as *Call Me a Cab*. However, with the majority of the famous *Carry On* crew appearing, Anglo Amalgamated wisely suggested that Peter Rogers release it as part of the *Carry On* series.

Kenneth Williams had been approached by Peter to star in *Call Me a Cab* before the change in title. According to his diary entry for Friday, 1 February 1963, Kenneth was not happy with the writing: 'Read the script of the Peter Rogers film, *Call Me a Cab*, and hated it. Wrote and said I didn't want to do it.'

Peter was upset but not surprised: 'Oh, dear Kenny was always complaining about the scripts. After *Carry On Cruising*, he said categorically that he wouldn't do another *Carry On*. Yet he made about another 20 after that. I was sorry he wasn't in the film [*Carry On Cabby*] and I rather missed Joan Sims too. She did want to be in it, but was just too busy.'

Carry On Cabby was to prove a vital bridge between the Hudis and Rothwell eras. As well as ushering in Talbot Rothwell as writer, and Eric Rogers as composer and musical conductor, the team were joined for the first time by the fresh-faced, energetic talent of Jim Dale as the frantic father-to-be. Jim had been on tryout in several cameo parts for Peter, and now his time had come to join the *Carry On* team. The series had found its perfect juvenile lead and handsome hero, and had set the seal for the Swinging Sixties and many of the finest films in the *Carry On* canon.

The *Carry On Cabby* film also proved a useful excuse to drag Charles Hawtrey back to the *Carry On* series in an undercover manner. Peter recalls:

'I was severely disappointed that Charles Hawtrey didn't see my way of thinking over *Carry On Cruising*, but I had no choice about the matter and had to recast that film. I didn't want to lose him completely from the team, however. I always considered him a very good artiste and I used him on a number of occasions before and outside the *Carry On* series – in *To Dorothy a Son* and *Please Turn Over*.

'Although I don't think there was any particularly bad feeling about the *Carry On* series, the *Cabby* film gave me the perfect opportunity to bring him back into fold. I cast him as Terry Tankard, a bumbling loon who staggers through the film clumsily breaking things, crashing vehicles and generally causing all sorts of misfortune. The relationship between the characters played by Sid James and Kenneth Connor rely heavily on a previous friendship in the army. Charles was also helpful in terms of filmgoers' and television watchers' memories from his army-based work in my *Carry On Sergeant* and Granada's *The Army Game.*'

As it happened, Charles Hawtrey was happy to return to the series and remained with the *Carry On*s non-stop until *Carry On Abroad* in 1972. The tales of Hawtrey, during the filming of *Carry On Cabby*, are legion because, like John Gregson in *Genevieve*, the actor couldn't even drive before filming began. Peter recalls the farcical situation:

'It never occurred to me to ask Charles if he could drive. I suppose, in my own defence, I should say that the script featured Hawtrey's character as a novice driver at the start and it's only much later in the film that he's seen driving. Anyway, we had to have Charles actually driving on location in the Black Park area and around Pinewood Studios so, before shooting, we brought someone in to teach him to drive.

'Unsurprisingly, it was a case of lock up your front bumper during those few days. Talk about a crash course ... poor Charles was all over the place. But to give him his due, he did learn to drive with reasonable efficiency and certainly with enough skill to get away with the making of the film.'

The usual six-week shooting schedule – ironically finishing on the very day when Talbot Rothwell's hero, music hall legend Max Miller died – came to a close under budget, and still the film was due for release as a non-*Carry On*. But, thankfully, the men with the money recommended the title change. Peter was more than happy, and the cast and crew, of course, had no say in the matter.

Charles Hawtrey was back in the *Carry On* team. And, if you listen very carefully to the theme music, from composer Eric Rogers, you can hear that the original title served as the basis for the tune. Sing 'Call Me a Cab' to the music, and you'll see what we mean. Besides that, 'Call me a cab' is the film's final line, repeated into infinity by a cheery

Charles Hawtrey as he tries to hail one for his guffawing boss, Sid James.

Everyone appeared to be having a great time. The script was up-beat and brisk, the actors were working well with the lines, and the new style of music was catchy. Peter's new composer, Eric Rogers, was delighted to be part of the team. Speaking in an interview in 1964, he said:

'I suppose I must possess one of the most enviable jobs it's possible to have. You don't believe me? All right, answer me these questions. Do you enjoy your work more than anything else you do? Are you doing the job you've always wanted to do ever since you were about eleven or twelve years old? Do you work for (and with) the sort of people you would choose to eat and drink with in your leisure hours? Well, do you? Perhaps you don't. But I certainly do. Just in case you don't know what on earth I'm talking about, let me hasten to tell you that I'm referring to my job as composer and music director for Peter Rogers and his team of film-makers. And who could work for a nicer bunch of people than Peter and Gerald Thomas and all those who surround them at Pinewood?'

Carry On Cabby was a great success and Peter was aware that he had now found a way of keeping the *Carry On*s going. Talbot Rothwell was a different type of writer, but a change in style was needed if the series was to survive in the changing world of the 1960s. Peter explains:

'There was a difference between the two writers. I could tell Norman that I wanted a tear-jerk ending, rather like the Chaplin films, and he would achieve that. Tolly was a different kettle of fish. I realized that he was the type of writer who would go out on a gag. I forgot about tear-jerkers and embarked on a series of films that relied entirely on gag and innuendo, with only the slightest thread of a story. I had a long relationship with Tolly. He was very easy to work with.'

Certainly Peter was to have more problems with the censors on Talbot's scripts than any others he had produced, but he felt it was well worth the extra time he spent on the phone to the British Board of Film Censors. Peter was nothing if not shrewd, and a game developed very early on between him and the censor:

'We would leave in certain risqué gags that we knew he would reject so that we could keep others we really wanted. We never had any real battles, it was more like old-fashioned, traditional bartering. In general, the censor appreciated the films and considered them to be well made.'

Tolly Rothwell's style of writing suited the audiences and that was worth fighting for. The late John Trevelyan, who was secretary of the BBFC during the most successful years of the *Carry On*s, admits that they did have one or two problems with Peter and his films. Speaking in 1964, he said:

'Some years ago, a well-known critic, when writing about one of the *Carry On* pictures, described it as "innocent vulgarity", and I think this is a very apt phrase. They are based on the old and great traditions of music hall, which has now largely disappeared as public entertainment. Perhaps this partly explains the popularity of these pictures. I cannot pretend that these pictures are always free from censorship troubles. But, so far, they have never given us problems that have no satisfactory solution, and I think Peter and Gerald can now anticipate our reactions with considerable accuracy, which is most helpful.'

With Tolly firmly on board as part of the Peter Rogers Productions set-up, original writer Norman Hudis was still under contract and still writing. His finest hour had been the second film, *Carry On Nurse*. Norman's final film for Peter was another restrained burst of medical madness starring Juliet Mills as a gentle district nurse in the comedy drama *Nurse On Wheels* in 1963.

Talbot Rothwell, meanwhile, had been hard at work perfecting his very first notion for Peter Rogers, the screenplay which was now dubbed *Carry On Sailor*, but which would eventually be released to cinemas as *Carry On Jack*. In many ways this film was a major departure for the *Carry On* series, not least in that it was the very first time the series had embraced the idea of historical costume.

In retrospect, it can be argued that the films were at their very best when mocking history and historical drama. *Carry On Cleo, Carry On ... Up the Khyber* and *Carry On Henry* would certainly get on most people's top-ten list, even if *Carry On England* and *Carry On Columbus* wouldn't – but, at the end of 1963, it was a brave experiment indeed. Not only that, but Peter's early sixties production line had been literally awash with seafaring comedies – with *Watch Your Stern* and *Carry On Cruising* appearing in quick succession.

Finally, Peter chose to cast a stolid background of established and experienced straight actors to heighten the realistic elements of the Spanish Armada, and the real sense of danger conveyed in the narrative. Bernard Cribbins was cast in the sort of bumbling innocent role of Kenneth Connor, and later Jim Dale was selected as the leading actor.

Of the regular cast members, only Kenneth Williams and Charles Hawtrey found themselves involved, with the relative newcomer, Jim Dale, stealing an early scene as he hoodwinks poor naive Cribbins into travelling in a sedan chair with no bottom. The rest of the cast was admirably fleshed out with scenery-ripping performances from Donald Houston, Percy Herbert and Cecil Parker.

Following her appearances in Peter's *Twice Round the Daffodils* and *Nurse On Wheels*, the part of the leading lady fell to Juliet Mills – her only *Carry On* film. Although he had been delighted with her performances in the other two films, Juliet was not Peter's first choice. It was to have been Liz Fraser, who had been groomed as the ideal *Carry On* leading lady, and who had appeared in four of Peter Rogers' films since 1961. But Liz had talked her way out of the team in an idle conversation with Anglo Amalgamated boss, Stuart Levy.

Discussing the popularity of the *Carry On* films and forcefully commenting on how the series could be better marketed, she had upset Stuart, who had immediately telephoned Peter Rogers, saying that he didn't expect an actress, involved in a series of films to be so opinionated about distribution and presentation. Peter Rogers was less than pleased:

'Liz spoke out of turn and that was that. As a producer, your credibility has to remain intact at all times. I would love to have used Liz in more films, but when your distributor picks up the phone and tells you not to use someone, you have to have a very good reason for going over their heads. Unfortunately, it was time to find a new leading lady.'

Location filming took place on Frensham Pond, just near Pinewood Studios, and for Bernard Cribbins it was one of his happiest experiences: 'The weather was beautiful and the laughs went on from morning till eve.' Even Kenneth Williams, delighted with his flamboyant central character role, had a whale of a time and, swallowing his pride, cheerfully played along with the comic exploits on the water. A rickety boat was found and the disgruntled cast of actors – Cribbins, Williams, Hawtrey and Mills – were set adrift, with a friendly cow for company. Thirty years later, Peter would be dragging Cribbins back, in the same boat, on the same pond, with Jim Dale, for *Carry On Columbus*.

That *Carry On Jack* succeeded at all was as much a testament to the pulling power of the *Carry On* title as it was to the film itself. For, clearly, the cast and the traditional atmosphere that a *Carry On* audience had grown to expect was very different in this film. Even Talbot Rothwell's *Carry On Cabby* had had that cosy, black and white edge of familiar, contemporary innuendo – albeit it served up with a much darker, harder edge of reality. *Carry On Jack*, on the other hand, was a seriously historical venture, packed with great swathes of nearly straight dialogue to set the context for the comedy.

Naturally, with the success of *Cabby* and *Jack* under his belt and a very clear idea as to how the *Carry On* series was developing – plus the meteoric popularity of the James Bond films – Peter decided that the abandoned script for *Carry On Spying* needed to be resurrected. It could then be stripped of Norman Hudis's serious pontificating, and choked full instead with corny one-liners and innuendoes *à la* Talbot Rothwell.

Taking the original draft from his shelf, Peter Rogers offered the tantalizing idea to his new writer. Tolly, already exhausted after the intensive toil on his first two films for Peter, drafted in his friend and fellow scriptwriter, Sid Colin, to help with the espionage film. The two had worked together on scripts for Arthur Askey and the BBC radio series *Educating Archie*, while, much later, after scripting all the television episodes of *Up Pompeii*, Tolly would step aside to allow Sid Colin to pen the 1971 feature film spin-off, starring Frankie Howerd and Bernard Bresslaw.

The *Carry On Spying* script that the two upbeat gag writers finally produced was a stunning piece of work. Interestingly, it was influenced as much by an earlier generation of films and film-makers (Carol Reed's *The Third Man*, Michael Curtiz's *Casablanca*, John Huston's *The Maltese Falcon*) as anything from Cubby Broccoli and his early adaptations of Ian Fleming's spy novels. Indeed, filmed as it was in black and white, it was only fleetingly akin to the gloriously colourful world of James Bond.

The result was an innuendo-packed comic film noir which utilized a smaller number of core team members than usual, and allowed the limp-wristed flamboyance of Kenneth Williams and Charles Hawtrey to let rip. Bernard Cribbins and Jim Dale provided some degree of good-looking, good-natured spying skill, while the major acquisition was in the tiny, bubbly blonde package of Barbara Windsor. After losing Liz Fraser – and not entirely happy with Juliet Mills for *Carry On* purposes – Peter knew he needed a strong bubbly blonde character to replace them. Peter remembers:

'We saw Barbara in the television series *The Rag Trade* with Peter Jones, and thought she was a very fine artiste. She was perfect for the *Carry On*s, in that she had just the right amount of cheekiness. Plus, of course, she was an excellent comedienne. She had been working in a revue with Joan Littlewood's company, so her pedigree was impeccable.'

Barbara had, in fact, just finished making the film *Crooks in Cloisters* with Bernard Cribbins and immediately latched on to the star of *Carry On Jack* for moral support. She dearly needed this during her first encounter with Kenneth Williams. Ever the joker on set, Kenneth was often deliberately hurtful to new actors on the films. After all, he practically considered the *Carry On* series as his own property and, out of protection for the films, could often be prickly company for new, unproven faces.

During the filming of the Café Mozart sequence with Miss Windsor's 'china plate' mate, Bernard Cribbins, Kenneth – with full black disguise beard in place – bemoaned the fact that the naturally nervous Barbara Windsor mucked up her lines on the first take. Stopping short, he cried, 'Oh dear … do try and get it right!', and gave her a filthy look. Barbara, aroused and ready to take care of herself after Bernard Cribbins' warning about Kenneth's practical jokes, let rip with a torrent of insults, complaining that he shouldn't have a go at her with 'Fenella Fielding's false minge hair round his chops!'

That seemed to do the trick. Kenneth broke into gushing enthusiasm for the spiky young lady and the rest of the film went without a hitch – or, at least, there were no more personality clashes between the cast. One of the lead cast members, however, and the high-flying production team were less than amicable during the filming of the climactic chase sequence, deep within the bowels of the headquarters of the notorious Dr Crow (played with Bondian bizarre eccentricity by Judith Furse).

For this sequence, a crop of glamorous models and wannabe actresses were done up as slinky, sexy Amazonian guards, while another crop of men (including the actor boyfriend of Joan Sims, Anthony Baird) were similarly kitted out in dark uniforms. The scene entailed the hapless heroes – Kenneth Williams, Charles Hawtrey, Barbara Windsor and Bernard Cribbins – running down a corridor and avoiding the bullets from the guards' guns.

Naturally, plastic bullets were being used for the shoot, but as the four principals were running away petrified, Bernard Cribbins suddenly stopped short, turned round and started to rant. One of the plastic bullets had ricocheted off the wall of the corridor and hit him on the back of the neck. Now, although not exactly agonizing, these plastic bullets can hurt quite a lot, thank you very much, and Bernard was protesting in screams and shouts.

Gerald Thomas was less than impressed and Peter Rogers was distressed: 'I understood how Bernard felt, but neither Gerald nor myself could tolerate that sort of bad behaviour on set. It shows a lack of control and undermines the authority of the director. It was unprofessional, and we both felt that our films could do without Bernard Cribbins in the future.'

Indeed, Peter's films did do without Bernard Cribbins for the next 30 years. The two didn't work together again until, with mass displeasure in the ranks of core *Carry On* team members who were either offered very minor roles or left out of the productions altogether, Bernard Cribbins was gleefully grabbed for a leading role in the ill-fated *Carry On Columbus* in 1992.

However, for some cast members, the production team was more than willing to bend over backwards to help. Kenneth Williams, undoubtedly the star turn of *Carry On Spying*, and a vital part of all the films – bar one – at this stage of the game, was treated with mock dignity and sincere affection on the set. In one of the *Carry On Spying* scenes, when Kenneth is bumbling about in the office with steely authority figures, Eric Barker and Richard Wattis, he had to put his hand through a glass-panelled door, look embarrassed, and make a swift exit for his Vienna rendezvous.

Kenneth, a physically proud and very vocal coward of the highest order, refused point-blank to do the stunt and with some glee, Peter remembers:

'I told Gerald that Kenneth would bolt at the idea. In fact, I remember having quite a laugh with Gerald at the very thought of poor Kenneth's reaction. On the set, Kenneth was adamant that he wasn't going through with it even though Gerald insisted that the glass was totally safe – it wasn't real glass but sugar glass, a soft convincing-looking substitute.

'Gerald insisted there was no danger and put his own hand through to prove it. Kenneth, convinced by this act of bravery, agreed to do the scene as long as he could wear a protective knuckle-duster and a flesh-coloured protective glove. We shot the scene, everyone was happy, and that was the moment when Gerald brought out the hand he had smashed through the glass – it was cut to shreds and bleeding quite badly. Poor Gerald, he certainly had trouble eating his lunch that day, but he was happy. He had the scene in the can and what's more, it was very funny.'

Charles Hawtrey, not being adverse to a spot of over-indulgence on the liquid refreshment front during lunch breaks, would often reappear for work a little worse for wear. He was still a brilliantly technical comedian and worth his weight in gold to the *Carry On* series, but he could hold up production on the smooth–as–silk organized schedule. Money was tight – and it didn't always help matters when one of the cast members was as well.

'Hawtrey was outrageous on *Carry On Spying*,' Peter recalls. 'There was a lot of technical business going on with gadgets and the like, and this, combined with hot studio lights, was taking its toll on some of the actors.'

The scene that day involved a complex and intricate system of crushing machinery, sharp cutting implements and, finally, a host of huge metal vats containing boiling, steaming acid. Now, in reality, there was little danger – the machinery was fake and the hot acid was cold water   but both Williams and Hawtrey were less than keen to film the sequence. When the time came for shooting, all the principal actors were harnessed up and the cameras started rolling:

'Unsurprisingly, Kenneth was complaining with mock indignation about being treated like a human prop, but, equally surprisingly, Charles was looking completely relaxed with the set-up. The scene was shot and Charles was still perfectly calm. In fact, if anything, he looked a little bit too relaxed. It transpired that he had passed out cold. The medical assistant was called on set and, with total innocence, asked, "Have you tried giving him a nip of brandy?" Kenneth looked aghast and muttered, "That's the last thing he needs, dear!"'

If the actors suffered for their art on the set of *Carry On Spying*, then at least the technical staff seemed to be having a ball. Alan Hume, the much-respected director of photography, who started out as cameraman on the first four *Carry Ons*, and subsequently went on to work with great success on the James Bond films, happily got into the film noir vision of Gerald Thomas.

A man of great talent and humility, Alan was also a great giggler and, to the pleasure of everyone involved, constantly broke up during the filming of various *Carry On* productions. For an important narrative scene in the spying film, the cast (including Kenneth Williams, Charles Hawtrey and Victor Maddern) were called into Pinewood for a night shot from three in the morning.

The scene, set in a darkened warehouse and featuring a dying double agent (Maddern) answering the team's cross-examination with a series of groans and grunts, proved so hilarious that Alan was forced to hide behind some large crates with a handkerchief stuffed in his mouth. Well aware that his suppressed laughter could both ruin the take and get the actors corpsing, he was forcing himself to keep a straight face, but there was something about Maddern's comical plight that proved irresistible. Peter recalls:

'Gerald was most insistent that, although laughter on and around the set was fine for a comedy film, when the cameras were rolling it was straight down to business. This scene, however, was obviously affecting everybody badly. Alan, feeling another attack pending, dived behind the crates once again and came face to face with somebody else having a fit of giggles, with a handkerchief stuffed in his mouth – it was Gerald!'

If the making of *Carry On Spying* was plagued with humorous set-backs, then the actual pre-production history was so complex that a lesser producer would have scrapped the project. Spoofing James Bond was one thing, but Peter quickly realized that Cubby Broccoli and, in particular, Harry Saltzman had little sense of humour. With the *Spying* idea fermenting in his brain – and *Dr No* having done wonderful box-office business – Peter could have been forgiven for paying the ultimate tribute to the Bond producers by considering a parody.

Carry On Jack, a film made on a budget which would have just about covered Saltzman's bar bill, had done extremely well and, indeed, on a ratio of budget against profit, even better than the massively successful Bond film. Peter remembers:

'Saltzman caught my eye in the bar at Pinewood and said, "Congratulations on your picture. That was marvellous. You know, Cubby and I have been thinking, we might like to make a comedy." To which I replied, "I was under the impression you already had!", which didn't please him very much. The seed of *Carry On Spying* was well and truly planted that lunchtime!'

Legal difficulties prevailed over the use of James Bond terminology, and although Charles Hawtrey does get to play a character called

Charlie Bind, with the code number 000 (as in 'Oh! Oh! Ohhh!'), originally it was planned to have him named Charlie Bond, with the code number 001-and-a-half. The Bond bosses said no.

Chapter Eleven
The Empire Strikes Back ... But Only Just!

Legality, ownership and threatened courtroom action also plagued the next entry in Peter's seemingly endless line of comedy hits, *Carry On Cleo*. One of the all-time greats of British films, it was a more than timely parody of that darling of the Nile, Queen Cleopatra. Peter was constantly amazed at the huge fortune that Twentieth Century Fox was throwing down the drain during its lengthy, problematic filming of *Cleopatra*, and a parody was just too good an opportunity to let slip by.

The press seemed more concerned with the on-off romance between Elizabeth Taylor and Richard Burton than the film budget escalating to a multi-million-pound level. Finally, the Hollywood company had had enough; it decamped from Pinewood Studios, left the hugely expensive Roman sets in place, in Buckinghamshire, and journeyed home with its Ancient Egyptian tail between its legs.

Twentieth Century Fox had worked out that it would be more cost-effective to leave the sets to rot where they stood, rather than actually removing them for later use. For the canny mind of Peter Rogers, this was too tempting. Hence, the palaces of Caesar and Cleo in his finished film had a grandiose quality that was severely lacking in most of the other entries in the *Carry On* series.

The interiors were equally impressive. Victor Maddern, who was playing the sergeant major, second in command to Sid James as Mark Antony, had bought the sets from a London production of *Caligula* that he had recently appeared in. The play had folded, and the stunning luxurious sets were left unwanted. Maddern asked what would happen to them and was told that they had been earmarked for sale at £150. The cost of making them was a huge £40,000. Maddern offered £150 and the deal was agreed.

Almost immediately after settling his new purchase in an old coach house in the grounds of his home, the actor heard through the grapevine that Peter Rogers was making *Carry On Cleo* at Pinewood. He contacted the art department and hired the sets out for £800. So, not only did he get a juicy job and a profit from his purchase, but 'the set was very familiar to me!'

However, it wasn't only the set that was familiar. With the public fascination over the behind-the-scenes and in-front-of-camera romance, and the cost for *Cleopatra*, Peter Rogers wanted to embrace as much of the familiarity of the serious drama as he could for his cheeky little comedy: 'My basic thought was, goodness, this is film-making gone mad. I really could make a *Carry On* version of this story in the time that it took Twentieth Century Fox to erect their scenery. My goal was simple – to do just that, in six weeks, under budget.'

Talbot Rothwell pulled out all stops and, although the funniest line – Kenneth Williams screaming 'Infamy, infamy ...', you know the rest – was borrowed from the radio series *Take It from Here*, by Frank Muir and Denis Norden, the major influence came from the hugely success-ful stage presentation of Steven Sondheim's *A Funny Thing Happened on the Way to the Forum*.

The stage cast was awash with familiar *Carry On* faces or *Carry On* faces-to-be, including Frankie Howerd, Kenneth Connor, Charles Hawtrey and Jon Pertwee. Indeed, most of these were recruited for *Carry On Cleo*, and Rothwell's original draft for the film is subtitled 'A Funny Sort of Screenplay'.

Amazingly, even at this stage, the budget was still making provision for a flat fee payment to Norman Hudis, presumably because his seven-year contract was just coming to an end, and his exclusive deal with Peter Rogers dictated that he should profit from any film with the *Carry On* title attached.

Thanks to his historic tragedy *Antony and Cleopatra*, even William Shakespeare got a cheeky 'based on an idea by ...' on the writers' credits for *Cleo*. However, although a host of writers, including Peter Rogers himself as usual, contributed ideas, lines and inspiration to the screenplay, the barrage of playful puns, witty observations and tragic-comic convention was the brainchild of the ever-fertile, ever-barrel-scraping imagination of Talbot Rothwell.

This writer, who had a keen interest in history and Ancient Egyp-tology in particular, revelled in the chance to resurrect some really old jokes for this sparkling film. More than 30 years later it still ranks as not just one of the best *Carry On*s, but one of the finest comic screenplays ever produced.

The shoot was quick, successful and enjoyable. The problems came during post-production. Desperately trying to poke as much affection-ate fun at Twentieth Century Fox as possible, Peter went as far as spoofing the elaborate poster artwork for the Elizabeth Taylor film. This featured Elizabeth reclining on a sumptuous divan, while Julius Caesar, in the person of Rex Harrison, and Richard Burton's Mark Antony are crowded around her. In the *Carry On* version, these illus-trious film stars were replaced with caricatures of Amanda Barrie, Ken-neth Williams and Sid James, with a cheerful-looking Charles Hawtrey thrown in for good measure, peeping out from under the divan.

The problem was that, unbeknown to Peter Rogers, the Twentieth Century Fox poster wasn't an original piece of artwork for the *Cleopa-tra* film, but an image based on an original Cleopatra portrait, painted by Howard Terpning – and the studio owned the copyright. By pro-ducing a mockery of the original, Peter had infringed copyright law, and the next comic stage on which the *Carry On* team was destined to play was the stage of law and order in the High Court. According to Peter:

'It was all hugely entertaining. Funnily enough, we cast our legal team in the same way as we cast the *Carry On*s. I selected Lord Hail-sham to represent us. He had that delicious twinkle in his eye, a real sense of theatre and an eccentric, extroverted edge to his character which made him our perfect choice. And Twentieth Century Fox, I believe, had Sir Andrew Clark – and the leading man, the Sid James of the piece, was Judge, Mr Justice Plowman. I'm glad to say that every-body seemed to enjoy the high spirits of the session, everyone was terribly polite and pleasant to each other and we ultimately agreed wholeheartedly to change our poster design.'

The old poster, which is still in circulation, remains the rarest image for fans to collect. The compromise, featuring Sid James as the face of the Sphinx, proved even more popular. And, besides, the legal battle merely added more fuel to *Cleo*'s fire and helped to make the film a huge box-office success. But that wasn't the only legal battle facing Peter over his new film.

Following the press screening of *Carry On Cleo*, one newspaper film critic telephoned Marks & Spencer to say that the new Peter Rogers comedy was taking the mickey out of its world-famous, much respected stores. The sequence, featuring the flamboyant slave-traders, Markus and Spencius (played with wry charm by Gertan Klauber and Warren Mitchell), set up the narrative for Kenneth Connor and Jim Dale (as captured Britons) to be picked up for the lion's arena or worse

– life as the plaything of some overfed, sex-mad woman (Peggy Ann Clifford).

The Roman joke on the name of Marks & Spencer was typical Rothwell humour, and not the problem in the eyes of the store. No, the problem was blamed on the set-design department and Bert Davey, the art director for the film. Peter explains:

'Marks & Spencers were, apparently, very fussy over the use of their trademark colours – green and white. To be honest with you, I didn't even notice the use of the colours when I first saw the film and I certainly didn't understand the importance of the colours to Marks & Spencer. Obviously someone, very laudably, had done their homework and used the official colours of the store to heighten the joke. It wasn't done out of malice, simply out of professionalism and good-natured humour. Still, we were very nearly sued over the scene.

'I am convinced to this day that if the Sieff family [owners of Marks & Spencer and therefore the people reacting to the *Carry On* "insult"] had employed an independent lawyer, like Twentieth Century Fox, we would have been over a barrel. There was no way the film could be re-cut, and we would have had to pay substantial damages. Thankfully, in the event, Marks & Spencer opted to use an in-house lawyer and all I was asked to do was write a letter of apology to be published in the *Daily Express*. I was never told *why* the *Daily Express*.

'But, in the end, it didn't really matter. The letter was never published anywhere! It wasn't even passed on to the paper for publication. After I had sent it to Marks & Spencer to be approved, they decided to forget about the entire thing. Besides, thanks to my film, Marks & Spencer have had nearly 40 years of totally free television advertising every time *Carry On Cleo* is screened!'

Despite the huge success of *Carry On Cleo*, the start of 1965 was a time for Peter to lick his legally bitten wounds and reflect. For the first time in 18 months, his thoughts turned to a film which, although destined to be a comedy in the *Carry On* style, would actually challenge his cast and crew, present a more narrative-based style of humour, and be peppered with the essence of innuendo which his audience had come to expect and lap up.

The script for the film, which would eventually become *The Big Job*, had been around forever and a day. Almost every writer in Peter's company had had a bash at turning it into a workable screenplay. The idea, a weary old chestnut involving a bank robbery which goes wrong, dated back years earlier. The 1935 film version, *A Fire Has Been Arranged*, seemed a tad dated and old-fashioned at the time, so what chance would Peter have, some 30 years later, of turning out a contemporary hit?

At one time or another, Norman Hudis, John Antrobus, and Spike Milligan were all put to work on it. Throughout the early sixties, Peter had wanted to resurrect the idea without much success. In the light of *Cleo*'s problematic post-production history, the time seemed right to try again. Naturally, Talbot Rothwell was recruited to put his unique slant on the idea, and he came up with a fresh, hilarious, well-paced screenplay which Peter Rogers and Gerald Thomas filmed in the spring of 1965.

The *Carry On* series was certainly not dead – merely resting – when Sid James was signed up as George Brain, the Great Brain, head of the bumbling criminal gang; Joan Sims was cast as the blowzy, flirtatious landlady; and Jim Dale as the face-pulling, naive and dogged policeman on the trail of the scheming jailbirds.

Filmed cheaply and quickly – and for the last time on a Peter Rogers film in black and white – the familiar cast were eagerly backed up by a familiar brigade of backroom boys. Eric Rogers composed the music, Jack Gardener was the assistant editor and Alan Hume the photographer. It could have been called *Carry On Stealing*, but what was the point? By now, Peter had proved that he really didn't need the *Carry On* title to make a hit movie. It certainly helped, but with enough familiar stars from the *Carry On* team he had created, a rose by any other name smelt as sweet and set the box-office turnstiles spinning with renewed vigour.

However, it was back in the saddle, quite literally, when Sid James and the *Carry On* team were sent way out West for the 11th film in the official series, *Carry On Cowboy*. 'That remains an ironic carbuncle on Gerald's and my unblemished track record. It was the only time we went over our planned shooting schedule for films – some 40 productions – that we worked on together. The problem was that much of the film had to be shot outside, in nearby Black Park, just at the back of Pinewood, and at Chobham Common, just a little bit further out in Surrey.

'It rained on the first day of production and absolutely nothing could be filmed. It was a lost day that, try as he could, Gerald could not make up. As a result, we overran the schedule by one day. Mind you, we saved a fortune by not going to America. Why bother? We had acres of field and Sid James in a black cowboy hat – the field was the prairie, he was our villain. We even had a totally convincing Western settlement, built on the back lot at Pinewood. Our film was the only time a Western town had a right-hand turnoff when the buildings were finished. Usually, you would see a great expanse of uncivilized land-scape. If we had revealed what was behind that last house, you would probably have seen the Pinewood canteen!'

The scenes involving the stagecoach transporting Jim Dale and Angela Douglas to the terrorized Stodge City involved a little help from a Pinewood property man. To give the impression of a dirt track with the coach spitting up clouds of dust, one brave chap was positioned on the coach with a powder-gun spraying Brian Rawlinson, the driver, with some instant Western effects.

All the regular cast were delighted with their roles in *Carry On Cowboy*. Sid James considered it a long overdue return to the more meaty parts he had been playing in British films before 'all this light comedy stuff'. Kenneth Williams grabbed his crusty character part with both hands and employed the abrasive vocal traits of the legendary Hollywood producer, Hal Roach, the man who brought Stan Laurel and Oliver Hardy together. Joan Sims was given the ultimate glamour role of Mae West-style saloon owner, Belle; and newcomer Angela Douglas caused red-blooded males' temperatures to soar as the ultra-fanciable Annie Oakley.

Peter could not have been happier with the casting: 'It was one of those occasions when, even though you know who would fit the part, you are still pleasantly surprised when the result is as good as it is.

'*Carry On Cowboy* was a delight from start to finish. The boys were playing Cowboys and Indians, and the girls added feisty glamour among the dirt and dust. Sid was ideal as the Rumpo Kid and Kenneth's voice was a scream, although he claimed he was in agony after a few days' shooting, having to put on that drawl – something to do with his jaw going slightly out of alignment. Mind you, by then, it was too late. If you start with a voice on the first day of shooting, you have to keep that accent throughout. As for Joan, she was beautiful. I never saw her look more sexy or confident.'

Two other actors, Peter Butterworth and Bernard Bresslaw, made their *Carry On* début in this movie, and proved to be so successful that even though the series was a third of the way through its final tally, they were both to clock up an impressive number *Carry On* appearances. They both fitted the bill for the *Carry On* tradition and, perhaps, even more importantly, completely settled in with the ensemble requirements of the team. Peter Rogers is adamant that it's not every actor who can play *Carry On* comedy – it's an actor of rare talent who can become an instant and valued part of the recognized team:

'You have to be an experienced professional performer to stand the heat of making the *Carry On*s. We had our own unique way of doing things and doing things on a tight budget. Unprofessional behaviour couldn't be tolerated because it would put the entire film in jeopardy. The artiste has to have the basic acting ability, has to capture the character, facial expression, relationship and humour of a scene as often as not in the very first take and very early in the morning. There was no room for egos, just hard, good-humoured work.'

Peter Butterworth and Bernard Bresslaw were definitive examples of Peter's requirements.

Peter Butterworth who proved very popular with his eponymous children's programme *Peter's Troubles* had scored many successes in supporting film roles for director Val Guest, and had worked extensively with the Goon generation of comics on radio. Bernard, on the other hand, had found comic fame very early and very young when, at the age of 23, he landed the role of Private Popeye Popplewell in *The Army Game*.

In a conscious attempt to escape the mantle of the gormless recruit, Bernard practically started afresh with Shakespearean stage roles. His call back to comedy came with his towering Indian brave opposite the diminutive camp Charles Hawtrey playing his father. Peter recalls:

'Bernard was working less and less because of his refusal to play the gormless giant he had became famous for. Although we allowed him to play straight roles within our films on occasion, it was always very rewarding to bring back the familiar comic character for the *Carry On*s. Talbot Rothwell was a huge fan of *The Army Game* and delighted to have Bernard in the cast. He would often include Bernard's familiar catchphrase, "I only arsked!", as part of the script. It was his tribute to Bernard's past.'

In *Carry On Cowboy*, the huge 6ft 7in frame of Bernie – as he was affectionately known – was given a baptism of fire by director Gerald Thomas. Although a huge man in every sense, Bernard was notoriously terrified of heights and the loud crack of gunfire. Ironically, the script called for him to make his first appearance in the film – his very first *Carry On*, don't forget – from a wooden platform high up in a tree in Black Park, firing a Winchester rifle. He had to climb some 50 feet for his scene and lean far enough out to spot the impending arrival of the local bad lads, played by Sid James and Percy Herbert. Peter remembers the scene well:

'Gerald had obviously seen the intense fear in Bernard's eyes during his ascent of the tree. It was a very precarious operation involving a rope ladder and a difficult step on to the wooden platform we had erected in the tree. The problem was that Bernard was very unsure of himself, but once he was up there he was professional enough to grit his teeth and play the scene.

'The unfortunate thing was that Gerald, having not noticed it was well over the time for a break in filming, called a stop to production and instructed the cast and crew to get their tea. There was nothing Gerald could do, it was time for a break and that was that. We organized a winch system to get some tea and a cake to Bernard so that he didn't have to come down the rope ladder and do the whole terrifying ascent again.

'Of course, by the time the break was over, Bernard, having got used to the situation, was much happier with the height, and gave a wonderful performance. However, he was convinced that Gerald and I had played a joke on him – and I'm sure he continued to think that till the day he died. I remember him mentioning the incident to me on one of his last trips to Pinewood in 1990 or 1991. But we really weren't. Gerald knew a break was needed and we did our best to make Bernard feel welcome. Tricks *were* played, but we wouldn't have done that – not to a new artiste and certainly not one of Bernard's capabilities.'

Having suffered, with great dignity, the legal attempts to restrict his *Carry On Cleo* film, Peter again faced a problem over a sequence for *Carry On Cowboy*. This involved the first appearance of Charles Hawtrey as the Indian brave, Big Heap. In the original script he was to emerge from his tepee singing a snatch of the 'Indian Love Call' from the Jeanette MacDonald and Nelson Eddy musical *Rose Marie*. The image of the tiny Hawtrey warbling 'When I'm calling you!' tickled Peter Rogers pink:

'We had given Charles a song – 'There's No Place Like Rome' – in *Carry On Cleo*, and I thought a song would work equally well in *Carry On Cowboy*. Unfortunately, the people who owned the rights to the song in America refused to play ball, so we had no option but to drop the idea. I still think it would have been very funny, but it's too late now, isn't it!'

Although, having come to an understanding after the debacle over his billing on *Carry On Cruising*, life with Charles Hawtrey on the *Carry On* set still proved troublesome at times. 'He continually commented that I was drunk with power,' complains Peter. 'But if anybody was drunk on those *Carry On* sets, it certainly wasn't me. And, besides, I have no use for power of any kind. I do my best to make a film on time and under budget, that's all.'

Despite excellent work in the previous films and an agreement with Peter never to have anything less than third billing on a *Carry On* – an agreement that Peter wholeheartedly kept to, although, it should be noted that he was never given anything above third billing either – Charles was not originally destined to be used for the next film, *Carry On Screaming!*

This idea for a *Carry On* mockery of the teeth–and–claw Hammer horror epics, from Bray Studios, was an inspired one; and with his brain finely tuned to a Sherlock Holmes investigation, scriptwriter Talbot Rothwell constructed a grim, darkly funny pastiche. Peter recalls many happy hours chatting with the head of Hammer:

'Dear Jimmy Carreras used to say to me, "You make the comedy. I'll make the horror." It may appear unfair that I tackled his line of business, but he was perfectly free to put "Matron Has Risen From the Grave" into production. I certainly wouldn't have minded!'

As for Charles Hawtrey, the simple fact was that there did not seem to be a place for the actor in the cast of this particular film. In the absence of Sid James, who was struggling with a very heavy workload on his hit ITV situation comedy, *George and the Dragon*, Harry H Corbett was drafted in to play the not so great detective, Sidney Bung; and Kenneth Williams held the *Carry On* fort as the superior, undead Doctor Watt – a manic mad scientist cum vampire figure.

Hearing that Hawtrey wasn't to appear, the respected film journalist C H B Williamson wrote a small but pithy article in the popular magazine *Today's Cinema*, expressing his distress at the news and pondering whether the absence of Hawtrey, one of the film's leading lights, would severely affect the potential earnings of the new film. Peter remembers:

'Stuart Levy, I believe it was, contacted me after his attention had been drawn to the article. Of course, the film didn't need Charles Hawtrey for it to be a success – *Carry On Cruising* had proved that – but Stuart was nervous that the article could strike a chord with people in the industry. It also satisfied his mischievous sense of humour for me to counterbalance the piece by including Charles in the film, and then publicly dismissing the article as nonsense.'

As a result, Sydney Bromley, who had played Sam Houston the cattle rancher in *Carry On Cowboy*, and who had now been cast in the minor role of Dan Dann, the Lavatory Man, saw his place filled by Charles Hawtrey in an eye-catching cameo. 'And I don't mind admitting,' confesses Peter, 'that Charles brought something very special to the role. I remember he enters the scene as a group of artistes [Harry H Corbett, Jim Dale and Peter Butterworth] are desperately trying to discover clues. Most actors would do everything they could to make the most of their limited screen time, but Charles knew differently. He was a very experienced film comedian. He came into shot, carrying a huge pile of towels which he held high in order to obscure his face. It was only as he came into close-up that he lowered the towels and revealed his face. It worked brilliantly.'

There was also an alleged threat of strike action on the part of the actors, although this is a story was blown out of all proportion at the time. Norman Mitchell, a familiar character actor from films such as *Carry On Spying* and *Carry On Cleo*, was involved in a night shot for *Carry On Screaming!* Playing the hansom cab driver, he remembers: 'The whole thing [the night shoot] went on and on. And when we were changing in the dressing-room, Jim Dale said, as a joke, "We ought to go on strike!"'

From this innocent moment between two actors, suffering for their art, word of a threatened strike reached Peter Rogers in a matter of hours. At six in the morning, Jim Dale was on the telephone to Norman Mitchell explaining that his agent, Stanley Dale, had been on at him about bringing the actors out on strike, and that Peter Rogers was furious. Peter recalls the incident:

'There was a rumour that Jim was causing problems on the set, complaining about filming in bad weather conditions. I couldn't have that sort of behaviour, so, yes, I did contact his agent and expected an immediate response.'

Peter was waiting by his phone for Jim to apologize for his actions and Jim was in a panic. Norman Mitchell assured him that he had understood that what he had said was a joke and that he would say that to Peter Rogers. Norman wryly comments: 'I didn't work on a *Carry On* for over 10 years after that!'

However, in terms of lead cast members, Peter was delighted with Fenella Fielding: 'We had used her very briefly in *Carry On Regardless*, and my wife Betty had employed her on several *Doctor* ... films. But I never felt we had got her finest performance until *Carry On Screaming!* She was a wonderful revue artiste and had worked with Kenneth Williams on the London stage. She had this real eccentricity about her, which I think we captured.

'I remember one occasion when we were filming on location in Black Park. Fenella and Kenneth were sitting in a hansom cab that Bernard Bresslaw was apparently driving. It was a two-shot, and needed the two artistes to sit very close together in order to get them on camera. In manoeuvring himself, Kenneth had obviously pushed up against Fenella, who, without missing a beat, purred, "Darling, why is your bum so hard? Do you leave it out at night!" There was no answer to that, even from Kenneth, who for once remained miraculously silent!'

Despite the critics dismissing *Carry On Screaming!*, the horror comedy has gone down as one of Peter's finest films. It also, importantly, proved to be the end of one chapter in his life and the beginning of a new, even more successful one.

When, in 1966, Anglo Amalgamated campaigner Stuart Levy died, the bottom seemed to fall out of Peter's world. Nat Cohen, the surviving partner of the company – and a close friend of Peter's and Gerald's, and a strong supporter of their profitable string of comedies – made it clear that he regretted his association with the *Carry On*s. In spite of the fact that he liked to boast in company that it was down to him that the *Carry On* films were made, he suddenly took Peter to lunch one day in 1965, and announced that he didn't want to do them any more. Peter was dumbfounded.

The films had been – and were continuing to be – exceptionally popular. More importantly, they were making good money – very good money. Later, Peter was told that Nat's children were ashamed of the films and repeatedly told their father that the series was a load of rubbish. Nat was apparently suffering from 'a touch of culture up his arse', as Peter refers to it, and wanted to make what he thought were significant films. He cited more artistic, important films such as John Schlesinger's *A Kind of Loving* and Michael Powell's *Peeping Tom* as the sort of fare he wanted to concentrate on, and bemoaned the fact that several high-profile film critics would immediately condemn anything from Anglo as simply another film from 'the *Carry On* company'.

'I was shocked and wondered if he would have made that decision if Stuart Levy was still alive. It was Stuart who told me that because of the *Carry On*s Anglo had got its first million pounds in the bank. I know that Nat's daughter was often moaning that her father continued to distribute the films and this seemed to offend her cultural susceptibilities.'

Peter's upset turned to anger: 'I honestly believe that he thought I was going to beg him to finance more. He never used his own money anyway. The Film Finance Corporation provided all the backing. There was no way I was going to beg for money. I just had to take the bad news in my stride and decide what to do next.'

Ironically, Anglo Amalgamated had just celebrated Peter's and Gerald's 21st film for the company, with a huge party in London.

While Peter was at his lowest ebb, theatrical agent Michael Sullivan tried to take advantage of the situation. The question of how much the actors were paid had often been a thorny issue, and Sullivan's plot was to headhunt as many of the *Carry On* team as possible, claim them as clients, and then ransom Peter into paying bigger fees for them. If Peter refused, Sullivan would refuse him access to his actors, and force the producer to face the impossible – to try, after almost 10 years at the top, to recast the entire *Carry On* team that was so firmly embedded in the minds of both the industry and the country's cinema-going public.

Sullivan already had Sid James, Charles Hawtrey and Kenneth Connor on his books. His aim was to tempt both Kenneth Williams and Joan Sims away from the much-respected Peter Eade and lay claim to representing the 'core *Carry On* squad'.

Peter was soon made aware of Sullivan's plans: 'Yes, what he was up to was brought to my attention, but I was powerless to do much about it at the time. I could not be seen to be getting involved in personal fights with an agent. You can imagine what the industry would have made of that. Besides, I had one or two other pressing things to take care of – such as finding a new distributor for the *Carry On*s!'

In the long run, Sullivan's notion would, doubtless, have been a better bet as far as the actors were concerned. Peter always insisted that he paid what the agents asked for. There was never any negotiation, and, although any room for negotiation would have been very tight indeed, if one agent had the control of so many important actors he would have become a powerful player in the *Carry On* story.

As it happened, though, both Kenneth Williams and Joan Sims refused to leave Peter Eade, and Sullivan was forced to accept the usual payment for his clients or face the prospect of them being phased out of the series all together. Reluctantly – with Hawtrey continually fighting to keep his place in the films, and Connor temporarily out of the series pursuing his West End stage career – he had to accept that Sid James was his only major coup.

So, the attempted takeover bid fizzled out and life went on as normal. Well, as normally as it could with no company distributing Peter's movies. Besides, within a matter of hours of Anglo dumping the *Carry On*s, Peter had secured a deal with the prosperous Rank Organisation which was more than keen to sign up Peter Rogers and his group of comic actors. Peter explains:

'After lunch with Nat, who waited until the end of the meal to break the news, I went directly to Rank in Wardour Street and offered them any future *Carry On*s, and all I can say is that they jumped at the idea. Jumped in my direction, that is!'

The problem was the *Carry On* name. Rank wasn't prepared to take over a highly successful series of films and promote them as its own. Whatever the quality or familiarity of the films, the *Carry On*s were clearly associated, in the eyes of the industry as a whole, with Anglo Amalgamated. Rank was not happy about being branded as a second-choice distributor or, even worse, being completely ignored. Many people, it assumed, would still think that any future *Carry On* was an Anglo product. The solution was simple, albeit a little silly:

'They dropped the *Carry On* title!' laments Peter. 'I was totally confused by their reasons, but what could I do? They wanted my films. The director, scriptwriter, crew and cast were identical. We had done films in the past with much of the *Carry On* feel – without using the name – so why not do it again? Besides, I was in no real position to complain.'

And there was always Betty: 'She helped me through that very difficult time in my life when we were, after all, comfortably off. I remember one glorious sunny day when I had stripped down to my shirt-sleeves and was tending to our front garden. I must have looked a bit hot and sweaty because I had been working for some time. Just then, a huge car drove along the road, pulled up, and this well-to-do lady stepped out and beckoned to me. "My good man," she said haughtily.

"How much do they pay you for doing the garden?" "Nothing," I replied, "but I get to sleep with the lady of the house!" With that, she gave me a shocked look, darted back to her car, and quickly drove away!'

And so it was that, after almost two decades, Betty and Peter found themselves making films for the same distributor. Previously, of course, Peter's films had been shown at ABC, while Betty's were shown at Odeon cinemas. On their weekend jaunts to Kent to see Peter's family, they would both study the queues outside cinemas as they drove through south London. But it was all a game. There was no rivalry. Peter couldn't even judge the results because he was driving. But, magnanimously, it seemed always to be a draw.

Chapter Twelve
Rank Stupidity

The first film under the new regime was a pet project of Talbot Roth-well's. Revelling in the fruitful world of swashbuckling romps once more, he came up with a *Carry On* treatment for the French Revolution. This film, starring Sid James as the dashing Black Fingernail, battling against the anti-aristocratic exploits of the dreaded Citizen Camembert, played with typical pomposity by Kenneth Williams, was released as *Don't Lose Your Head*. Peter recalls: 'The film marked a special mile-stone for Gerald and myself. It was our 25th film together.'

Stunning location filming was secured at Waddesdon Manor, some six miles from Aylesbury. The house, the only genuinely designed French chateau in England, was originally built for the Rothschild family and found itself used for film-making for the very first time. It was on this location that Kenneth Williams started playing up after a falling out with Joan Sims. What started as a bit of messing around, Peter says, got blown up out of all proportion:

'Kenny would often play up to guests who came to visit us on the set. The problem was that sometimes he thought he was just being himself, but to the uninitiated he came over as being quite rude. On this particular day, he had been a little rude to a few of Joan Sims' guests. She quite rightly tried to have a word with him about it afterwards, and he took umbrage and wouldn't talk to her. We thought he was just play-ing hard to get, but it went on for three days. In the end I had to take him to one side and have a few words with him. After that, he was as nice as pie. He could be like a scolded child sometimes who just needed a little reassurance.'

Peter always got on with Kenneth Williams. They were both artis-tic men with a love of literature and classical music. They both liked their privacy and, indeed, Kenneth was the only member of the *Carry On* cast who regularly received invitations to dine with Peter at his home. Considering Kenneth's distaste for the films, many who knew him assume that the main reason he continued to make the *Carry On*s was because of his long and enduring friendship with Peter.

In *Don't Lose Your Head*, Dany Robin played the sweet innocent French maiden who catches the roving eye of Sid James. She was, in fact, married to Sid's agent, Michael Sullivan, and took part in a cheeky piece of British cultural referencing with her serenading of the French troops under the evil Kenneth Williams. While plucking a Haydn symphony out on her harp, the energetic chorus of 'Yeah! Yeah! Yeah!' pays fine homage to the 1963 Beatles classic, 'She Loves You'.

Earlier, with Kenneth Connor's hero mobbed by a collection of groupies in *Carry On Cleo*, the essence of pop culture had also been embraced. It was the nearest Peter Rogers came to fulfilling a dear wish of Beatles' manager, Brian Epstein. Brian, who was a fan both of Peter's films and Peter himself, had approached Peter in the early days of the Beatles' fame and asked if the Fab Four could make an appearance in one of his films. The suggestion was that they could be playing music and singing in the background of, say, a bar or restaurant scene.

Unfortunately, although Peter would have been more than happy to oblige, it was one of those magical ideas that never quite happened: 'It wasn't that I didn't like the idea. It was just that the film I was working on at the time was *Twice Round the Daffodils*, which, being all about tuberculosis, was hardly suitable for popular music accompaniment. By the time I had a film in production that we could have slotted the Beatles into, they were unavailable.'

With Peter now firmly in historic-film mode and fully sensing the potential of these innuendo-packed celebrations of quality drama and stirring adventure novels, Talbot Rothwell was set to work on another. Also a *Carry On* in all but name, the new film, *Follow That Camel*, was based around the P C Wren masterpiece, *Beau Geste*.

Peter's usual collection of familiar character stars was gathered together, with Jim Dale perfectly cast as the hapless handsome hero, B O West. Within the plot, he is tricked by the dastardly Peter Gilmore, disgraced and dishonoured, and faces up to his shame by joining the French Foreign Legion. His companion, assistant and little bit of England, Simpson, is played by Peter Butterworth, while Kenneth Williams is allowed to furiously overact as the Germanic camp commandant, and Charles Hawtrey minces around as his equally camp second-in-command.

As with *Carry On Screaming!*, the head of the *Carry On* 'family', Sid James, was again unavailable for the film. This time it was much more serious. Having been hard at work on the television series *George and the Dragon*, Sid had suffered a heart attack and was ordered to rest.

For Peter, this was an opportunity to experiment and try to bring in an international 'draw' to attract American audiences, instead of another star of British comedy.

Not since Norman Hudis had given the world the immortal daffodil-up-the-backside sequence in *Carry On Nurse* had Stateside warmed eagerly to *Carry On* comedy. A huge effort had been put into the promotion of *Carry On Teacher* and *Carry On Constable*, but with little success. The films were too rooted in English eccentricity to appeal across the board to the diverse cultures of America.

It had become common practice for British film-makers to import American stars to improve their chances of distributing a film to the widest possible number of countries. In the 1930s, Constance Cummings had journeyed to England to appear in such films as *Channel Crossing*, while the fledgling Hammer Studios at Bray had signed up Universal's horror star Bela Lugosi to add star attraction to their creaky *Mystery of the Marie Celeste*. The full-blown Hammers of the sixties continued this trend: Ursula Andress, Bette Davis, Joan Fontaine, and other notable Hollywood names, were employed on the films.

Peter Rogers had always considered it a trend worth bucking because, for him, it felt like letting down the unique style of British film: 'I never felt our films needed these big Hollywood stars to make them work better. Certainly, our film [*Follow That Camel*] wasn't funnier simply because we had an American in the cast. If anything, it affected the quality. The team couldn't relax.'

True as that may have been, Peter had bowed to pressure on more than one occasion previously, particularly in the casting of Shelley Winters in his early fifties comedy *To Dorothy a Son*, and burly American actor Alan Hale Jr in the sixties' 'homage' to British steam engines, *The Iron Maiden*.

Press releases of the day hinted that, with Sid James out of the production, the Rank Organisation had been seriously considering the hip new comedian Woody Allen as its star turn. This, Peter Rogers strongly denies, but Rank was indeed looking for someone with an interesting and successful international track record. The star it finally selected was the legendary vaudevillian and Broadway player, Phil Silvers.

Unfortunately, despite the huge success of Silvers as the classic television comedy creation, Sergeant Ernie Bilko, his fame at home was diminishing. *The New Phil Silvers Show* had flopped on television and the star was reduced to cameos and supporting roles in other people's pictures. Peter Rogers recalls: 'Phil Silvers was a big star in England. His Bilko shows had proved very popular, but, then again, these shows were 10 years old even then. He didn't have the clout that the big bosses at Rank thought he had.'

Apart from that, the American star turn proved to be problematic from the outset. During the making of *Follow That Camel* in the spring of 1967, Phil Silvers was feeling extremely unwell and suffering from traumatic domestic dilemmas. He was hardly in the best of spirits to skip through a tight, quick-shooting schedule on a *Carry On*.

He was also having great difficulty with his eyesight and, as a result, was forced to wear his trademark thick glasses and some painful contact lenses. It was a common sight to see him – aided and abetted by Peter Butterworth and Jim Dale – crawling around on all fours, searching the sands of Camber Sands and Rye, Sussex, where the film's location work was being shot, for one of his lost lenses.

Naturally, with a film centred in the middle of the desert and needing a great deal of location filming, the cast and crew were forcibly thrown together in their Sussex hotel. Phil Silvers, uneasy and in pain, avoided the rest of the cast as much as he could. After a day's filming, he would creep back to his hotel room and stay there. With Kenneth Williams and Charles Hawtrey holding court in the hotel bar, many of the team considered Phil Silvers rude and unsociable. He was, after all, the star of the film and, more to the point, a guest in somebody else's successful series of film comedies.

Not surprisingly, different cast members reacted in different ways to Phil's American brashness. Peter remembers Kenneth Williams' reaction to having Phil Silvers on the film: 'To be honest, Kenneth hated anybody new on the series, because he always felt it detracted from the close-knit community spirit of the *Carry On*s. But perhaps Silvers did have ideas above his station. I certainly wasn't happy with him being in the film. I had continually told the distributors at Rank that the *Carry On*s didn't need an American to make them work and that, in any case, Phil Silvers was not the person who would make a difference in that market. I'm glad to say that, in the end, I was proved right, although I would rather have made the film I wanted to make than to turn round and say, metaphorically, "I told you so!" I say metaphorically because I wouldn't have lowered myself to say it to their faces. They knew they were wrong in the end.'

Without Sid James on the film, Kenneth Williams took pole position in the cast of regulars, and took it upon himself to teach Phil Silvers the methods for making a *Carry On* film. Silvers, obviously considering himself the biggest star in the film – which, indeed, he was – could often come across as brash and unpleasant. He was full of long-winded stories of his days working with Dean Martin, Frank Sinatra, Jerry Lewis, Gene Kelly and Bing Crosby in Las Vegas, on Broadway or in Hollywood.

He was also suffering from short-term memory loss. His stories, although fascinating on the first telling, were repeated over and over again. Jim Dale remembers having dinner with Silvers and Kenneth Williams during the filming and having to suppress his laughter as Williams made a non-stop string of faces and whispered comments. In the end, his laughter having blurted out, Jim had to explain to Silvers: 'You've told us this twice already!', but the star carried on regardless, repeating the shaggy dog story for a third time.

Silvers also boasted that he could host an entire television show in America – an hour-long variety programme – without knowing one single line of dialogue. Williams, the professional to his fingertips, wasn't impressed with that and nor, in a quieter way, was Jim Dale: 'I thought, well, that's nothing to be proud of really!' Williams reacted with more vigour explaining that, in England, learning your lines was a sign of the true professional and if you merely read your dialogue on a set of idiot boards you couldn't possibly find the true character you were playing.

Notwithstanding this indignant advice from Williams, Silvers insisted on filming his scenes for *Follow That Camel* with an assistant holding up his lines just beside the camera. On a particularly difficult day, with sand getting into the sandwiches and the camel spitting at everybody except Charles Hawtrey (whom the creature, Sheena, adored), Peter Rogers remembers Kenneth Williams throwing a tantrum:

'He rushed over to me after a scene had gone wrong and started complaining about his co-star. Now this was the sort of behaviour I didn't usually tolerate in an artiste, but when Kenneth Williams complained, I always seemed to see his point of view – and couldn't help agreeing that he was right. Phil Silvers should have learnt his dialogue like everybody else on the picture. As it happened, though, I didn't need to intervene in this incident. I simply told Kenneth to behave himself, that Mr Silvers was our guest on the *Carry On* series, and that he should be treated with respect. I wouldn't normally tell my artiste off on location, but Kenneth needed to be told. I told him that he may not like the way Phil Silvers was acting, but he had no right to condemn him – although I did secretly agree with his point of view.

'Anyway, Phil, who had got wind of what Kenneth told me, departed after the day's filming and hid himself in his hotel room as usual. The next day – when we were shooting more material with Phil, Kenneth and others – Phil Silvers arrived on the set knowing every word of his day's dialogue. Typically, Kenneth was the first to beam with delight and congratulate him. So, he could do it after all, you see!'

The usual mixture of high jinks and low gags of the *Carry On*s allowed jokers like Kenneth Williams to run riot as per usual. Although he disliked the unprofessionalism of Silvers, he thought nothing of pulling a few fast ones on the film's leading man, Jim Dale. It was, after all, his prerogative. Peter explains:

'Kenneth could be very naughty. I remember I had cast Jim Dale and Peter Butterworth as a sort of British double act in *Follow That Camel*. They were in almost every scene and had a lot of intricate, two-hander dialogue together. Kenneth, in one of his mischievous moods, had gone up to Jim Dale and explained that Peter Butterworth hated his style of acting, didn't care for him as a person very much either, and planned to steal all the scenes from right under "that Jim Dale bloke's nose"! Throughout the filming, Jim kept a constant eye on Peter, trying to work out what he was up to and desperately trying to act him off the screen. What Jim didn't realize was that Kenneth, typically, and with that wicked charming glint in his eye, had gone to Peter Butterworth at the start of filming and given him a friendly piece of advice – that Jim Dale hated his style of acting, didn't much care for him as a person, and aimed to steal every scene they played together.

'But that was Kenneth. It was a real pleasure to have him on the films and I missed him dreadfully when he was not on call. I still miss him to this day.'

Although a practical joker, Williams always got down to business with an air of steely professionalism. He only played jokes on cast members he trusted, liked and warmed to. Often a guest actor on the films would look forward to being dragged into Kenneth's mind games and jokes – and that was certainly more appealing than the cold shoulder he usually gave them. Jim Dale was a prime candidate for Kenneth's boyish antics. Peter Rogers recalls:

'I think it was during the making of *Follow That Camel* that Gerald and I had lunch and heard a rumour that Jim Dale was facing hard times. As we were paying him an adequate amount for his work, we found it hard to believe that an artiste of his popularity was suffering in that way. But the rumours had swept through the studio and, indeed, when Jim appeared for work, everybody kept asking if he was all right, if he was managing to look after himself.

'I wasn't the least bit surprised at Jim's surprise. Kenneth Williams had been round to his house while Jim had been redecorating, and the place had been in a right royal mess with just the bare sticks of furniture in place. Instead of taking on board the additional problem of preparing a cooked meal, Jim had taken the easy option and purchased a huge, delicious pork pie. He apologized to Kenneth for the state of the place, but Kenneth – knowing a great gag when he saw one – had immediately told the Pinewood regulars that Jim Dale was on his uppers and had nothing to eat but a stale pork pie!'

Although *Don't Lose Your Head* and *Follow That Camel* did very good business, the great British public was not fooled that these were not part of the *Carry On* series, and Peter was definitely eager to resurrect his 'star' – the title itself – as soon as possible. Finally, after a year in which he made two films with the Rank Organisation, he managed to convince the money-men that reinstating *Carry On* as a prefix would immediately improve box-office business. The two historical romps were then re-released with the *Carry On* name appended to posters, and much more was made of their *Carry On* roots, stars, writer, production team, and so on.

That partially satisfied Peter. But he was far more concerned with moving on and bringing his series back with a vengeance on the occasion of the 10th anniversary celebration of the films. This, in effect, would reinvent them for a whole new generation. Having decided on the archetypal subject that had paid off dividends in *Carry On Nurse*, he set Talbot Rothwell's comic wit to pay homage to all the familiar bedpan humour and men's ward antics of the earlier film. There was even time for a cheeky tribute to that immortal daffodil gag which had set the world laughing in 1959.

Although enthusiastic about his idea – and actually rather proud that his long-running series could comment on its own history in this way – Peter was slightly concerned that John Davis, the head of the Rank Organisation and, more to the point, his wife, Betty E Box, might be distressed at the thought of *Carry On Doctor*. Davis, however, was cheerfully dismissive of Peter's doubts. As far as he was concerned, both Peter and Betty were the uncrowned royalty of Pinewood, and were making a string of huge successes in next to no time and next to no budget. He grinned and said, 'You had better fix it with your wife!'

Following the 1954 classic *Doctor in the House*, Betty had, of course, made a string of successful *Doctor* ... comedies. And by the time *Carry On Doctor* was a gleam in Peter's eye, she had chalked up a further five films in the series. Her latest, *Doctor in Clover*, starred Leslie Phillips (late of *Carry On Nurse*) and Joan Sims (a current member of the *Carry On* team). In the circumstances, it was not surprising that Peter thought Rank may not take kindly to another producer muscling in on one of its hottest properties: 'I wasn't worried that the word 'doctor' in a title was the copyright of Betty – after all, the BBC did that science fiction thing [*Doctor Who*], and never gave her a penny! It was simply common courtesy for me, as a fellow producer, rather than as Betty's husband, to check things out.'

In the end, Peter got a huge thumbs-up from Rank and kept his wife happy by insisting she receive a percentage of the film's box-office takings. As well as celebrating his own *Carry On Nurse* in *Carry On Doctor*, Peter included an in-joke dedicated to Betty's *Doctor* ... series. Sharp-eyed viewers will spot a portrait of James Robertson Justice – the fine Scottish actor who played respected surgeon Sir Lancelot Spratt in all the *Doctor* ... films – just between the lifts in the hospital foyer.

Carry On Doctor was an important film for many reasons. Its very reliance on an audience's shared knowledge of previous comic films set the seal for the code and conventions of this type of entertainment. Also, as with *Follow That Camel*, the film was blessed with an unfamiliar comic guest star – Frankie Howerd. However, this time, the guest was perfectly in tune with the *Carry On* tradition, and took to the series like the clichéed duck to water.

Frankie, having served with Benny Hill in camp concert shows during the war, was a legend in British comedy at the time. With more comebacks than Frank Sinatra, Frankie had first found national fame with the radio series *Variety Bandbox*. Film and television work had followed, but, in the early sixties, his career took a nosedive and, for the first time in his life, the performer seriously considered giving up the business before the business gave up him.

Salvation came in the shape of the hip young comic genius Peter Cook, who invited him to wow the London set at his exclusive Establishment Club. Ned Sherrin then asked Frankie to comment on the Chancellor's Budget for the trendy satire show, *That Was The Week That Was* and that, as they say, was that. Back in favour, scriptwriters Ray Galton and Alan Simpson penned a BBC television series for the star and he headlined the 1966 comedy *The Great St Trinian's Train Robbery*. Peter Rogers remembers: 'Frankie was the ideal person for the *Carry On*s. He had this unique way with an audience – a likeability that came across on the screen. It was strange really. The man was so lacking in charm that he almost charmed you – he grew on one "like friendly moss!" '

The saga of how Frankie became involved in the *Carry On* series is a long one. Originally, Peter Rogers had offered him the plum part of Francis Bigger – faith healer, old moaner and central figure in the film. Indeed, Rothwell had pretty much written the character with Frankie in mind. However, Frankie, preferring the buzz of a live audience – which theatre, radio and, in the main, television gave him – initially turned down the film. He still had bitter memories of when he and Tommy Cooper had struggled through Michael Winner's *The Cool Mikado* in the bad old days of 1962.

In the meantime, Kenneth Williams was less than pleased by the character role he was offered – Dr Tinkle – a part he considered a mere cameo in comparison to others in the film – notably the character Frankie Howerd had been offered. With Frankie less than keen, Peter offered the lead role to Kenneth, who immediately accepted. However, not long after accepting the part, Kenneth got cold feet about taking the central role, and, in effect, being expected to carry the film with supporting turns from the other *Carry On* regulars. He asked Peter if he could possibly play the original role of Dr Tinkle instead.

By this time, Frankie Howerd had agreed to take on the star role and, bingo, Peter Rogers enjoyed the prospect of employing both actors in the film. As a matter of fact, with all the uncertainty over the casting, Peter Rogers and Gerald Thomas only realized the quandary that that particular casting could have put them in at the very last minute. Peter explains:

'With two comedians who used camp to great effect in their

performances, both Gerald and I were concerned that a clash of styles could happen. Ultimately, Frankie and Kenneth could cancel each other out and that would never do. In the end, we came up with a solution. We cut back on a lot of dialogue between the characters, Francis Bigger and Doctor Tinkle, and allowed Frankie and Kenneth only a handful of scenes together. Frankie was then restricted to mainly working opposite Joan Sims and Jim Dale, who both contrasted his camp comedy perfectly.'

Having accepted the role, Frankie Howerd wasn't exactly the most tactful of men when he arrived at Pinewood Studios for his first day's filming. Peter, having injured himself while working in his garden, was walking towards the mansion house with the aid of a stick. Frankie's first words were, 'Hello Peter – what did you do? Trip over your wallet?' The star was shocked by his own comment, but Peter took it in his stride: 'I thought it was a very funny ad-lib! But Frankie was like that. If you were offended by what he said, that was your lookout. He was one of the best people to tell a joke or a funny anecdote to. He was a great listener and always gave you the impression that he really cared about what you were saying.

'I remember telling him about the time when Betty and I were spending Christmas in Venice. We were dining at the Gritti Palace Hotel with a devout Catholic Italian lady. As often happens, she screamed, "Peter, do come and sit with us and make me laugh!" Just because I make funny films people insist that I be funny too. Anyway, I asked her if she had seen the Pope's Christmas message. She answered in the negative, and I commented that it was, "Don't come all ye faithful!" She didn't speak to me after that. Frankie loved that story.'

Frankie Howerd's inbuilt insecurity and professionalism sometimes expressed itself in an air of distant aloofness not dissimilar to Phil Silvers'.

On the set he could appear detached from the rest of the *Carry On* team or throw himself into the antics. A familiar co-star from several television shows was Joan Sims and the two together sparked an insane comic chemistry, which caused countless hours of laughter.

During the filming of the scene featuring the bizarre marriage between Frankie and Joan, with deaf vicar Peter Jones performing the service, and frustrated Bernard Bresslaw acting as best man, the unrestrained laughter affected everybody. The cast and crew were in fits, director Gerald Thomas was chuckling, and even people from other parts of the studio were wandering past and being caught up with the hilarity. The only person not laughing was Peter Rogers:

'Frankie was a joy to be with, but I didn't take kindly to artistes breaking up on the studio floor. Time really was money on the *Carry Ons* and I had to keep the film under control. I walked on to the set, tapped my watch and rather confidently said, "We have got to be finished by 5.30 p.m." The laughter stopped immediately and we got the scene in the can!'

One very special member of the team, Sid James, was welcomed back with open arms. Returning to the *Carry Ons* after his heart attack, Sid suitably played bedridden patient, Charlie Roper, allowing the actor to spend the majority of his comeback comfortably tucked up in bed. Peter was delighted to have Sid back in the company:

'Sid was a unique actor and a very fine artiste. He loved doing the *Carry Ons*, and didn't care if he played big or small parts. He was always the same – always wonderful to have on the set. Sid was determined to get back to work as soon as possible and that's why I gave him the comparatively small role in *Carry On Doctor*. Needless to say, Sid was excellent – and it's down to his unique ability to draw you in that you fail to realize that, first, he is not in much of the film and, secondly, he plays most of his part in bed!'

The actor remained with the films, without a break, from then until *Carry On Dick* in 1974.

Chapter Thirteen
Right Up the Censor's Nose

Given the quick turnover of Peter's films, the *Carry On* crew was already hard at work filming the next entry in the series when *Carry On Doctor* was released. The 16th film in the series, *Carry On ... Up the Khyber*, would in years to come be considered the crowning glory of *Carry On* comedy. Justly considered to be Peter Rogers' masterpiece, this particular film saw all the elements come together perfectly:

'Many people say I always quote *Carry On ... Up the Khyber* as my favourite because it was such a huge box-office success. But that's totally untrue. Of course, it's always very gratifying to have one of your films do well, but I just feel that Talbot Rothwell came up with a wonderful script, the cast were working brilliantly well together, and Pinewood Studios had never looked so good!'

With the back of the familiar mansion house utilized as the Regency home of Sir Sydney Ruff-Diamond (played with typical rough-diamond charm by Sid James), Pinewood Studios did, indeed, look stunning. However, as well as the buildings and grounds of Pinewood, many of the regular team, such as Kenneth Williams and Charles Hawtrey, who had been with the series from the outset, were amazed that Peter Rogers was actually taking the crew on location – and a location that was further afield than the usual Maidenhead or Slough retreats.

This time, in order to capture the sweeping mountain regions of the Karakoram ranges of British Imperial India, the *Carry On* squad were decamped for one whole week to Snowdonia, North Wales. This location had just been used for another film – the Gregory Peck adventure *The Most Dangerous Man* – which had used the place to double up for China.

It was typical of the *Carry On*s to do things as economically as possible, with the producer quite literally sitting down to figure out the easiest, most cost-effective way of making a film in the shortest time possible, with the least amount of money being expended. But Peter Rogers is adamant that this particular location was just as convincing and acceptable as spending huge fortunes on filming in the Karakoram ranges of India:

'I could easily have spent a million pounds and made *Carry On … Up the Khyber* in the actual mountains of India, but what would have been the point? The audience wouldn't have laughed at the film any more vigorously just because the scenery was accurate!'

On *Carry On … Up the Khyber*, Peter was – categorically – proved correct in this belief. Following the film's successful release, the usual fan letters started to arrive at Pinewood – and one actually arrived for Peter. It was from a man who had served in the British Army during the latter days of the Raj. Waxing lyrical about the memories the film had brought back to him, he finished his letter by saying: 'I know exactly the mountains you were filming in. I served there for two years. Thank you for bringing back such happy memories for me.'

To this day the letter still makes Peter laugh: 'Well, I could hardly tell the old bugger that we had shot the thing halfway up Snowdonia!'

The mistaken identity didn't stop there. Shortly afterwards, Bernard Bresslaw – who had given a towering performance in the film as Bunghit Din, the Indian warrior – was appearing in pantomime in Newcastle upon Tyne. Popping into a local Indian restaurant for a curry after the show, the proprietor greeted him flamboyantly with, 'Mr Bresslaw, I love the *Carry On*s – especially *Carry On … Up the Khyber*. It was so good to see my country again!' 'So,' says Peter, 'the locations were very convincing indeed!'

However, it was back 'home' at Pinewood Studios where, arguably, the most famous *Carry On* anecdote was played out between tongue-in-cheek lovers Kenneth Williams and Joan Sims. It has gone down in British film history, but, from the horse's mouth, Peter Rogers explains it best of all:

'We were filming after a lunch when, as usual, Kenneth Williams had got into the restaurant before anybody else and had stuffed his face. Back on the set, poor Joan Sims, in an intimate embrace with Kenneth as the turbaned Khasi of Kalabar, was just getting started on her romantic motions and going on about Oriental passion and the like. Then, just after Joan's emotive dialogue, Kenneth broke wind rather violently. Not surprisingly, Joan was completely put off her stride, and moaned to Gerald that it was disgusting behaviour and how was she expected to play a love scene with that sort of thing going on? Kenneth, grinning with that mischievous schoolboy look of his – and desperately trying to defend his action – haughtily commented that the great Latin lover Rudolph Valentino used to break wind all the time. Now, the famous pay-off has been attributed to several people, including Gerald and Joan, but it was, in fact, me who blurted out, "But Kenneth, those were silent films. We've got your fart on the soundtrack!" '

By common consent, the finest moment in *Carry On ... Up the Khyber* – and, indeed, the finest moment in the history of the series – is the hilarious climactic sequence as the grand Regency abode of Governor Sid James is blown to bits by Kenneth Williams, Bernard Bresslaw and his revolting Burpa tribesmen. Peter Butterworth, as the bemused and terrified clergyman, looks on with mounting disbelief at the strength of the British stiff upper lip when faced with times of trouble.

Peter remembers the scene with great affection and is proud that it is often referred to as a classic of British film: 'Roy Castle was our guest for that one, standing in for Jim Dale I seem to recall, and he was delightful company. When we were filming the dining-room scene with Joan Sims and the rest, we actually used real food – boiled ham and the like – which was gradually joined by bits and pieces of fuller's earth, which was doubling for falling debris. It must have been quite a revolting concoction. Gerald kept encouraging the artistes to keep going and keep acting, and what with the mock explosions and puffs of smoke all over the set, the crew gradually disappeared. Gerald left them all talking and acting for what must have been minutes before they realized that he had gone off to join me for lunch. We laughed heartily all over the dessert!'

Peter's ongoing strong but cheerful battle with the British Board of Film Censors came to a head with this classic film. There were several notable suggested cuts from within the screenplay, with Cardew Robinson's variety stage comedian-styled Fakir being the butt of one particularly forthright innuendo. In order to appease the censors, Peter changed the Bernard Bresslaw line from 'He's just a travelling Fakir!' to 'Fakir ... off!' 'The way Bernard delivered the line,' Peter explains, 'meant there was sufficient gap between the word "Fakir" and "off" to get away with the instruction – and just enough of a pause to calm down John Trevelyan at the censors' office.'

Ironically, it wasn't the British Board of Film Censors but the Rank Organisation – the company which was distributing Peter's films – that almost instigated the most ridiculous *Carry On* cut of all. With several important, high-flying, chinless friends of friends on the Board of the Rank Organisation, several old-timers took an immediate dislike to the title *Carry On … Up the Khyber*. Considering it out of character for the fine dignified tradition of J Arthur Rank's majestic empire, they approached Peter with an alternative idea for the title. 'You may not believe this,' Peter chuckles, 'but they wanted to call it *Carry On the Regiment*. How was I expected to sell a film with a title like that? Ridiculous!'

If *Carry On … Up the Khyber* is the critics' choice for the best entry in the series, the one that even the most diehard of anti-voices tip their hat to is the following film, *Carry On Camping*, which became the definitive saucy classic for an entire generation of red-blooded males. For most of us, Barbara Windsor vigorously doing her exercises under the studious guidance of a snooty Kenneth Williams was the first flash of female nudity happily experienced by pubescent teenagers across the country. Life on the *Carry On*s would never be the same – bare flesh had been exposed and it was a journey further downmarket from then on.

After the comparative luxury of a Wales location, *Carry On Camping* was reassuringly straight back to tat's corner. The furthest the cast and crew travelled for this one was Maidenhead and, for the majority of the rain-sodden shoot, the fields around Pinewood Studios served the camping-site purpose perfectly. The nightmarish filming conditions – it was made in the winter of 1968 for the summer season market the following year – have become a vital part of the *Carry On* legend. And most of the stories are perfectly true.

The muddy fields were indeed sprayed green to make them look like grass. A fishing line was indeed attached to Barbara Windsor's bikini top for that immortal bra-popping moment. Peter Rogers, however, is convinced that his artistes, particularly Barbara Windsor and Kenneth Williams, who have both voiced their opinions in print, were never suffering as much as they claimed:

'Yes, it was cold and, yes, it was wet. This was, after all, the middle of November. But our team are professional people and most of them made the best of a less than desirable job. Actors like Bernard Bresslaw and Sid James just knuckled down and did the job. I remember Terry Scott wrapping himself in a fur coat before tentatively whipping it off for a scene in which he wore only a short-sleeved shirt and a pair of shorts. He was a real trooper – and he was suffering from piles at the time!

LEFT: Peter and Betty on the terrace of the Gritti Palace hotel in Venice in the 1960s.

BELOW: Gerald Thomas and his wife, Barbara, join Betty Box to celebrate Peter's 70th birthday at the Dorchester Hotel, London.

Peter gets to grips with his cast; with
Barbara Windsor (left) after a press
showing in the early 1970s and (above) on
the set of *Carry On ... Up the Khyber*
with Kenneth Williams (1968).

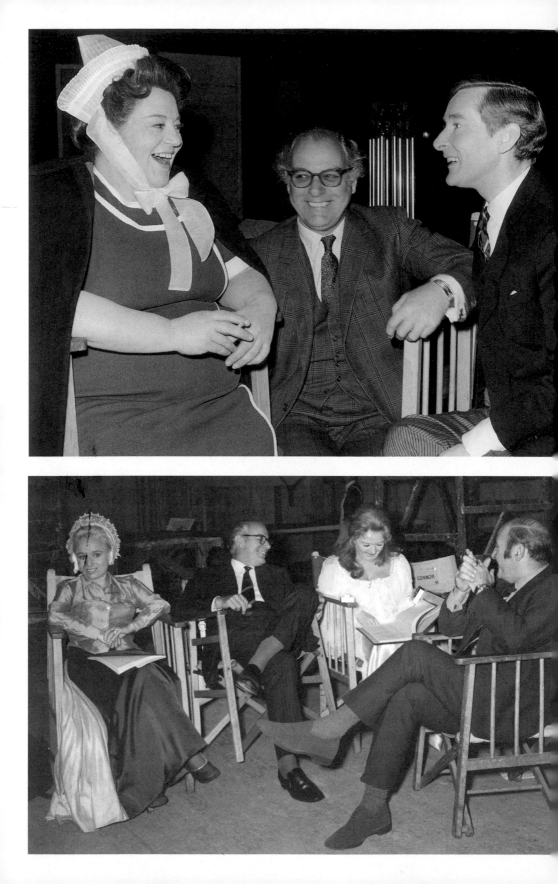

TOP LEFT: Peter enjoys a relaxing moment from *Carry On Again Doctor* (1969) with Hattie Jacques and Kenneth Williams.

BOTTOM LEFT: *Carry On Henry* (1970) – Barbara Windsor, Peter, Joan Sims and scriptwriter Talbot Rothwell.

RIGHT: International star, Elke Sommer, visiting Peter's home during the filming for Betty Box's *Deadlier Than the Male* (1966).

BELOW: Good friends Peter and Kenneth Williams clown around on the set of *Carry On Abroad* (1972).

OPPOSITE: Head of the *Carry On* 'family', Sidney James, discussing his 'motivation' on the set of *Carry On Abroad* (1972) while Bernard Bresslaw seems more interested in the *Daily Telegraph* crossword.

ABOVE: The 'gospel' according to St Peter on the church set for *Carry On Dick* (1974).

OVERLEAF: Peter and his beloved dog, Heidi, in the gardens of Pinewood Studios in the year 2000.

'I read something Barbara Windsor wrote about me during the making of *Carry On Camping*. She said something along the lines of me turning up on location when all the artistes were freezing, and me stepping graciously out of a huge chauffeur-driven Rolls-Royce, with a bottle of champagne in one hand and a jar of caviar in the other. I flamboyantly waved and cried, "Jolly good ... carry on! carry on!", and was promptly driven off to lunch. I mean, that's nothing like how I would react ... I would never drink champagne in the middle of the day!'

Actually, after her most famous moan on the *Carry Ons*, Peter got his own back on Barbara. With her little feet sinking deeper and deeper into green-painted mud, the actress was furious with the way she was being treated. She ranted at Kenneth Williams that the cast were being treated like sheep. She even, in the heat of the moment, threatened that she would never do another *Carry On*. Enough was enough, this filming episode had broken the camel's back. Unbeknown to both of them, Kenneth Williams' tie microphone was still in place and every word had been caught on tape.

Peter recalls: 'Gerald played the very heated conversation back to me. Barbara was almost acidic in her opinion of me, and the vocabulary she used was so vast and vulgar it was almost impressive. I thought she should be treated to a kindly lesson. After viewing the previous day's rushes with some of the cast and technical crew, I invited her to stay behind and watch some further footage with me. She looked a little frightened. Then, over a scene between Kenneth and Barbara, I played the tape and she left the screening room somewhat shamefaced. A few months later, when Barbara turned up at the studios to start work on *Carry On Again Doctor*, I jokingly commented, "I thought you had decided not to be treated like rubbish any more!" '

Being treated like rubbish or not, many actors were happy to return to the *Carry On* fold. Jim Dale, for instance, after scoring with a string of successful television and theatre appearances, returned after just a year's absence, to take the leading role as Doctor Jimmy Nookey in *Carry On Again Doctor*.

Less of a retread and more of a rethink of what made the medical antics of *Carry On Doctor* so popular, the emphasis in this film shifted from the trials and tribulations of the patients on to the trials and tribulations of the hospital staff. For Jim Dale, it was his last *Carry On* encounter until he returned some 23 years later, in 1992, to rediscover America in *Carry On Columbus*, while Patsy Rowlands chalked up her first appearance in the series as Miss Fosdick, ever-faithful secretary to the snooty Kenneth Williams.

Although Sid James, Kenneth Williams and Charles Hawtrey were billed above Jim Dale, there's no denying that Talbot Rothwell's glorious barrel-scraping screenplay puts his energetic performance at centre stage. Capitalizing on his proven skill at stunt work, falls and slapstick comedy, Jim suffered for his art. He flew down a flight of stairs on a hospital trolley, and fell through a dodgy hammock. Peter Rogers recalls Jim's performance:

'He insisted on doing all his own stunts – and on that particular film he had a lot of stunts to do. I remember Gerald telling him to look round in the direction of the camera before falling through that hammock at the shack that was Sid James's house – just to prove to the audience that it really was Jim Dale actually doing it. That was, after all, the point. We had great fun on that film – plastering Jim with cream and cakes for the finale of his accident-prone crusade through the hospital, and so on.'

Barbara Windsor approached the film with some trepidation. Having exposed her right breast to the viewing public – albeit very briefly – in *Carry On Camping*, this film called upon the actress to show a lot more. Once the eager *Carry On* audience had seen a bit, they were ready for another eyeful and that meant four strategically placed heart shapes positioned to cover her vital statistics – but only just. Peter recalls Barbara's problem:

'The first shot was of her coming in on a trolley after supposedly having had an accident during a publicity shoot for an imaginary product called Bristol's Bouncing Baby Foods. She was wearing these hearts, which didn't leave much to the imagination, and Jim Dale was meant to take one look and say, "Yes, I can see the connection."

'Barbara was worried about looking too fat and, unbeknownst to Gerald and me, had gone on a strict diet. The first time we saw her slimmer form was as we were shooting. Gerald called "cut" and went over to ask her what she had done. She explained her nervousness about being seen with so little on, and told us about the diet. Gerald exclaimed in disbelief, "Well, that's the joke about bristols out of the window." In all fairness, I think Barbara looked fine. She was a great sport for stripping down that far in the first place.'

The poster slogan screamed that the *Carry On* squad were 'poking their diag'noses' into other people's business' again, and the film cleaned up at the box office. It was the last release in the Swinging Sixties and ushered in a new more permissive attitude for the Saucy Seventies. Indeed, cinema itself was, once again, being threatened by the ever-present goggle-box in the corner of most living-rooms. Peter Rogers had always been very shrewd when it came to television. Right back to the very first film, *Carry On Sergeant*, which had recruited William Hartnell, Charles Hawtrey and Norman Rossington from *The Army Game*, he had wisely cast familiar faces from popular television comedy shows. He had used both *Steptoe and Son* (Wilfrid Brambell and Harry H. Corbett) for *Carry On Again Doctor* and *Carry On Screaming!*; Dandy Nichols from *Till Death Us Do Part* for *Carry On Doctor*; and television favourites, such as Phil Silvers, Bernard Bresslaw and Barbara Windsor, had also been gleefully plucked for the group.

For December 1969, Peter Rogers took the full plunge and made his very first made-for-television *Carry On*. The result, *Carry On Christmas*, was given a seasonal screening and proved to be one of the biggest audience-pullers in the ITV schedule. Broadcast at 9.15 p.m. on Christmas Eve, the show attracted over eighteen million viewers and hit the number one spot in the Christmas week Top Ten. Peter recalls:

'It was a gamble to try our series on television but all the artistes, particularly people like Terry Scott, Hattie Jacques and Sid James, had vast experience of working in situation comedy. They knew, by instinct, how to time lines for a television audience and could bring this knowledge to their playing of a *Carry On*. For Frankie Howerd, it was like a duck to water. He had always been troubled by film-making, only fully coming to life when he could get the technical crew laughing at what he was doing. For the television show, he was in his element with an invited audience to entertain.'

The success of the first Christmas special, with Sid James as a chuckling Ebenezer Scrooge being visited by three seasonal ghosts, led to a long line of specials, series and stage show spin-offs for the *Carry Ons*. Thankfully, however, the main business at hand was still feature films, which – being made back to back with the small screen offering – retained guest star Frankie Howerd. The team were happy to be back at Pinewood to make *Carry On Up the Jungle*.

This time around, Peter's dilemma over having two equally camp, flamboyant performers in one film – namely Frankie Howerd and Kenneth Williams – was avoided. Although Peter was desperate to cast Kenneth, the actor – due to a rigorous writing timetable, with John Law, for his BBC television variety series, *The Kenneth Williams Show* – was unavailable. Peter regrets that he couldn't get Kenneth back:

'We had wanted Kenny to play the lead role of the Professor of Ornithology opposite Sid James as the great white hunter. Unfortunately, Kenneth was preoccupied with other work. Frankie Howerd was the ideal replacement, but I still wanted Kenneth in the film. I offered him the tiny part of the King, who doesn't have any dialogue until right near the end of the film, but Kenneth turned this down on the grounds that he still wouldn't have time to film the role. More to the point, however, he was rather upset that I had offered him such a small part. We recast with Charles Hawtrey.'

There was, of course, an added complication to the hiring of Frankie Howerd for a return visit to the *Carry On*s. Almost all of his scenes were to be played opposite the haughty Lady Evelyn Bagley (played with sexual elegance by Joan Sims). Peter Rogers remembers: 'It never occurred to me until the very first day of filming, but there we were with a repeat performance of the studio hilarity that we had experienced on *Carry On Doctor*. Frankie and Joan were in almost every scene together, and the entire place was a giggling confusion. But it was worth it.'

The other casting problem facing Peter was for the central role of the bumbling Jungle Boy – the Tarzan-styled anti-hero of the film, who woos his fair maiden, bungles rescue attempts, and has a nasty habit of crashing into concealed trees as he swings through the jungle on his vine. This was a familiar trait to any reader of the American cartoon strip *George of the Jungle*.

As always, having a fair idea of who he wanted to cast – and, working on the assumption that all his usual team of rep players would be willing to appear – Peter had originally wanted Jim Dale for the role. It was a fairly energetic part requiring the young servant of Joan Sims – played here by *Carry On* débutante Jacki Piper – to fall hopelessly in love with him and his jungle abode. It seemed an ideal role for the popular, handsome hero of the *Carry On*s, and the script was sent.

Jim Dale, however, having experienced quality theatre and musical comedy, decided that the time had come to move away from the *Carry On*s before more challenging career opportunities started to disappear. For the actor, the part that was being offered was not, anyway, in the same league as the previous roles he had enjoyed in *Carry On Cowboy* and *Follow That Camel*. Peter was disappointed:

'If you were part of the team, you were expected to play whatever part you were offered. Sid James and Charles Hawtrey were always happy just to be included in the films. Jim complained to me that the role was nothing more than a lot of nonsensical grunts, ughs and face-pulling. Well, so is Frankenstein's monster – it's up to the actor to bring the best out of a role. In my opinion, the jungle boy character had a lot of potential for a performer who was as adept at physical comedy as Jim Dale clearly was. But he was adamant. The role wasn't good enough for him, so we recast. I consider Terry Scott's performance an excellent one.'

Notoriously, Terry Scott revealed a bit more of his talents than the original screenplay had intended him to do. He was on the jungle set in the Pinewood sound stage, lying on the ground with Jacki Piper. Gerald Thomas called 'action' and off Terry went with his lines. In the background, both Terry and Jacki were aware of giggling which was extra-ordinary for two reasons. Firstly, Gerald always insisted on absolute silence during filming to prevent the need for redubbing of sound later on; and, secondly, neither of them thought the scene was that hilarious. Peter takes up the story:

'What dear Terry didn't realize was that he had inadvertently fallen out of his loincloth and we had suddenly found ourselves with another cast member on set! Gerald called "cut", pointed out the cause of the hilarity to Terry, and proclaimed, "If we knew that was going to make an appearance, we would have got make-up to come and put powder on it!" '

The 'Jane' to Terry's 'Tarzan' – although the names were never included because of copyright trouble from the estate of Edgar Rice Burroughs, the author of the original Tarzan book – proved to be the first of four *Carry On* roles for Jacki Piper. Having been spotted in a theatre production, Peter invited her to meet with him and Gerald Thomas and promptly gave her a three-year film contract, which expired in 1972. Nobody else, not even Sid James and Kenneth Williams, was ever put under contract by Peter Rogers.

The title for the film, as originally written by Talbot Rothwell, was *Carry On Jungle Boy*, and, even though that was sensibly changed to *Carry On Up the Jungle* during post-production, criticism was still levelled at Bernard Bresslaw's blacked-up manservant performance as Upsidasi. Within the innuendo-packed environment of a *Carry On* – and, in addition, Laurence Olivier's rendition as the violent Moor,

Othello, on the London stage – it could hardly be rated as racism. If it was good enough for a distinguished theatrical knight of the realm to black up, it was certainly good enough for Bernard Bresslaw.

Indeed, the actor was delighted with his role – a kindly, quick-witted, slightly naive and misunderstood historical character for a change, instead of his usual sword-wielding baddie. Even more importantly, Bernard was determined to imbue his characterization with as much authenticity as possible. Realizing that he would be filming several sequences which featured him dishing out instructions to a group of African carriers, he decided to learn a few instructions in a recognized African language.

As luck would have it, Bernard's older brother, Stanley, spoke Ndebele, the tribal language of the Rhodesians, and taught his acting brother a smattering of rudimentary commands. The dialogue in Tolly's script was merely gibberish and, although plenty of the 'dickey-nookey' talk between Bernie and Sid James is prevalent throughout the film, the interspersed scenes, where he addresses his helpers in 'real' language, are 100 per cent genuine.

Unfortunately, this effort was completely wasted. All the performers were from the West Indies and didn't have a clue what Bresslaw was talking about. At least Sid James, being a native South African, knew it was the genuine article.

'There were so few films around that week I thought – Oh, my goodness. If I'm not careful, I could end up having to review a *Carry On.*' That legendary snub to the comic success story of Peter Rogers was rumoured to have been heard at the 1976 press showing of Oscar-winning film *Network*.

Coming in the immediate wake of Peter Rogers' lacklustre army comedy, *Carry On England*, the critic who muttered it could be forgiven, but it also highlighted the less than high esteem in which the series was held.

Even after some 28 films – the majority of which were box-office hits – the *Carry On*s were still perceived as nothing more than vulgar pieces of cheaply made trash. Peter Rogers, however, was laughing all the way to the bank. This 'trash' was making him a fortune and, following the Christmas television spectacular and the *Jungle* picture, the series was at the peak of its commercial popularity.

It isn't difficult to imagine that, with both Peter and Betty making as many films as they did, and with most of them being highly successful, the couple had quite a tax problem. The last thing Peter would ever have considered doing was to leave the country as so many of his show-business counterparts did when the tax rates on the rich hit 98 per cent. Peter jokes now that many of the exiles came back in later years and were duly honoured, in one way or another, for their contribution to the country.

Betty certainly had enough fur coats and jewellery, which Peter enjoyed bestowing on her. They had wonderful holidays, a large house and the staff to operate it, although, with both working so hard, neither spent a lot of time there – only late evenings and weekends. They probably spent more time at Pinewood than they did in their actual home. According to Peter's accountant there was only one extravagance that was allowed under the business rules – and that was cars. Betty enjoyed driving Aston Martins and Peter opted for Rolls-Royce:

'Betty was inclined to hang on to her cars, but I changed mine every year. I had 35 Rolls-Royce cars in all and would have continued with them if they hadn't started to play up. There is no truth in the myth that a Rolls-Royce never lets you down, otherwise I would still be driving them.

'The reason I changed cars so frequently was because the second-hand price, if you looked after the vehicle, was equal to the new price. This was because there was such a long waiting list for the cars. By having a regular order, I didn't have to wait, so my initial down payment never increased. As a matter of fact, I had two at a time – a saloon and a convertible. It was pure indulgence and the tax man could do nothing about it.'

Peter bought his first Rolls-Royce for £17,500 in 1955 and reckons he has hardly paid a penny more since.

Carry On film number 20 was *Carry On Loving*. Made in 1970, its suggestive title stretched the boundaries even further, and ensured that a whole new generation of couch potatoes would be watching innuendo on television – the *Carry On*s only started to receive terrestrial broadcasts from 1969. With TV viewers and the regular army of cinema-goers intrigued by the risqué title, this new film proved to be the biggest instant money-spinner of them all.

The time was perfect for the series to embrace a bit more than gentle necking in the local Odeon. This film was the ultimate 'nudge-nudge, wink-wink, say no more' feast with jokes aplenty and a brand new crop of young actors brought in to supplement the established cast. London Weekend Television (LWT) was working along similar themes with its comedy series *The Mating Machine*, which took individual cases from a back catalogue of stories, centred round couples brought together by a dating agency. In cinemas, the New York sophistication of the George Segal and Eva Marie Saint film, *Loving*, was also pushing out boundaries. All Peter Rogers did was stick his two favourite words in front of the theme and, bingo, *Carry On Loving* was born.

It was the age of the more open-minded comedy film. The *Confessions…* series and full-frontal nudity were just round the corner and, in 1969, America had unleashed the partner-swapping shenanigans of *Bob & Carol & Ted & Alice*. If Peter's effort was more like Sid & Hattie & Kenny & Charlie, then so be it.

Although the familiar old faces were very much to the fore, *Carry On Loving* recruited a clutch of younger talent, with Richard

O'Callaghan and Imogen Hassall joining the already established Jacki Piper as part of the team. Naturally, the subject matter – with fresh-faced young things finding love, romance and sex for the first time – warranted these new recruits, but Peter Rogers denies that this was a new *Carry On* team waiting in the wings:

'We never planned anything beyond the next film, or, at most, two *Carry On* films ahead. There was never that kind of arrogance – that, "Oh, we may last another 10 years, so we had better have some suitably trained-up actors to take over when the team starts dropping off its perch!"'

Tragically, as it happened, Imogen Hassall died at the very early age of 38 in 1980, just two years after the *Carry On* series itself was pretty much dead in the water. The more forthright sexual encounters of *Carry On Loving* had led, indirectly, to the hugely successful series of *Confessions* ... films and signposted the trend for British comedy films to move away from mere innuendo to a more permissive attitude to sex.

For Peter Rogers, *Loving* was a short-lived experiment and, although Richard O'Callaghan would reappear for one more film in 1971, he never became that elusive Jim Dale replacement that several actors had tried to be right up to the actual return of Jim Dale himself in *Carry On Columbus*:

'Richard was – and is – a delightful chap. He had the right sort of naivety I was looking for in the character he played in *Carry On Loving*, but, when it came to dashing hero types, he was less believable. We did need a Jim Dale type for the seventies, but Richard wasn't quite it.'

Peter recalls that the most memorable part of filming *Carry On Loving* was when the team shot the climactic slapstick fight with real cream and buns from the Pinewood canteen. It was getting to be something of a tradition for the series to go out with a bang, and this time the bang was aimed right at Kenneth Williams:

'Everybody was to get covered in cream and, for one sequence, we wanted dear Jacki Piper to throw a cake at Joan Sims, who was to duck out of range so that the missile would hit Kenneth Williams bang in the face. Obviously this was a difficult shot to do in one take, so we decided to break it up. The final shot was simply to be Kenneth receiving the cake full in his face. Well, no one could actually hit him for what seemed like an age. Gerald had everybody – good cricket players such as Julian Holloway, Bernard Bresslaw, the lot – all getting into a line to take aim at Kenneth Williams, but without success. Kenneth, of course, was loving the attention and crying out that he was unhittable! He was screaming "Williams the Conqueror!" just as someone – and no one can quite recall who – got him square on. That taught the bugger a lesson!'

Even while such jolly antics were taking place, Peter and his script-writer were already discussing ideas for the 21st *Carry On* film. With British industry in a mess and union power taking control, capitalist Peter decided to launch a comic attack on the ideals and attitudes of left-wing union bosses. It was, of course, all done within the *Carry On* tradition – problems at a lavatory factory – but the notion lacked the biting satire of *I'm All Right Jack* and attacked with a somewhat misconceived bite.

The film was due to go before the cameras under the rather frank title *Carry On Comrade*, unless a better idea came along. A better idea did: 'I had wanted to do a *Carry On* based on the life of King Henry VIII as early as 1966. At that time I had imagined Harry Secombe – a fine artiste and very underused by cinema – to play the monarch. I loved the idea of him composing and performing madrigals as part of the film and the time was right. Robert Shaw had just played King Henry in *A Man for All Seasons*.'

This idea was resurrected in 1970, but the madrigals did not become a part of the *Carry On* mythology until they surfaced in the 1972 *Carry On Christmas* television special, and were featured again as an interlude in the stage show *Carry On London!* By then, Harry Secombe had lost the role of Henry VIII to the only man for the job, Sid James.

The timing, however, still proved to be perfect for a right royal *Carry On* – Richard Burton had just starred as the King in *Anne of a Thousand Days* – and, before *Mind My Chopper* was chosen as the cheeky alternative title to *Carry On Henry*, full deference was made to this serious production with the *Carry On* subheading *Anne of a Thousand Lays*.

During the early 1970s, Pinewood was at a very busy period in its history. James Bond was popping in every other year for the latest adventure and during the making of *Carry On Henry* director Ken Russell was painstakingly putting his actors through torture on the set of *The Devils*.

Although often condemned for their saucy content, the carryings-on in the *Carry On*s were as nothing compared to what was going on during the Russell sessions. Barbara Windsor, who was exposing her best-known assets for the umpteenth time, still insisted on a closed set, and one props man was amazed: after all, full nudity and all sorts of bizarre goings-on were happening next door for anybody to have a look at.

Ken Russell, despite being a long-standing and vocal dismisser of the *Carry On*s, employed Barbara Windsor's sassy charms for his big screen treatment of Julian Slade's *The Boyfriend*. He did this even though, as late as 1998, he branded the *Carry On* series as 'crap' in *Carry On Darkly*, a programme which was part of a lacklustre celebration weekend on Channel 4.

Ironically, although considering himself a serious actor at the time, Oliver Reed had a change of heart about the *Carry On* films in the early 1970s. He recalled making *The Devils* over a period of several months and bumping into actor friends such as Sid James and Peter Butterworth at Pinewood. On one occasion he suddenly realized that Sid was wearing a different costume and was amazed to be told that in the period Ken Russell was still to be found agonizing over the shooting of one film, the *Carry On* crew had already started on another one. His respect was a long time coming, but sincere and lasting.

Commenting on Ken Russell's attitude, Peter Rogers says, 'He should have my troubles! I make a film in five working weeks and it makes a fortune. I wouldn't criticize his work, but this business is a business and I haven't done too badly out of it. And neither have those who have worked for me.'

One thing that often annoys Peter about the public's reaction to his films concerns the amount of money they cost, or, more to the point, the lack of money he spends:

'Just because I don't spend a fortune, some people consider them cheap rubbish. Well, that isn't so. The worst thing is when people actually look upon us as if we are a charity case. My job as the producer has always been to make sure the film comes in on budget and on time. There is no room for sloppiness in the editing or tantrums from the cast. More to the point, I do all this within the boundaries of a working studio and a working film unit.

'People have accused me of begging and borrowing costumes, which is simply not true. Sid James does, indeed, wear the same cloak that Richard Burton wore, but it wasn't a case of that production company making the garment and my film using it for nothing. We all hire costumes from Berman's in London. Whether you are making an epic film or a 15-second commercial, they have one King Henry VIII coat.

It just happened that the person to use it before Sid was Richard Burton. We paid the same amount of money to hire the damn thing as anybody else!'

Although Peter still prided himself on keeping costs down, *Carry On Henry*'s budget was a far cry from *Carry On Sergeant*'s in 1958. *Henry*'s budget weighed in at £223,000, which, although cheap by anybody else's standard, simply underlined the escalating cost of these types of films. With the majority of the box office coming from the home-audience market, the *Carry On*s, if not struggling, were finding that it took a little longer each time to recoup the production costs.

Regardless of the slower turnover, the *Carry On*s were fighting back and winning. So much so that, in early 1971, Peter resurrected his union comedy idea under the new, much improved title of *Carry On At Your Convenience*. The title – reflecting the toilet manufacturers at the film's heart – would prove totally nonsensical to an American audience so, in the States, it was released as *Carry On Round the Bend*.

A long time after the glory days of *Carry On Nurse*, *Carry On Round the Bend* – irrespective of its change of title – did as badly as ever in America. The most surprising thing of all, however, was that home-audiences tended to stay away as well. The problem was a misreading, for the first time, of his audience. Peter, without thinking, had mocked the union movement which protected the interest of his most loyal and vocal band of followers – the working-class, beer and chips audience that formed the never-crumbling spiritual backbone of Britain. Peter explains:

'There was never any intention of dismissing these people's opinions. I was just making another film and I hoped that people would find it funny. There was never any question of trying to cause offence. However, to this day, I still strongly maintain that *Carry On At Your Convenience* is a very good film, and it did make a profit for the distributor, so someone must have gone to see it!'

Peter is certainly not in the minority today. For many, *Carry On At Your Convenience* is a definitive example of all that is great about the series – a healthy roster of familiar team players, acting to type, plenty of dubious lavatorial gags, and a day trip to the films' spiritual home of Brighton.

For once the weather was kind to Peter and the crew during the shoot. It was the spring of 1971 and, while not hot, the warm sun beat down on the shingle beaches of the south coast. As always, much had to be crammed into a day's filming. The cast had only a few days to get everything in the can, so, by the end of the day, most of them were exhausted. They were all put up in pleasant hotels and Jacki Piper says that, if she stood on top of the toilet and looked very hard into the distance, she even had a view of the sea!

The days were long and hard work, but the atmosphere was as relaxed as ever. All were happy apart from a rather shamefaced Bernard Bresslaw. Before finally casting the film, Peter Rogers had looked at the script and obviously seen Bresslaw as the perfect, clumsy, bumbling Bernie Hulke. And Talbot Rothwell had tailor-made the role for Bernard Bresslaw to play. The role, however, required the actor to ride a motorbike and, as a matter of course, Peter had enquired if Bresslaw could handle those scenes. Bernard, a dab hand at riding an average bicycle, said yes, and immediately forgot all about it. His agent was contacted, Bernard signed for the film, and the shooting began.

The day before the filming of the big motorbike scene was due to take place, Bernard suddenly clocked the huge biker's machine at the studios, and went cold. He couldn't face the thought of getting on it, let alone riding it! He met Peter in the Pinewood bar and bought him a huge drink. The producer gratefully accepted, but then listened, ashen-faced, as Bernard gingerly explained that he couldn't ride a motorbike:

'I was outraged to be honest. When I had asked Bernard if he could ride, he had said yes. Naturally I believed him. If I had known he couldn't ride the bike, I would have cast someone who could. It was as simple as that. He was a fine professional actor and I was rather disappointed with his admission, but it was far too late to get angry, we had to resolve the situation. The son of our production manager, Jack Swinburne, could ride brilliantly, so it was off for a few quick lessons – just like Charles Hawtrey in *Carry On Cabby* all over again!'

Bernard learned to ride the bike, but only in a straight line. He couldn't turn corners, so the burly figure of David Bracknell, the first assistant director, was used in long shots. Bresslaw simply had to jolt the machine to a halt, get off and hand his mate, played by Kenneth Cope, a pair of trousers. The problem was that, what with juggling the bike, the trousers, propping the machine up and knocking on a door, he struggled to get his actions right. In the end, the scene went to a mind-blowing 17 takes to get the comedy and prop-handling right and, as Peter Rogers laughs, 'In the end, most of the footage was cut from the released print of the film anyway!'

Sadly – and mainly because of word of mouth concerning the comic depiction of union members and unionist doctrine – the film failed to make much headway in the British cinemas of 1971. And even as late as 1976, after television and world sales, the film was still struggling to make a profit. However, with money in the bank and another script already commissioned, the Rank Organisation wasn't fretting too much. Besides, Peter was no fool, and – having made one error of judgement – he wisely galloped straight back to subject matter he had total faith in – hospitals.

With a freer hand in the more permissive climate of late 1971, Talbot Rothwell could incorporate all those weary old medical jokes that had been deemed a bit near the knuckle in the 1960s and, more to the point, could set his entire screenplay for *Carry On Matron* within a maternity hospital. Thus, there was a whole new area of contraception and pregnancy gags just longing to be included. Sid James again headed the cast, with Hattie Jacques resuming her most celebrated role as Matron, and Kenneth Williams as the all-superior head surgeon, the aptly named Sir Bernard Cutting. Charles Hawtrey provided the flagrant camp, Kenneth Cope the drag, and Barbara Windsor the bristols.

Life was back to normal at the *Carry On* headquarters and the film cleared up at the box office, making back its production costs in a matter of weeks: 'We wetted the baby's head with champagne!' recalls Peter.

The 'baby' was not the only one to get champagne out of *Carry On Matron*. Although it was to be the last contribution to the series from the under-rated *Carry On* stalwart Terry Scott, the film ushered in a new boy, Jack Douglas, who would stay with the team until the bitter end of *Carry On Emmannuelle* – and even further – returning for *Carry On Columbus* 14 years later.

Jack Douglas explains that his introduction to the *Carry On* series was something of a double-edged sword: 'My agent telephoned me and said, "Jack, I have some good news and some bad news." Well, being an optimist, I said, "Fine, tell me the good news." He said, "I've managed to get you a small part in the next *Carry On* picture at Pinewood." I said, "Oh, that's wonderful, thank you ... but what's the bad news?" He said, "Well, brace yourself. You're not getting paid!" I said, "What do you mean, I'm not getting paid?"

'He explained that Peter Rogers had already cast the picture, the budget had already been worked out, and that he had got me a tiny role at the very last minute. There was no more money to pay me but, if I did this role as a favour, you never could tell: I might get involved in the series on a long-term basis. I decided it was worth the risk, turned up for my one day of filming, met Sid James and Kenneth Connor, who were immediately welcoming to me, the new boy, and that was that.

'A few days later I was working in my garden when a chauffeur driving a Rolls-Royce pulled up outside my house, and said, "Mr Douglas?" I said, "Yes?", and he presented me with a crate of Dom Perignon champagne. There was a note which said, "Welcome to the *Carry On* team", and it was signed Peter Rogers and Gerald Thomas. So, I was launched with champagne and never looked back!'

Peter Rogers remembers the occasion somewhat differently: 'We did indeed send Jack 12 bottles of champagne. He was a very good artiste and we were keen to have him as part of the *Carry On* team. It was a decision of mine, which I think worked very well. He was an excellent member of the squad and very funny. But, as for giving him the champagne instead of a payment, that's absurd. Even if I had wanted to avoid paying him – which I didn't – I couldn't have employed an actor on a feature film on that basis. The Equity people would have had a field day!'

With Jacki Piper's contract coming up for renewal and her role in *Carry On Matron* reduced to just a few scenes opposite Hattie Jacques and Sid James, it seemed the best time for the actress to part company with the series. Besides, ironically, after working for six weeks at playing a Sister on a maternity ward, she discovered she was pregnant: 'Something must have rubbed off during the filming,' she explains, 'because certainly nothing else was going on!' Peter Rogers is tickled that, for the second time, his medical films had had that effect:

'First, it was Shirley Eaton getting pregnant during the making of *Carry On Nurse* and then dear Jacki Piper when we were filming *Carry On Matron*. Maybe there is something magical in the water at Pinewood – don't look at me, I was there to produce films and nothing else!'

However, it was certainly Peter who turned the *Carry On* fortunes around in the space of just one movie. With the unhappy reaction to *Carry On At Your Convenience* completely forgotten, his loyal, forgiving audience returned to the cinemas in droves.

Away from innuendo, Peter was happily experimenting with executive-producing credits on hard-hitting, thought-provoking dramas such as the child-kidnapping nightmare of *Revenge,* and the science fiction romance of *Quest for Love* directed by Ralph Thomas. And, indulging in his passion for music once again, he composed the theme for *Quest*.

Indeed, Peter's film career was blossoming in all manner of ways. Having been one of the shrewdest film producers in the country when it came to the threat of television, Peter noticed with wry interest that the cinema was gaining the upper hand and presenting big screen versions of the nation's favourite television situation comedies. It was a throwback to the days when companies such as Hammer were making film versions of popular radio shows (*PC 49*, *The Man in Black*), and even television comedy shows such as *The Army Game*, which was filmed as *I Only Arsked!* with Bernard Bresslaw and Charles Hawtrey in 1958.

This trend, kick-started once again by the Monty Python boys and their film *And Now for Something Completely Different* in 1971, would radiate throughout the decade. Film versions of *Dad's Army*, *Up Pompeii*, *Porridge*, *Man About the House*, *Are You Being Served?*, *On the Buses* and, finally, in 1980, *George and Mildred* and *Rising Damp*, would prove hugely popular.

As always, Peter Rogers was well ahead of the game when he secured the film rights to ITV's favourite domestic sitcom, *Bless This House*. It made perfect sense as the star of the show, Sid James, was the undisputed star of the Peter Rogers film empire. Dave Freeman, having written for the television *Carry On*s and many episodes of the *Bless This House* series, was commissioned to write the screenplay for Gerald Thomas to direct.

The *Carry On* connection was enhanced with the casting of Peter Butterworth as Sid's next-door neighbour, Trevor – replacing the original actor Anthony Jackson – and new neighbours were brought in to be played by that familiar sitcom married couple, Terry Scott (immediately after his last *Carry On* appearance) and June Whitfield (immediately after her first return to the series in almost 15 years).

As for the central roles of the family, television stars Sid James, Diana Coupland and Sally Geeson were all retained, but instead of Robin Stewart, who starred as Sid's son Mike in the series, Peter decided to recast the role and brought in a young actor by the name of Robin Askwith.

Askwith had previously appeared in one episode of *Bless This House* – 'Things That Go Bump in the Night', ironically scripted by Dave Freeman – and had made an impression on the British film industry in Lindsay Anderson's *If* in 1969. After playing the lead role of Timothy Lea in the *Confessions ...* film series of the mid 1970s, Anderson brought him back to quality cinema in the 1982 satire *Britannia Hospital*. Peter Rogers insists:

'Although Sid probably had more influence with Gerald and myself than he did with his bosses at LWT, there was no way that Sid's influence would affect my casting of a film. He didn't have that sort of clout with us.'

But, in fact, Sid did seem to have that sort of clout with the *Carry On* people. When Askwith proved so popular, Sid pushed for a role for him in *Carry On Girls;* and, even before that, Sally Geeson and Carol Hawkins (having played Askwith's girlfriend in the film version of *Bless This House*) found themselves as the central pair of young dolly birds in *Carry On Abroad*. Whatever the reasoning, *Bless This House* proved to be a popular spin-off film production, and, although there was the injection of a bit more risqué subject matter and slapstick comedy crossing into *Carry On* territory, the film still retained the flavour of the television original.

Peter explains that the film was 'an enjoyable experience, but I wasn't planning to do a whole run of these films. I know Hammer did very well with their *On the Buses* film [Hammer's highest grossing picture in its entire history from British box-office receipts] and made several more [two sequels followed – *Mutiny on the Buses* in 1972 and *Holiday on the Buses* in 1973], but that was never my intention.'

Indeed, *Carry On*s remained Peter's main concern. *Bless This House* was his only non-*Carry On* film as producer in over seven years – since filming the Sid James heist comedy, *The Big Job*, in 1965 – and no sooner had his fourth medical theme film, *Carry On Matron*, hit the cinemas than he had dreamt up an idea for his next one, *Carry On Abroad* – a comic satire at the expense of the popular short package holiday breaks to the sunny Mediterranean.

Talbot Rothwell seized upon this idea, an almost full company of *Carry On* stars was assembled, and *Carry On Abroad* went before the cameras from April 1972. By now, of course, all the regulars were well aware that no foreign location filming would be included in the budget and seemed fairly resigned to the fact that a spot of filming in Maidenhead would be their lot. June Whitfield, however, returning to the series for the first time since *Carry On Nurse* at the end of 1958, was less clued up about the *Carry On* way of doing things. When her agent said she had been offered a part in the latest *Carry On Abroad*, she excitedly wondered where they would be sent for the film. She – and everybody else – ended up in the car park at Pinewood Studios.

Fun and games were still rife during the making of *Carry On* films and, on one occasion, the ever unflappable Sid James almost got into a flap after a trick was played on him by the property department. For the early scenes of Sid and Joan Sims arriving at the offices of Wundatours Ltd, Sid is seen lugging a couple of heavy suitcases. Of course, in reality, the cases weren't heavy at all – or weren't supposed to be. When Sid was filming the second part of the scene, he had to pick up the cases again and board the coach. Expecting the usual lightness of empty cases, he got the full shock of a dead weight, and almost collapsed on the floor from the sudden heave. Some wag had filled the cases with weights! Like the trouper he was, he play-acted a bit of mock outrage before joining in with the universal laughter on the set.

There was less laughter when Charles Hawtrey was due to be on set for filming. Although he had been a constant presence in the *Carry On* series since returning for *Carry On Cabby* in 1963, the problem over his drinking was coming to a head. Peter explains:

'I had always maintained that a film could wait for no man. To keep these films on budget, it had to be a complete team effort with no slacking on anyone's part – whoever they may be. Charles was drinking in the mornings, and half asleep for work after more drinking during lunch. He was holding up the production.'

Despite the problems, Hawtrey's performance in *Carry On Abroad* is as wonderful as ever, and earned him the by now standard third billing below Sidney James and Kenneth Williams. *Carry On Abroad* was, however, destined to be the actor's last association with the series. When Peter and Gerald Thomas were casting for the 1972 television special, *Carry On Christmas*, they had included Charles Hawtrey in the team and the script was written accordingly. However, they couldn't get a final answer concerning Hawtrey's involvement because of the old, old question of billing.

With both Sid James and Kenneth Williams uninvolved in this small screen special, Hawtrey naturally assumed that he would get top billing. Peter and Gerald, however, considering the television pulling-power of Hattie Jacques, thanks to her role in the BBC situation comedy *Sykes*, offered him second billing below her. This was quite an extraordinary decision when you consider that Hattie was, in fact, billed as eleventh in the latest film, *Carry On Abroad*, under guest stars such as June Whitfield and Jimmy Logan. Peter's decision, though, was final:

'There was no question that Charles Hawtrey was going to hold me to ransom. We offered him second billing and that was that. He wanted time to think it over, which we gave him, but we needed an answer. On the final day, Gerald was eventually able to contact Charles, who was having lunch at the department store Bourne and Hollingsworth. Gerald once again offered him second billing and Charles refused.'

Peter had to frantically recast at a time when most performers suitable for the *Carry On*s were already tied up with pantomime commitments. In the end, Peter selected Brian Oulton – who had appeared in *Carry On Camping* four years earlier – and Norman Rossington – absent from the series since *Carry On Regardless* in 1961 – as replacements for Hawtrey's camp characters:

'There was no way that we could trust Charles Hawtrey after letting us down like that, so we never used him again – although he was considered for a couple of the films we planned to make in the 1980s. It would have been nice to have had him back.'

Indeed, it would have been nice to have had him back for the very next film, *Carry On Girls*, a rather rushed though enjoyable attack on the feminist movement's reaction to Miss World and other such branded cattle markets. The film saw Sid James keeping the British end up as June Whitfield's burn the bra brigade stormed through the seaside fun. Jimmy Logan, recruited after his sterling Scottish lad role in *Carry On Abroad*, gamely struggled with the sort of ultra-camp cameo that Hawtrey could have played in his sleep.

More to the point, the film returned to the glorious seaside town of Brighton and fully utilized the on-screen chemistry between Sid James and Barbara Windsor. The two would later work closely together for the stage revue *Carry On London!* at the Victoria Palace – the home of the Crazy Gang shows, a generation earlier. Peter remembers:

'The idea for the show was brought to me by Louis Benjamin, who suggested that a big London gala spectacular would suit the *Carry On* series, and would I be interested in gathering some of our cast together? Well, obviously, Charles Hawtrey wasn't in the running and Kenneth Williams refused almost immediately because he didn't like stage work at the best of times. But Sid James was happy to star and we roped in other fine stage performers such as Kenneth Connor and Peter Butterworth.'

The show previewed at the Birmingham Hippodrome and later transferred to the Victoria Palace, in London's West End, in October 1973.

During the run of *Carry On London!* at the Victoria Palace, London was suffering a spate of bomb threats. One evening a bomb was defused in a nearby street and the sound of the explosion was heard for miles around. Barbara Windsor was on stage at the time, singing one of her numbers in the show. She heard the noise and exclaimed, 'I'm not as bad as all that, am I?'

A second alert, as Peter recalls, was more serious: 'The police decided that the theatre needed to be evacuated. The show was stopped while the cast was in the middle of a sketch revolving round a Boy Scouts' outing. We all hastily made our way to the gathering point, which happened to be the pub across the road. The landlord refused to serve the stars because they were dressed in Boy Scout costumes. He thought it would look bad!'

It is a little known fact, but, at that time, five of the big theatres in London had their hydraulic systems, used for moving scenery, powered by the flow from the River Thames. The Victoria Palace was one such theatre. Among the scenery that was powered by the water was the safety curtain, which has to be exceptionally heavy for the job it has to do – to protect the audience or backstage from a fire on the other side. One night during the performance, the level of the Thames had dropped to such an extent that the water being pumped to the theatre was not enough to keep the system running properly. As Peter remembers:

'Suddenly out of the corner of his eye, Jack Douglas noticed that the safety curtain was slowly coming down. Barbara was singing again and he was hissing at her: "Get over here quickly, get over here." She didn't really know what was going on, but slowly edged towards him, narrowly avoiding being struck by the curtain as it came down, which could have been very nasty indeed. Being the pros that they are, they made a comedy performance out of it, with Jack lying down on the floor trying to see the audience and so on. That's the only time the curtain has come down on one of my shows while the actors were still performing!'

The threat of bombs in the capital did not put Peter or Betty off and they made regular visits to the ballet. It was one of the few occasions they managed to spend time together. They were great ballet fans and regular visitors to Covent Garden, where the barman became a personal friend and always had champagne and a tray of smoked salmon sandwiches ready for the couple during the interval. The only problem about travelling into town was the horrendous parking conditions, a problem which Peter explains resolved itself purely by accident:

'We were driving around Covent Garden one evening, looking for somewhere to park, when a man with one of those boat-shaped coster-monger barrows was just pulling out after a day's trade. I moved into his place and he enterprisingly stopped and asked if we were going to visit the Opera House. When I told him we were, he said that he would keep the space open for me again if I could tell him when we were coming. This pleasant arrangement lasted for a long time.'

Peter, never one for hiding his feelings, disagreed with the good reviews that he had read of Macmillan's *Anastasia* during its run in the 1970s. He wrote to the director and told him how much he felt he had got it all wrong: 'I don't suppose he cared about reviews any more than I did, but I couldn't resist writing. At the same time, I suggested that he should make a ballet of Claude Anet's story *Mayerling,* and mentioned the music and the book that told the story in a very straightforward manner. He wrote and thanked me for my suggestion and said he would consider it – which he did. In fact, he made it.'

This ballet was such a success that Peter couldn't even get tickets to go and see it. He tried writing to Macmillan to see if he could help. 'I wrote to him several times but he never replied. It's a shame, because I wanted to interest him in a ballet version of *Winnie the Pooh.*'

The stage show of *Carry On London!,* meanwhile, ran successfully until the middle of 1975, and remains one of the biggest money-spinners for the Victoria Palace Theatre.

Chapter Fifteen
His Way

A lot of hushed speculation has mounted over the years concerning the romance between Sid James and Barbara Windsor, but Peter Rogers is adamant that he saw nothing untoward going on during the filming of *Carry On Girls* or the rehearsals for the stage show, *Carry On London!*:

'Sid was as professional as he always was. He certainly wasn't the lovesick, drunken wreck of the newspaper articles and reports that have been published after his death. He was the head of the *Carry On* family of actors and enjoyed his position. I have nothing but fond memories of him.'

The situation allegedly came to a head when the 26th film, *Carry On Dick*, was put into production in early 1974. According to the candid diaries of Kenneth Williams, everybody – including the ever-cheerful Gerald Thomas – was decidedly fed up with the films by this stage. Everybody, that is, except Jack Douglas:

'*Carry On Dick* was a wonderful film to make – and, in fact, my personal favourite of all the series. It was lovely doing those scenes with Kenneth Williams and Sid James, and I can only suppose that Kenneth's diaries, as always, enclose the hidden thoughts of this very unique and private man. That is just Kenneth being Kenneth. On the set, he was as great company as always. And Sid, I can honestly say, looked wonderful. I had never seen him so fit and well. So, all those stories about him arriving on set drunk, haggard and depressed are totally untrue. Either that, or he was a far, far better actor than anybody has ever given him credit for! He was on top form.'

It is possible that the gang were becoming jaded. They had the pressures of a long-running film series to keep up, the competition (notably Val Guest's box-office-busting *Confessions of a Window Cleaner*) biting at the *Carry Ons*' ankles, and, more to the point, six of the *Carry On* regulars were spending all day filming and all evening working on stage together. Jack Douglas categorically disagrees:

'If anything, that stage show brought me closer to people like Sid and Bernard Bresslaw. We were having a wonderful time. We really bonded – all of us, Kenneth Connor, Peter Butterworth – all of us, so when we got together for the film, it was even more fun and easy.

'It's true that sometimes the thought of seeing your old mates again – after being away from them for six months or a year – was part of the fun. Don't forget, only a few of us were actually in the stage show. We had the extra bonus of meeting up with friends like Joan Sims, Hattie Jacques and, yes, Kenneth Williams, for the filming at Pinewood.'

Despite the impression given in Kenneth Williams' diaries, then, the atmosphere does seem to have been as much fun as usual. Nevertheless, in many ways, *Carry On Dick* did prove to be a watershed film. Although Peter had never actually sat down to work out what he would do, and who he would cast, when his familiar team started getting older, the time had come for some changes in the familiar *Carry On* line-up. At 37 Barbara Windsor, for one, was considered – and, indeed, considered herself – too old to keep playing the flirty, busty glamour girl, and was mooted to be someone who was to be removed from the team. Peter explains: 'It wasn't so much a case of dropping Barbara completely, but moving her on to other roles within the series. She was, after all, a character actress at heart and could play almost anything.'

However, in reality, this proved to be Barbara's last character part in a *Carry On* film – although she did return to co-host, with Kenneth Williams, the compilation picture, *That's Carry On*, in 1977.

Even more to the point, rumours were flying around in the industry that Sid James was now considered too old to keep playing the eternal laughing letch. Peter again recalls:

'Many cruel things were said about Sid, and one critic said frankly to me that Sid James had become so boring that my films would do much better without him. I dismissed this as nonsense and, of course, after Sid's death that same person said to me, "You know, Peter, the *Carry On*s just aren't the same since good old Sid died!" That's human nature. But there certainly comes a time when you have to offer actors different roles.'

In actual fact, for *Carry On Dick*, Peter achieved the perfect contrast, allowing Sid to play the more mature, restrained vicar character as well as his typical, lusty alter ego as the notorious highwayman Big Dick Turpin. What with his long-running television situation comedy, *Bless This House*, the actor himself was concerned about being overexposed. But there is no truth in the rumour that Sid James was dropped from the series. Peter comments:

'Believe me, I didn't listen to any whispers from within the industry. Sid James was the head of our "family" of actors and he would get a role in any film I made if I could get him. People tend to forget that Sid did star in several of our *Carry On Laughing* shows, and was only kept out of the next film because of his stage commitments.'

Although no one knew that *Carry On Dick* was destined to be the last appearances for both Sid James and Hattie Jacques, Peter was aware that one of his most important contributors, Talbot Rothwell, would have to bow out after this film went into production. Talbot, who had written all the *Carry On* films from *Carry On Cabby* back in 1963, suffered an unusual attack at the end of 1973. Having been in occasional poor health since his traumatic experiences in a PoW camp during the 1940s, Rothwell had also been overworking. He had feverishly scripted the Frankie Howerd situation comedy, *Up Pompeii*, in double-quick time and had been churning out up to two or three *Carry On* feature film scripts a year. The toil suddenly took its toll on him, as Peter recalls:

'Talbot had almost completed the screenplay for *Carry On Dick* when he had a bizarre mental block. He told me later that he simply sat down at his electric typewriter and stared at the keyboard in dumbfounded bemusement. The complete layout of the keyboard just seemed totally ridiculous to him. In a funny sort of way, it is. One gets used to it, but Talbot just couldn't understand what was going on. He could think up dialogue and could physically type, but it just didn't make any sense to him.

'Thankfully, most of the script had been completed and he got his daughter, Jane, to type up a fairly comprehensive copy. Gerald's oft-quoted response was: "Looks like you'll have to spend a few days at home next week, Peter!" That was my cue to take the "finished" script and add my own dialogue and structure to it. This was my favourite part of the filming process, as a rule. I am a writer first and foremost and I loved putting my own slant on scripts. But this one was less enjoyable. I felt dreadful about what had happened to Talbot. I kept his script intact and just added a few lines here and there – without credit, of course – to help the overall structure. I think we just about got away with it because it remains many people's favourite *Carry On*. Sadly, we couldn't use Talbot again.'

The writer, who had made such an immense contribution to the history of *Carry On*, died in 1981 and *Carry On Dick* was his epitaph.

Carry On Laughing, two batches of self-contained half-hour shows for Associated Television (ATV), cast a lot of familiar *Carry On* faces in various historical contexts – and Sid did, indeed, star in the first four to be broadcast. At the time he was quoted as being concerned that, with the decline of British cinemas and cinema-going, the actual *Carry On* film series would fold and be replaced by these television shows. But he also revealed that a new film was set for the start of 1975 and he was eager to star in it.

This film, *Carry On Behind*, was written by Dave Freeman and did include a tailor made role for Sid James – that of butcher Fred Ramsden, a part subsequently played by *It Ain't Alf Hot, Mum* star, Windsor Davies. Unfortunately, Sid was contracted to a starring role in the Australian stage tour of Sam Cree's latest farce, *The Mating Season*, and couldn't join his friends at Pinewood Studios. Kenneth Williams was signed up as the pompous archaeologist, Professor Roland Crump, and the glamour was provided by international star Elke Sommer.

Unlike Phil Silvers on *Follow That Camel*, Elke was immediately embraced by Williams and the team. Having worked with Betty Box on several films – including the sex romp *Percy* – she was a little more familiar with the ways of film-making in Britain. Indeed, it was Williams, who had been so adverse to Phil Silvers' attitude, who instantly warmed to the German beauty and brought her into the usual high jinks of the *Carry On* stable at Pinewood. Peter remembers:

'Elke is a very good actress, brilliant at the *Carry On* style of comedy and happy to behave as part of the team and not a star – which she undoubtedly was. She became a very good friend of both Betty and myself.'

Peter paid his own personal tribute to Betty, who made her last film, *Percy's Progress*, that year. He wrote the theme tune to *Carry On Behind*, a Scott Joplin-style number, with the music based on Betty's initials, BEB.

With the absence of Sid James for this latest film, and the rather lacklustre reaction to the television episodes, the series was facing an uncertain future. One episode, originally written for television, but hastily converted into a script for the 28th film, was a full-circle return to the army misunderstandings of *Carry On Sergeant*. Written by David

Pursall and Jack Seddon, and entitled *Carry On England*, the industry was less than certain about the film's potential earning power. Indeed, even certain actors approached for the film were uneasy about accepting.

Patrick Mower, the latest in a long line of handsome heroes, desperately trying to recapture the old magic of Jim Dale, was one of them. He accepted only because he was longing to do comedy – any comedy – and was a close friend of director Gerald Thomas. Other new faces included Melvyn Hayes, joining Windsor Davies from the hit military situation comedy series, *It Ain't 'Alf Hot, Mum*, Judy Geeson (the sister of *Carry On* starlet Sally Geeson) and Diane Langton, whose prime assets and chirpy cockney persona instantly presented her as the 'new Barbara Windsor'.

As well as new faces in front of the camera, the heart of the *Carry On* backroom boy brigade was ripped out. Even though Talbot Rothwell was now in semi-retirement, Dave Freeman found himself shunned for another *Carry On* script. Perhaps even more affecting for Peter Rogers, his faithful composer and close friend, Eric Rogers, wasn't involved on the new project either.

A slight disagreement about the number of musicians to be used on the film was at the root of this problem. As part of Peter's cost-cutting programme, Eric was offered the services of just 20 musicians instead of the 40 he was happiest with. He loved to give his *Carry On* scores a richness of texture, which he felt would be lacking if the number of his players were halved. He declined to work on the film and handed his baton over to his friend, Max Harris.

Only a handful of *Carry On* regulars were recruited, with Joan Sims and the cast from the 1976 stage show *Carry On Laughing* (Jack Douglas, Peter Butterworth and Kenneth Connor) helping to keep the film together. The atmosphere, for once, wasn't a cheerful one. The film went before the cameras on 3 May 1976, just a week after Sid James had opened at the Sunderland Empire in *The Mating Season* on 26 April, and died on stage. Peter Rogers was distraught:

'To lose any close friend is a dreadful feeling, but Sid was comparatively young and seemingly quite fit. He wasn't going to be in *Carry On England* because he was booked up with *The Mating Season* for much of the summer, but people have accused me of being heartless and uncaring. But what could I do? *Carry On England* was budgeted, the studio was booked, the actors were ready to start work. I couldn't abandon the project and, in many ways, I don't think Sid would have wanted me to do that. "The show must go on" may be a cliché, but it could have been written with Sid James in mind.

'I always said that the trouble with Sid was that he was such a young man from his neck down. Nevertheless, he could play any character you could write for him. He wasn't a man I could get very close to – he was obsessed with horses and gambling, so I couldn't imagine discussing music or literature with him as I did with Kenneth Williams, for instance. But, as part of the *Carry On* team, he really was irreplaceable. It was now just a case of having no choice but to try and go on without him.'

Not surprisingly, *Carry On England* wasn't popular at the box office and, in fact, at some cinemas it was taken off after just three days because business was so bad. It was a culmination of things. The nation was mourning the death of Sid James, the appetite for these cheeky, saucy comedies was failing in the light of more risqué films – such as the *Confessions* ... and *Adventures of* ... series – and, most important of all, the cinema chains were beginning to take over, and, as was often the case, American hits tended to block out homegrown efforts. The age of the film blockbuster had started – and small cinemas just couldn't attract big audiences. *Jaws* was packing them in and, in the next couple of years, *Stars Wars* and *Superman* overshadowed anything from Kenneth Williams and the *Carry On* gang.

In addition, *Carry on England* was the first of the series to go out with an AA certificate, meaning it was deemed suitable for viewers over the age of 14. In this film there was a considerable increase in the amount of female breast nudity. In the past, the nudity had only been implied – now it was there staring people in the face. While it may have been the sort of thing some films sold well on, it was not what *Carry On* audiences had come to expect. The film was hastily re-edited and re-released to slightly better audiences.

As well as the stress and strain caused by the death of Sid James just before production started on *Carry On England*, Peter's emotions were also seriously affected by the sudden death of his father, aged 92, in May 1976. For years Peter had longed to improve his relationship with his father and, during this final chapter of his father's life, he believes he did:

'I watched the coffin slowly pass into the crematorium then, following the service, I walked round the ground by myself. It was a time for reflection. I noticed the birds singing in the trees and the beautiful flowers growing in the garden of remembrance. I am convinced that, although I'm not a religious man, my father was sending positive thought-transference. I felt closer to him in that moment than I had ever felt before.'

Although Peter Rogers was determined that the series would not die with Sid James, and several new performers ('we considered Jimmy Tarbuck for a while') were mooted as possible members of the gang to plug the gap left by Sid's death, in the end the producer decided to do a complete U-turn and make a film in celebration of his beloved series. It wasn't planned as a tribute to Sid James, but that's what *That's Carry On* turned out to be.

An extremely cheap and cheerful film to make, it only employed two performers – Kenneth Williams and Barbara Windsor – and required Gerald Thomas to record new footage over a three-day period in a projection room at Pinewood. It proved an ideal chance to reflect. Although planned as the benchmark from where one *Carry On* era ended and another began, time was running out for Peter Rogers. The Rank Organisation was suddenly unhappy with the quality and performance of the series.

After *Carry On Dick* there had been a swift and sudden drop in popularity for the films. For the compilation *That's Carry On* – a co-production with EMI (which now owned the interests of Anglo Amalgamated) – the Rank Organisation controlled distribution, and Peter was 'outraged at the way they treated my film. It was very much a part of the *Carry On* series. We had got the idea after MGM had created a huge box-office hit by plundering its rich archives for *That's Entertainment!* In the same way that we had taken off from where serious films about spies, *Cleopatra* and *King Henry VIII*, had left off, our film was an answer to the MGM compilation. It wasn't a B-movie, but that's exactly how Rank treated it!'

Indeed, the film was sparingly screened countrywide and, on some occasions, only quietly crept out as the second feature to the Richard Harris thriller, *Golden Rendezvous*. For Peter Rogers this was the ultimate insult. After all, his films had kept money pouring into Rank for over a decade and now, in his opinion, with only a minor problem to contend with, they were preparing to leave him high and dry.

'I went to Rank with a few ideas for a new *Carry On* film, wondering which one they would want first. It turned out they didn't want any – ever. We had a script from Jonathan Lynn and George Layton, who had appeared in *Carry On Behind* and had been writing the *Doctor* ... television shows for London Weekend Television (LWT). It was a sure-fire hit called *Carry On Again Nurse*. It was 20 years since we had made *Carry On Nurse* and I thought it would be interesting to make the sequel, in much the same way that we had made *Carry On Doctor* 10 years after the first medical film. The other film was written by an Australian gentleman called Lance Peters and was a parody of the *Emmanuelle* films.'

Both these films were originally destined to spearhead the *Carry On* series into the X-rated market and, although old favourite members of the cast, such as Kenneth Williams, Hattie Jacques and even Charles Hawtrey, were being considered, the Rank Organisation decided to withdraw before any more of its money was invested. For Rank, the *Carry On* series was finished.

For Peter Rogers, though, it was just another beginning. Determined to carry on, as it were, he took the projects to other distribution companies and found an interested party in Hemdale. It had just released a spoof version of Sir Arthur Conan Doyle's Sherlock Holmes classic, *The Hound of the Baskervilles*. Starring Peter Cook and Dudley Moore, it featured Kenneth Williams as Sir Henry Baskerville and was designed to emulate the *Carry On* series. The director, Paul Morrissey, was a very vocal *Carry On* fan, and Hemdale happily agreed to take over the distribution of the *Carry On* series.

Settling on the *Carry On Emmannuelle* script (now with an extra 'N' in the title, which even Peter Rogers can't fully explain) – 'Maybe our film got an extra 'N' for naughtiness!' – the idea for an X-rated *Carry On* was abandoned. Hemdale preferred a return to the traditional style rather than competing with the sex comedy market on its own terms – especially as these films were, by now, running out of steam with the last *Confessions* ... comedy, *Confessions from a Holiday Camp*, doing only moderate business in 1978.

The *Emmannuelle* screenplay, which Lance Peters had presented to Peter Rogers, was completely rearranged and overhauled, and today the producer is prepared to admit: 'I totally wrote his dialogue out of existence. The script was, in effect, my own.'

However, even before filming began, *Carry On Emmannuelle* ran into trouble. Barbara Windsor was reported to have walked off the set in disgust. Peter explains:

'Barbara couldn't have walked off the set – she wasn't even on the set in the first place! Originally, the script did have several sequences where Kenneth Connor, Peter Butterworth and others dream of their ideal woman. And, as an idea for getting Barbara involved in the film, Gerald and I did consider her for these dream sequences – the ideal *Carry On* woman, if you like – but she was never going to play Emmannuelle. That part was always earmarked for Suzanne Danielle. She was perfect.'

Indeed, Barbara Windsor was approached for a cameo role in the film, read the script, rejected the idea, received further amendments and suggestions and rejected it again. Kenneth Williams was also less than impressed with the script, but his casting was even more important:

'Hemdale wanted Kenneth Williams in the film almost as badly as I did. To secure his services I did the only thing that would change his mind about doing the film – I paid him more money!'

Williams received a pay increase of £1,000, and was awarded a fee of £6,000 to play the French Ambassador to England, Emile Prevert. It was a role he disliked in a film that he hated but in a way it was fitting that for the very last film in the original run, Kenneth Williams returned to top billing and went out in a blaze of talcum powder and bum exposures. Peter remembers:

'Kenneth pushed for a car to drive him from his London home to the studios every day, but that's where I had to draw the line. It was a car or a pay increase. If he wanted a car, it would have to come out of his £6,000 fee. Kenneth quickly worked out that it would cost him a lot less to travel under an alternative arrangement.'

The film was made quickly – in just over a month – and released in November 1978 to a very lukewarm reaction. It clearly fell between two stools – too far removed from the old-style *Carry On* films for the faithful audience, and far too conventional for the followers of the *Confessions* … sex comedies. It was destined to be the last *Carry On* film for 14 years.

However, at the time, Peter Rogers refused to give up the ghost. For him it was a welcome experience to make the film: 'I still think it works very well indeed and it was lovely to have Kenneth Williams and Kenneth Connor together again. And Eric Rogers returned to compose the musical score shortly before his sudden and premature death in 1981.' Sadly, another key member of the *Carry On* team, Peter Butterworth, died at the tragically early age of 59 in January 1979. *Carry On Emmannuelle* was still on general release and the acting fraternity mourned the loss of one of its favourite sons. Speaking at the time, Peter Rogers said he was, 'a thoroughly nice bloke and a dear friend', but life went on and the *Carry On*s were still an active series in the producer's mind: 'Peter's death was tragic, but if we could go on without Sid James, we could certainly go on without Peter Butterworth. No actor could bring down the *Carry On*s – the series was the star!'

Although *Carry On Emmannuelle* had not exactly set the world alight, there was enough interest for Peter Rogers to push for another film. He had achieved what he had wanted to do, had brought the series to 30 feature films, and he approached Cleves Investments Limited to back his next production. This company, under the suitable production name of Thirtieth Films, had financed *Carry On Emmannuelle*. The film's budget of £320,000, though, was still very far from being cleared and it quickly decided against sponsoring another *Carry On* picture.

With the money-men gone, Hemdale dropped the series and Peter tried to find another distribution outlet for the *Carry On* films: 'I really wanted to make *Carry On Again Nurse*. I had paid for the script – a script I had total faith in – and I wanted someone to put up the money and provide distribution. But nobody seemed to understand that the stuff I was making could still make a fortune. No one wanted to know.'

The cast wasn't a problem. According to Peter, Hattie Jacques had already agreed to reprise her role as Matron, Kenneth Williams was happy to appear, and even Barbara Windsor and Charles Hawtrey were set to return to the Pinewood medical wards. The money never materialized. Although the idea never completely went away, and 1979 passed without a new *Carry On* going into production – the first year since the series started in 1958 which saw no new *Carry On* filming taking place at all – the series was considered a thing of the past.

When Hattie Jacques died of a massive heart attack at the age of 56, in October 1980, most people thought the idea for another medical *Carry On* was redundant. As it happened, the idea quickly resurfaced, but there's no doubting the shock waves that Hattie's death sent through the country. Nobody was more shocked than the *Carry On* producer himself. Peter speaks fondly of the lady who was often considered the mother superior of *Carry On*:

'She was a large lady in more ways than one – large in heart. She would sit on the set doing her *Times* crossword and all of the cast would gravitate towards her. If they had a problem they needed to talk about, Hattie would listen and quietly offer advice. She was never offended if you chose to ignore her advice, never boastful if you chose to follow it. She was simply Hattie, a tower of strength. Kind, understanding and generous to everybody.'

Chapter Sixteen
Columbus Sinks But Peter Swims

Peter could have been forgiven if he had abandoned all further ideas for *Carry On* films when Hattie Jacques died, but he still refused to give up. He did, though, thanks to Hattie's indelible mark as the archetypal matron, shelve the idea of another medical *Carry On*. That aside, thoughts of another *Carry On* were still very much alive. Just a few months after Hattie's death, Peter received a screenplay he had commissioned from writer Vince Powell.

With his late partner, Harry Driver, Vince had written the Sid James television hit of the 1960s, *George and the Dragon*, and Peter considered him the ideal person to write a *Carry On*. His script was designed to hit a nerve with every person in the country. At the time, the BBC had been showing *Dallas,* the flashy American oil business soap opera – and the current storyline had caught the public's imagination. Larry Hagman, starring as the devious cunning J R Ewing, had done one dirty deal too many and the question on everybody's lips was 'Who shot J R?'

The new *Carry On* seemed to be perfectly timed. Originally entitled *Carry On Texas*, the title was instantly changed to *Carry On Dallas* and Peter began casting. However, Peter's never-failing gut instinct was causing him concern. He was expecting trouble when he announced that he was planning to make *Carry On Dallas* and he got it. Kenneth Williams had been cast in the leading role of the J R Ewing parody, R U Screwing, Barbara Windsor was to play Lucy Screwing, Joan Sims was wanted for Miss Ellie, and Jack Douglas was cast as a twitching member of the Screwing family. Kenneth Connor and Bernard Bresslaw were also to be offered leading roles.

There was even a plan to pay tribute to Sid James, the late star of the series. Jimmy Tarbuck and Mike Reid were being considered to help plug the gap left by Sid's cockney charm, but the actor was to be involved – if only in spirit. The opening scene was to be the funeral of the head of the Screwing family, Jock. In later scenes, a portrait of the late Screwing would be featured. The face in the portrait was due to be the unforgettable mug of Sid James.

The script, however, although a hilarious piece of work, was thought by some people in the business to take the innuendo too far and Peter was persuaded to change the central family's name from Screwing to Ramming. The joke was less effective than the rhyming parody, but Peter reluctantly agreed. But it all proved fruitless anyway. Lorimar Productions, the makers of *Dallas*, got wind of the plan for a *Carry On* spoof and immediately threatened Peter with legal action. Unlike his battles some 20 years earlier over *Carry On Spying* and *Carry On Cleo*, Peter was not prepared to take on the TV giants.

He was very disappointed to miss the *Dallas* boom boat, but keen to get the *Carry On*s back into the cinema before a damagingly long gap developed between the release of *Carry On Emmannuelle* and a new film. After all, almost three years had passed since his ill-fated sex comedy had been released. But the opportunity to further the reputation of his beloved *Carry On* series came, ironically, not from the cinema chains but from the eternal threat to British film-making – television. *That's Carry On* – the 1977 film of classic *Carry On* moments linked by Kenneth Williams and Barbara Windsor – had received its television première on bank holiday Monday at the end of May 1981, and had pulled in a more than respectable 11 million viewers for ITV.

This successful airing prompted one TV head to approach Peter with an idea: 'Naturally we were busy trying to sell another *Carry On* film, which was proving more problematic than I could ever have imagined. We were trying to sell a proven commodity, after all. But no matter. Suddenly I was approached by Philip Jones, the head of Thames Television, who made those wonderful Benny Hill shows I admired so much. He said *That's Carry On* had been very popular and asked if we would consider doing a series of half-hour compilation programmes for the ITV network.'

The programmes were not planned to be new shows, but classic clips cut together without any need of linking material. Always happy to return to the scene of an earlier crime, Peter and Gerald accepted the commission and got straight to work sifting through dozens of hours of material to pick the best clips with which to put the shows together.

At the same time they had to consider cohesion. The programmes couldn't just be a series of one-liners – some building up of gags was required. Before the advent of video – and therefore the ability of some fans to literally get to know films backwards – there could be no assumption then, as now, that the average viewer would know just by looking what a scene was all about or if it was funny in relation to something that appeared earlier in the film.

To prevent having to film linking material – which would have slowed the shows down as well as putting the price of production up – Peter hit upon the idea of theming the programmes. Some were based on the medical *Carry On*s, others on the historicals, and another on the films' holiday exploits. By not cutting across the themes – and, therefore, the types of clips shown – the half-hour shows could sit very well as comic pieces in their own right.

The first series took some six months to cut together. Veteran editor Jack Gardner was brought in to help cut these vintage sequences into shape, to rearrange the musical work of his late friend, Eric Rogers, and to ensure that the scenes didn't seem too slow for the vicious appetite of the small screen.

The work was made slightly easier by the fact that they could only use clips from *Carry On* films for which the ITV network currently held a licence to broadcast – around half of the 30-strong series. The rights to the others were currently owned by the BBC. *Carry On Laughing*, which started its run on the last day of 1981, was an instant ratings' winner. The first show was watched by a staggering 16.5 million people, which made it the second most watched programme of the Christmas and New Year week.

The moral argument concerning Peter's use of film performances – some dating back 15 years – without either the permission of the actors involved or further payment for the privilege, still rages to this day. However, there is no doubting that the compilation shows -which were, as often as not, slipped into the schedules before the nationally popular *Coronation Street* – proved to be the perfect format for *Carry On* in the early 1980s. This format – namely 25-minute tasty chunks – was guaranteed to make the viewers laugh with familiarity and, more to the point, appreciate the sterling work from the likes of the late Sid James.

Peter Rogers also quickly turned out a BBC compilation series, *What a Carry On*, using the films which the BBC held the rights to, and a special Christmas version of the ITV show was presented by Kenneth Williams and Barbara Windsor in December 1983. What concerns Peter about this feverish workload in the early 1980s is that the majority of audiences and critics tended to dismiss it out of hand:

'The compilation programmes that Gerald and I worked on didn't just happen overnight, you know. People tended to think that just because we stopped making the films in 1978 the *Carry On* series was over and, more to the point, I remained bone idle. I didn't, I can assure you. It didn't just take five minutes to put these shows together. There were literally miles and miles of film to view and the entire process could often take up to a year to finish. So I was hardly lazy during those years!'

Peter had other things on his mind too. His wife Betty had retired in the mid 1970s following a falling out with the Rank Organisation, which had withdrawn support for her projects, forcing her to make the last three films of her career at Elstree Studios. Her health had begun to deteriorate with the onset of hip and knee trouble, and her problems had caused the couple to move out of their magnificent home. The great distances in the house at Drummer's Yard, with its long corridors and wide staircases, meant it was time to look for something smaller and more compact:

'It was 35 yards from the butler's pantry to the sitting-room. I know butlers' pantries don't exist much today, but that's what the room was called on the original plans and that's what we always called it, although it was mostly used for feeding the dogs. We found the house we wanted and installed a stair lift. We couldn't have done that at Drummer's Yard. We would have needed a model railway!'

Both Peter and Betty were fast approaching 70 years of age, and it really was time to slow down a little and spend more time together. As husband and wife they had recognized very early on in their relationship that they were not only married to each other, but also to their work. However, it was not a marriage of convenience – far from it – it was a marriage of understanding. They loved each other throughout every minute of their 50 years together. By mutual decision there had been no children. Their parental love had been spent on their animals, which required far less responsibility and created far less guilt when they were spending so much time away from home filming. They had made time for holidays over the years, and occasionally Peter had made a trip abroad to visit Betty while she was filming on location:

'Betty would naturally be busy, so it wasn't really a break. She would be working very hard with her director, Ralph Thomas, while I was supposedly on holiday, making it quite lonely. The shooting days were long and everyone was obviously tired in the evenings, with no one feeling particularly relaxed. Ironically, when there was time for a real break, Betty and I would go away with Ralph and his wife, Joy, sometimes to places where they had been filming. Then it felt like a proper holiday. We spent many happy times away with Ralph and Joy.

'We never went away with Gerald and Barbara Thomas – somehow that was different. I suppose they had a young family and that changed things. I believe Jack Douglas, though, visited Gerald in the south of France on more than one occasion.'

Peter, himself, loved the south of France. He and Betty would fly there and have their car delivered by a driver. Their favourite spot was the privately owned and secluded La Réserve in Beaulieu. They also adored the Hôtel de Paris in Monte Carlo. It was adjacent to the Casino, and symphony concerts were held there:

'We made a trip there one November, but never left the building because both Betty and I were hit by a flu bug and the doctor had to visit us every day. We also took holidays in Cairo and Alexandria, and many in Cyprus, which – before it was divided – became our favourite. We only went back once after the invasion and didn't like it very much. After that, we took to touring France – covering hundreds of miles on some days. But I mustn't forget Venice, which we loved to visit during all seasons, even when it was flooded!'

An opportunity to spend more time together arose from an invitation they received to become joint presidents of the Cinema and Television Veterans (CTV) in 1983. This organization, with its hundreds of members, held many of its events at Pinewood Studios. Peter was still based at the studios with slightly less to do, and the opportunity gave Betty a reason to revisit her 'second home' on a regular basis.

At the first CTV council meeting they attended, Peter suggested that for the next annual event for the veterans they should hold a dinner and dance instead of the usual dinner with a guest speaker, who would, Peter felt, just bore the pants off everybody with his life story. Peter said he would engage the famous Joe Loss and his orchestra to play popular vintage music for the oldies to dance to. A gasp of horror echoed around the room. Oldies dancing? How preposterous! Peter was asked to think again. He insisted that the veterans would like it and also pointed out that older members only made up part of the organization and that there were many younger men and women who qualified as veterans only because they joined the film industry in their teens, and membership was based on service not age.

So outraged were the CTV council members that they formed splinter groups to consider how to change Peter's mind about the dancing. Even John Davis, head of the Rank Organisation, got involved, as did future film commissioner Sir Sydney Samuelson. But Peter was not to be moved. He had meetings with Joe Loss and the plans went ahead for a veterans' dinner and dance.

Everybody loved it and everybody danced. John Davis admitted to Betty that he had been wrong and Peter had been right: 'He had his finger on the public pulse as usual,' he told her. The dinner dances became a regular event throughout Peter and Betty's seven-year stint as presidents – although, as Peter remembers, changes were made to the line-up:

'I had to change from Joe Loss. He was too loud and people at the tables could hardly hear themselves think, let alone speak. When I told him we couldn't continue with his orchestra, he cried – actually wept. It was quite embarrassing. He wouldn't admit his music was too loud. It wasn't so much the orchestra as the singers – four of them belting it out at separate microphones. We surreptitiously unplugged some of his amplifiers, but it was still too loud. We engaged the Glenn Miller Orchestra after that. They were a great success and we continued with them until the end of our tenure of office.'

Peter would happily have gone on – and the Committee was certainly happy for the couple to continue – but Betty wasn't feeling up to it. It was the beginning of the ill health that would dog her for the rest of her days. There was no more dancing for the veterans after that. It was back to the dinners and a guest speaker.

Peter still hadn't given up on the idea of making another *Carry On*. The success of the compilation shows was proof in his eyes that the country loved his product. He was, however, becoming more realistic about the changes in the industry and the chances of getting one off the ground. He started to use his spare office time to return to his first professional passion – writing – and wrote some novels, with impressive results.

However, throughout the 1980s he was quietly noting a growing cult popularity for the *Carry On* series: 'Every time I saw someone like Kenneth Connor or Kenneth Williams interviewed on television, the only subject people seemed interested in was the *Carry On* series. The most asked question always seemed to be, "Are they going to make another *Carry On* film?" As I was one half of the "they", I thought that could mean the time was right to try again'.

Following the 1987 launch of Video Collection International's classic *Carry On* range from the Rank era, Peter announced his intention to make another film. Again the film was destined to send up *Dallas*. The Vince Powell script was dusted down and slightly amended to reflect the current storylines in the American soap opera. The series had now been running for eight years to huge worldwide audiences and had spent a massive 146 weeks in the UK TV charts. Indeed, the series was so popular that over eleven million viewers were regularly tuning in once a week for the BBC1 screenings.

Ironically, repeat showings of the *Carry On* films during the same year were pulling in the same number of viewers. It seemed fated that the two should be brought together. However, once again legal action was threatened by the makers of *Dallas*. So Peter thought, why bother? He had another plan up his sleeve:

'It was rather amusing actually that I could get them so het up – as if a little British comedy could really hurt their viewing figures. I suggested to the writers that we call it *Carry On Down Under* and transfer the setting to Australia. The soap *Neighbours* had just started on television and had better ratings than *Dallas*.'

Australia had always been a good market for the *Carry On* films and when the news hit the country, immense interest was aroused amongst various Australian companies. Never one to travel unless he really had to, Peter stayed at Pinewood working out the details of production and working on the script, while Gerald made the trip to Melbourne to look for locations. The rest of this story is confused, as Peter tries to explain: 'Gerald discovered that there was no Australian money after all – £500,000 had apparently been put aside, but someone had run off with it. Floreat Australia!'

Gerald returned home and the idea was put on hold, only to be discarded altogether shortly afterwards. Peter was particularly upset because he had a lot of relatives in Australia and 'rather fancied meeting them on their home territory for the first time!'

Following this less than professional end to the potential hot release *Carry On Down Under*, Peter still had the bit between his teeth. The year was now 1988, a decade since *Carry On Emmannuelle* had sunk without trace in British cinemas, and Peter was only too conscious that, with his films now available on video, eager young fans were shelling out tenners to enjoy a *Carry On* in the privacy of their homes. Thanks to this, the *Carry On*s were reaching a new peak in their cult popularity.

Aware that 1988 marked the 30th anniversary of the release of *Carry On Sergeant*, his first *Carry On* film, and also the 30th anniversary of the filming of his second film, *Carry On Nurse*, Peter was determined to mark this special occasion, and announced that he was to make *Carry On Again Nurse*. The screenplay was not to be the unused X-rated idea that George Layton and Jonathan Lynn had penned nine years earlier, nor the treatment that Don Maclean had been commissioned to write. For this special occasion, a very special writer, Norman Hudis, was asked to deliver the script.

The film centred around a hospital due for closure and an oddball set of characters who went about saving the institution. The years hadn't dated Norman Hudis's ability to write about a bunch of incompetents sticking two fingers up at bureaucracy and winning. And the subject was particularly apposite at a time when National Health Service hospitals were closing across the country. People understood the subject because they were living through it.

One thing that age had brought Norman was the ability to write less sentimentally with more of the *double entendres* that had been prevalent throughout the Talbot Rothwell years. There were jokes about being circumspect: 'Blimey, at my time of life, I hope not. It wouldn't half hurt'; and a postman with diarrhoea: 'When did you first notice it? When I took my bicycle clips off.' Yes, it was subtle stuff – and very funny.

Parts had been written for surviving cast members, including Kenneth Williams, Charles Hawtrey, Joan Sims and Barbara Windsor. Some were approached, including Kenneth, and had accepted a role. There was a reminder of *Carry On*s past in a tribute to a former colleague, when the new matron, Joan Sims – after the hospital has been saved – turns round a photo, which shows Hattie Jacques in her Sister's outfit, and says: 'Well? Did I do all right?'

It was all wonderful stuff and Peter had pulled the money together to make it. The production date for filming was set for the first week of June 1988 – and then the news that no one wanted to hear, happened. On Friday 15 April 1988, a shocked country mourned the death of Kenneth Williams, the longest-serving *Carry On* actor of them all. He was only 62.

Having appeared in 26 of the 30 films made, the death of this prolific *Carry On* star made national headlines, and the nation mourned his passing. Peter knew the film had lost one of its major draws and the project had to be put on hold. Of all the deaths to afflict the *Carry On* cast, few would sadden Peter Rogers more than the passing of Kenneth Williams:

'I thought the world of him. He brought me so much pleasure over the years. I became good friends with him and, as people will testify, that wasn't always easy with Kenneth. He came to our house for dinner on several occasions over the years, and we would sit and talk on the most serious of subjects. He was always good company whether he was showing off or not.'

Just over six months later, in a nursing home in Deal, Kent, Charles Hawtrey died aged 73. And once again, Peter was rocked: 'I had known Charles for years and had used him in films even before we made the *Carry On*s. The secret of his success was that he was always the same. He was good, whatever the part. I once wrote a tongue-twister for him – in my film *To Dorothy a Son*. He was supposed to be a mechanic in a garage and was supposed to say to his boss, "Bloke's back brake light's broke." He never faltered on the take. I know many highly paid actors who would have taken all morning getting that line right. He was one of the best comedy actors this country has ever produced.'

Peter now knew that *Carry On Again Nurse* would not be made: 'We had lost two of its top stars – and other cast members were no longer keen to make a film. It was to have been a tribute to everything that had been before, especially to those who had already departed. The deaths of Kenneth and Charles, two actors who had made *Carry On Nurse* so funny in the first place, were just too fresh in everyone's minds. I had no choice but to halt the film'.

As well as the public tragedies that were befalling the *Carry On*s at this time, Peter also had some personal problems which were causing him a major headache. He was regarded throughout the business as a keen and shrewd businessman, but there was one thing which could upset his finely tuned ability to see a good deal, and that was friendship. Peter was – and still is – a philanthropic individual. He gives to a host of good causes without ever letting his donations be known. At Pinewood he would often help out in cases where help was needed. It is a subject he is embarrassed to talk about:

'One good thing about having money is that you can help people. If I heard of someone at the studios who needed help, I would send something. Nobody approached me or asked. I don't think I would have done anything if they had. It is a wonderful feeling, though, when you are able to help with no strings attached.'

Peter's beneficence, however, was almost his undoing. He came a cropper in the late 1980s when he decided to help someone who, perhaps on reflection, he shouldn't have done. What started as a small loan for a project escalated into quite prodigious amounts until Peter's accountants advised him to opt for bankruptcy, which, humiliatingly, he was forced to do. He lost a vast amount of money – some unsubstantiated reports place the figure at £500,000 – although Peter will not admit to any fixed amount:

'I lost a lot of money, that is all I can say. I was guilty of putting all my eggs into one bastard! My life didn't change all that much and I soon recovered. Betty was worried, of course, because she saw that I was worried. The most unfortunate aspect of the whole affair was that I lost someone who I thought was a friend – and a friend is worth more than money.'

Despite the abandonment of *Carry On Again Nurse*, Peter still announced more *Carry On* projects. This time, the idea was to make a series of four self-contained, hour-long *Carry On* films for television. The likes of Frankie Howerd, Kenneth Connor and Barbara Windsor were continually mooted as being involved. Annoyed, some of the artistes later complained that nobody asked them in advance before their names were automatically and, seemingly, officially linked to this new *Carry On* product.

Rumours of new *Carry On*s continued unabated throughout the late 1980s and early 1990s; in 1989, after a pause to show respect, Peter said he hoped to make *Carry On Again Nurse*, and in 1991 he revealed that he was about to put a half-hour series of *Carry On*s into production for the ITV network. All these plans came to nought. Thus, when in early 1992 a press report claimed that the cameras were due to start rolling on another film – *Carry On Columbus* – most people simply took it as another rumour.

What made this particular rumour even less likely to be true was that Gerald Thomas had recently left Peter Rogers to go off and explore the possibility of making his own films. As Peter explains: 'Gerald Thomas decided that he wanted to break away from me and try to make films on his own, but I'm afraid he didn't get very far. He made one, which he produced and directed himself, but it was never shown, in spite of a lot of ballyhoo about a charity première which never came off.

'There were one or two other abortive attempts after that until John Goldstone, a friend he had been working with, came up with the idea of

Carry On Columbus to celebrate the 500th anniversary of the year in which a certain man made the biggest mistake in his life – he discovered America and set the world drinking Coca Cola.'

John Goldstone, who was responsible for producing Monty Python film classics such as *Life of Brian* and *The Meaning of Life*, had indeed found the £2 million needed to finance the idea, but, of course, if he and Gerald wanted to call their project a *Carry On*, they couldn't do it without Peter's permission. So Peter was offered the title of executive producer.

Dave Freeman, who was commissioned to write the script, claims that he was given only a fortnight to complete it. Peter read the script and didn't find it funny, but he didn't blame Dave Freeman, who had produced several good works for him in the past. Another concern that Peter voiced was the lack of well-known *Carry On* faces in the cast. He was told that the financiers wanted new faces and had insisted on more up-to-date television personalities. Peter, however, felt that that decision was fatal:

'I felt sorry for them [the new faces]. They may have been names in television, but they had no connection with the *Carry Ons*. Most of them were comedians, not actors who could perform comedy – there is a major difference. A comedian tells jokes; an actor acts the lines and derives the humour from the situation. That's what was so brilliant about Sid and Kenny and all the others. First and foremost, they were great actors.'

Filming got off to a sad start. Frankie Howerd – one of the few names to set the fans' hearts pumping – died just days before filming on *Carry On Columbus* started. He had been cast to play the fretful King of Spain (a role eventually played by Leslie Phillips). If Peter was sad at that news, he became even more depressed during the production. Early every morning he viewed the previous day's rushes with producer John Goldstone. While Goldstone chuckled away, Peter remained silent. He couldn't see what was funny. On occasions he even asked what the joke was. He genuinely couldn't see the humour in what he was being shown:

'I never laughed at our own comedies, but I *knew* they were funny. The more I saw of *Columbus*, the more depressed I became. Gerald worked terribly hard on it and I felt sorry for him. I think he realized early on that there was not much teamwork among the new cast and he wasn't getting the performances he had hoped for. The only people who appeared at all real were the original *Carry On* players such as Jim Dale, Bernard Cribbins and Jack Douglas. Of the newcomers I would happily cast Sara Crowe and Julian Clary in any *Carry On* I might make. But none of the others.'

The film was not well received. Critics and fans alike dubbed it the worst film of 1992. It was a sad epitaph to the world's longest-running series of British film comedies, going out with a moan rather than a bang.

With what proved to be the final, ill-fated *Carry On* out of the way, 1993 saw the sad deaths of three key people involved in the series. Bernard Bresslaw, aged 59, died of a heart attack in his dressing-room as he was about to go on stage at the Regent's Park Open Air Theatre in June, and Kenneth Connor, aged 77, passed away in November after suffering from cancer. Peter remembers his two friends with great affection:

'Bernard really was a gentle giant – 6ft 7in of gentlemanly kindness. He was a lovely man and a great actor. Kenny Connor became a good friend too. He had a passion for sailing, and as a bit of a sailor myself, that endeared him to me. I believe his father served on the royal yacht – and I have always found that people who have dealings with the sea work at a different rate to the ordinary man. They are more reliable and their appreciation of life is different – no doubt something to do with coping with the sea in all its moods. You can't play about with the sea, you are too near to God. Kenneth was a very funny man who seemed able to assume the most extraordinary voices when telling his innumerable stories. He always kept us in fits of laughter.'

But fate had not yet played its last card against the *Carry On*s in 1993. November of that year was to bring to Peter the ultimate sense of loss that any one death associated with the *Carry On*s could bring. Just a few weeks before Kenneth Connor passed away, Peter received a phone call on 9 November to tell him that Gerald Thomas, his work partner, director and friend of 42 years, had died at home of a heart attack. He was 72. He had just finished work on the new compilation series, *Laugh With the Carry Ons,* for ITV. Peter was distraught:

'It was such a shock – he always looked so healthy and well – and had such energy and love of life and his work. I nicknamed him Speedy Gonzales because he went through the schedule like the Ferrari he used to drive. After just two days' shooting on a picture, people used to shout to him in the corridors at Pinewood, "How many days ahead now, Gerald – how many weeks ahead?" And that was Gerald, one of the best and most professional people I have had the pleasure to work with. He was often dubbed "The Headmaster" by the "schoolchildren" who made up the cast. But he loved those children, as he loved the films we made. In all the years we worked together I never saw him lose his temper on set. He was a good man, a good director, and most of all a good friend.'

Afterword

On 15 January 1999, Betty Box died peacefully in her sleep. She was 83 and had been suffering from cancer. This crippling illness had stolen the two most important ladies in Peter's life – his mother and his wife. Betty's funeral took place at Amersham on 23 January, with Peter surrounded by family and friends – among them people who had worked on Betty's films and his, from in front of and behind the cameras.

As well as tears there was laughter. Sir Donald Sinden reminisced with screenwriter Norman Hudis and Joan Sims locked walking sticks with Betty's former director, Ralph Thomas. Peter smiled bravely, but his grief was plain for everyone to see.

There were those who thought that for Peter – who would be 85 in just a few weeks' time – this would be the end. He had lost most of his favoured film cast, had lost his director, and now he had lost the most important person in his world. What was there left for this man to do?

Within a few days, Peter was back at Pinewood. Every morning in his office, pen in hand, he desperately tried to find the words for a novel, when all the time his mind was so full of pain and grief that he was hardly able to think, let alone write. With his house empty, Pinewood had granted him special permission to bring his Alsatian dog, Heidi, into the studios every day. So now, with no need or desire to rush home at lunchtime, as he had done for the past few years to check on Betty, he became a permanent fixture of the Pinewood restaurant. Slowly the black cloud of sadness started to lift.

The pain was – and is – still there, but it is becoming easier to cope with now. Peter has comforted himself with getting Betty's autobiography, *Lifting the Lid*, published. Betty had worked extremely hard on this project – writing it herself, during her last few years while she was mainly housebound. And, for Peter, there is still talk of more *Carry On*s – perhaps not a film, but a series of one-hour television shows. It's not out of the question. Is it?

The prospect of future productions is what keeps a spring in Peter's step – this, plus the endless fan letters that flood into his office, day in, day out, week after week. It never ends – and that is Peter's desire, to see the legacy of the *Carry On*s carry on. As long as there is laughter in this world, and videos and DVD players, and TV schedulers looking for something cheap, cheerful, and, most of all, popular, to broadcast late on a Friday night, no one will forget them.

But all that counts for little now. Peter would give it all up to have Betty back. But he accepts that cannot happen. For the first time, he is able to talk about his feelings about Betty's death:

'When Betty died, my world and, it seemed, my own life came to an end. We had been married for over fifty years, but had been friends long before that – and had spent our lives working in the film industry. So, how do you fill a gap like that? You can't, of course, and you shouldn't try. You live with an empty chair in your room. It's not easy. But Betty is there in the empty chair while I try to continue with my life and my writing. I have started a new career – writing novels. It keeps me busy, otherwise I'd go mad, which may not be so much of a change. So, my career has gone full circle. I started in the film industry as a writer and so this is where I came in.'

So for Peter, life now, although so much emptier than ever before, still has meaning and purpose. In effect, he wants more than anything to embrace those two words which he has made universally famous and, uniquely, his own… he wants simply to carry on.

The Career of Peter Rogers

AS A WRITER

★ *Thought for the Week*

A series of religious shorts made by Religious Films Limited and commissioned by flour merchant, film mogul and devout Methodist J Arthur Rank. Peter Rogers penned a selection of these five-minute productions throughout 1942.

★ *Human Straw*

A play performed – for seven days – at the Players' Theatre. The theme was unconsummated marriage.

★ *Mr Mercury*

The first comedy penned by the man who would keep an entire generation laughing, this play told the tale of an Australian who inherits a place in English high society. The laughs came from culture shock and a comedy of manners. Performed at the Arts Theatre, it ran for 10 days.

★ *The Man Who Bounced*

Another comic stage play from the struggling playwright.

★ *Mr South Starts a War*

A further dramatic stage piece.

★ *Cards on the Table*

A stage play which was successfully adapted for BBC Radio.

★ *Holiday Camp*

A compendium of stories based round various working-class families enjoying a relaxing time at a typical British holiday camp. In the section that Peter Rogers wrote, Dennis Price played the murderous, silky-smooth baddie who seduces the ill at ease, twittering Esma Cannon. Old maid Flora Robson discovers her blinded, long-lost wartime sweetheart, Esmond Knight, and crafty cockney John Blythe fleeces young and naive Jimmy Hanley. However, the most lasting element of the film remains the Huggett family. Headed by Kathleen Harrison and Jack Warner, the family included the ultra-sexy figure of Susan Shaw and went on to feature in several big screen spin-off productions.

With Hazel Court, Emrys Jones, Yvonne Owen, Peter Hammond, Diana Dors and Charlie Chester. Co-written by Muriel and Sydney Box, Ted Willis, Mabel and Denis Constanduros and Godfrey Winn. Produced by Sydney Box. Directed by Ken Annakin, 1947.

★ Here Come the Huggetts

The first feature-length spin-off for Jack Warner and Kathleen Harrison as *Holiday Camp* couple, Mr and Mrs Huggett. That crafty spiv, John Blythe, reappeared, as did Jimmy Hanley and Susan Shaw as their troublesome kids. A domestic soap opera with domestic dilemmas, youthful romance and plenty of working-class high jinks. The series continued with a political slant in *Vote for Huggett*, later in 1948, and the French trip in the 1949 film *The Huggetts Abroad*.

With Jane Hylton, Petula Clark, David Tomlinson, Diana Dors and Peter Hammond. Co-written by Mabel and Denis Constanduros and Muriel and Sydney Box. Produced by Betty E Box. Directed by Ken Annakin, 1948.

★ Up to His Neck

A bunch of British naval chaps get stranded on a desert island and meet up with the grass-skirted dancer of Hattie Jacques.

With Harry Fowler and Norman Mitchell, 1954.

AS ASSOCIATE PRODUCER

★ It's Not Cricket

Those great comic creations, Charters and Caldicott, as played by Basil Radford and Naunton Wayne, are resurrected as a couple of frightfully British chaps on the trail of a Nazi spy. Wonderfully entertaining comedy adventure, with notable supporting work from celebrated Rank glamour starlets Diana Dors and Susan Shaw.

With Maurice Denham and Nigel Buchanan. Written by Gerard Bryant, Lyn Lockwood and Bernard MacNab. Produced by Betty E. Box. Directed by Alfred Roome, 1949.

★ Don't Ever Leave Me

Jimmy Hanley, playing against type as a rather heartless abductor, kidnaps a young girl (played by the sweet and innocent Petula Clark), and faces home truths as the girlish captive falls in love with him. Rather daring for the time and contrasting a familiar Rank cast of young stars with a storyline of corrupted domestic drama based on the novel *The Wide Guy* by Anthony Armstrong.

With Edward Rigby, Hugh Sinclair, Linden Travers and Anthony Newley. Written by Robert Westerby. Directed by Arthur Crabtree, 1949.

★ *Marry Me!*

Light years before *Carry On Loving* came this four-part portmanteau relating the funny and pathos-driven tales of a quartet of couples from a marriage bureau. It may lack the 'Cor!' factor of the Sid James classic, but there is plenty of emotive drama and lightweight comedy in the script from Peter Rogers and the usual Gainsborough crew. David Tomlinson and Susan Shaw, fresh from *Holiday Camp*, star.

With Patrick Holt, Carol Marsh, Derek Bond and Guy Middleton. Co-written by Lewis Gilbert and Denis Waldock. Produced by Betty E Box. Directed by Terence Fisher, 1949.

★ *Appointment With Venus*

David Niven and his gang of trusty British servicemen rescue an invaluable cow from the Channel Islands, under the occupation of Germany during the Second World War. Kenneth More, a favourite actor of Peter Rogers, and future *Carry On* legend Peter Butterworth are among the supporting cast. The film is based on the novel by Jerrard Tickell.

With Glynis Johns, George Coulouris, Barry Jones, Noel Purcell and Bernard Lee. Written by Nicholas Phipps. Produced by Betty E Box Directed by Ralph Thomas, 1951.

★ *Venetian Bird*

Richard Todd stars as a dogged private detective trying to discover a neglected wartime hero-cum-petty-criminal in postwar Vienna. Shamelessly retreading similar ground to Carol Reed's masterly *The Third Man*, this dark and tense thriller includes a delightfully unconvincing Italian supporting turn from Sid James, and a blink and you'll miss an appearance by the producer herself.

With Eva Bartok, John Gregson, George Coulouris, Margot Grahame and Walter Rilla. Written by Victor Canning. Produced by Betty E Box. Directed by Ralph Thomas, 1952.

AS PRODUCER

★ *The Dog and the Diamond*

A 1953 Children's Film Foundation featurette. Hugely popular and finely crafted, the film won first prize at the Venice Film Festival. The cast includes the star of 16 *Carry On* films, Peter Butterworth.

Written by Peter Rogers, 1953

★ *You Know What Sailors Are!*

And yes, we all know what sailors are, and here star Donald Sinden helps to prove it. As well as producing, Peter Rogers wrote the screenplay for this slightly naughty nautical comedy.

Directed by Ken Annakin, 1953.

★ *The Gay Dog*

Radio star Wilfred Pickles stars in this sentimental comedy drama as a miner who trains his beloved pet greyhound to win races. The script was written by Peter Rogers, based on the play by Joseph Colton.

With Petula Clark, John Blythe, Megs Jenkins and Peter Butterworth Directed by Maurice Elvey, 1954.

★ *To Dorothy a Son*

A hapless handsome hero – played by John Gregson – is trapped by the amorous advances of a wild American film starlet, played by Shelley Winters. A rather risqué narrative – rumours of illegitimate children, comic blackmail and sexual politics – is balanced by the no–nonsense Englishness of Peggy Cummins. Released in America under the title *Cash on Delivery*.

With Alfie Bass, Wilfrid Hyde-White, Joan Sims and Charles Hawtrey.
Written by Peter Rogers. Directed by Muriel Box, 1954.

★ *Circus Friends*

Another Children's Film Foundation production, historically important as the first Peter Rogers production directed by his long-term partner Gerald Thomas. Peter also wrote the script. Carol White – later one of the crafty schoolkids in *Carry On Teacher* – and Alan Coleshill star as the emotional children who rescue an abused circus horse from certain death. Character star Hal Osmond dubbed the 13-year-old blonde bombshell Carol White as 'pure jail bait'. The *Carry On* connection was already being made. The music was composed by Bruce Montgomery and the editor was Peter Boita – later to work on both *Carry On Sergeant* and *Carry On Emmannuelle*.

With John Horsley and Sam Kydd. Directed by Gerald Thomas, 1956.

★ *Passionate Stranger*

Margaret Leighton plays the charming novelist, whose novel convinces her faithful chauffeur (Ralph Richardson) that she actually loves him, in this unique comedy produced by Peter Rogers. Filmed in black and white, *Passionate Stranger* includes the gimmicky touch of a sequence in Eastmancolor.

With Marjorie Rhodes, Thorley Walters and Frederick Piper. Written by Muriel and Sydney Box. Directed by Muriel Box, 1956.

★ *After the Ball*

Ambitious biopic of the energetic music hall artiste Vesta Tilley, with Pat Kirkwood taking the lead role.

With Laurence Harvey, Clive Morton and Jerry Verno. Written by Hubert Gregg. Directed by Compton Bennett, 1957.

★ *Vicious Circle*

That definitive hard-done-by, much-haunted hero of British cinema, John Mills, is perfectly cast as the hounded Doctor Latimer in this fast-moving, tightly constructed thriller. Based on the story *The Brass Candlestick*, by Francis Durbridge, the story tells of an ill-fated actress who is found dead in the poor doctor's flat. Even more damning, the murder weapon is discovered in his car and, on the run, the doctor needs to prove his innocence before capture.

With Derek Farr, Mervyn Johns, Wilfrid Hyde-White, Roland Culver, Lionel Jeffries, Noelle Middleton, Rene Ray and Lisa Daniely. Written by Francis Durbridge. Directed by Gerald Thomas, 1957.

★ *Time Lock*

The nearest that the Peter Rogers/Gerald Thomas partnership ever got to the Hitchcockian thriller they longed to make, this is a stunning minor British thriller classic which was based on a celebrated television serial from writer Arthur Hailey. The film tells the gripping tale of a small boy (Vincent Walker), who gets trapped in the overnight safe of a bank vault with a time lock system. Robert Beatty is the international hero and Sean Connery – as a lowly blowlamp operator – makes his big screen début. Alan Gifford – later the governor in *Carry On Cowboy* – also appeared, and the script was written by producer Peter Rogers himself.

With Peter Hennessy, Betty McDowall, Lee Patterson and Robert Ayres. Directed by Gerald Thomas, 1957.

★ *The Duke Wore Jeans*

Having been in the business for all of five minutes, Tommy Steele, British teen rock 'n' roll sensation, was given the ultimate honour, a film biopic called *The Tommy Steele Story,* produced by Herbert Smith. The writer was Norman Hudis. Never slow to miss a profitable film asset, Peter Rogers signed up the pop favourite for *The Duke Wore Jeans,* a reworking of *The Prisoner of Zenda.* In this, Tommy plays a dual role – a posh prince and a cockney singer. The two swap places *à la* Cinderella's principal boys and Tommy, the rockster, woos the prince's lady love, played by June Laverick.

   With Michael Medwin, Alan Wheatley and Eric Pohlmann. Music by Bruce Montgomery. Songs by Lionel Bart and Michael Pratt. Written by Norman Hudis. Directed by Gerald Thomas, 1958.

★ *Chain of Events*

John Clarke, an uninspiring sort of fellow, works in a bank, and one day, having boarded a bus on his way home, forgets to pay his fare. He is caught by the inspector and, while being questioned, gives the name and address of one of the bank's clients. In doing so, he sets into motion a violent chain of events involving blackmail, robbery and death.

   With Susan Shaw, Dermot Walsh, Jack Watling and Lisa Gastoni. Directed by Gerald Thomas, 1958.

★ *The Solitary Child*

The marriage of Harriet, a well-known London model, to Captain James Random causes a sensation. Just two years previously, Random was acquitted in dubious circumstances of the murder of his first wife, and there is still widespread doubt in the public mind as to whether he is the man who 'got away with it'.

   With Philip Friend, Barbara Shelley, Sarah Lawson and Julia Lockwood. Directed by Gerald Thomas, 1958.

★ *Carry On Sergeant*

A kind-hearted but hard around the edges army sergeant is about to retire and, confidently, agrees to a bet that his very last platoon will be his very first star platoon. A film which launched a thousand quips, or has got a huge amount to answer for, depending upon which side you are on. This delicious, spiralling, life-enhancing, fun-packed, roller-coaster runs through tired old jokes, creaky comic stereotypes, barrack-room companionship and sloppy romantic misfortunes, without taking a breath.

Bob Monkhouse and Shirley Eaton are the lovelorn newly married couple, immediately split up on their wedding day thanks to her husband's conscription. That side of things shovels sexual frustration and misunderstanding into the mix, but the actors who really captured the essence of life in khaki were those core members who went on to become *Carry On* legends.

There is the pompous, vowel-bending superiority of Kenneth Williams, the sickly, paranoid, doom-laden angst of Kenneth Connor, and the boyish, slightly camp bemusement of Charles Hawtrey. The latter, of course, had been a staple part of the cast of ITV's hit comedy, *The Army Game*.

William Hartnell and Norman Rossington are also part of the small screen squad and their presence in the cast did no harm at all to the success of the very first *Carry On* film. Hattie Jacques and Terry Scott – who makes the initial, plot-shaping bet with Hartnell – also crop up in this ground-breaking picture.

Sentimentality, fairly blue humour and bucketloads of feel-good factor became the norm for the Norman Hudis era, and this little film, making its small £74,000 budget back in a matter of days, started something so big that nobody involved from the outset could have guessed.

With Eric Barker, Bill Owen, Terence Longdon, Gerald Campion and Dora Bryan. Written by Norman Hudis. Directed by Gerald Thomas, 1958.

★ *Carry On Nurse*

Lightning does strike twice and it struck again for Peter Rogers and the *Carry On* crew for this second bite of the innuendo cherry. Basically, it is life and love in the corridors of a typical men's ward in a National Health hospital. Terence Longdon and Shirley Eaton go through the romantic motions as the painstricken, bedstricken local newspaper reporter and the glamorous blonde bombshell staff nurse. However, as with *Carry On Sergeant*, the pathos-ridden core of the comedy comes in a very bad second to the slap-and-tickle, grin-and-bear-it community of the ward itself.

Nostril-flaring, authority-baiting swot Kenneth Williams gets all hoity-toity again, Kenneth Connor takes a different direction with his hard-man boxer reverting to nervous energy as his dignity and boxer shorts are whipped away, and Charles Hawtrey – playing away from the gang for the majority of the time – is happily locked within his own mini-universe through his radio headphones.

Carry On favourite Joan Sims makes her début, and the script fully utilizes the wealth of hospital stories provided by the screenplay writer's wife, Rita Hudis. For the most part it's a fairly carefree and unstructured romp through medical misunderstanding, camp crusading and raffish charm – the latter brilliantly brought to life by Leslie Phillips – but there's real heart at work in the sentimental comedy. Williams gets to play the gamut, from pompous outrage to sheepish enchantment, opposite Bohemian nougat-fancier, Jill Ireland.

And, stomping and storming into view through the corridors of Pinewood Studios, Hattie Jacques is upgraded from the supporting role of medical officer from the first film to bellowing, ground-shaking matron here. Her place as a *Carry On* regular was assured.

The climax, persistent patient Wilfrid Hyde-White unwittingly having his rectal thermometer replaced by a daffodil, has gone down in cinema history. This gag – used to promote the film with the use of over two million plastic flowers – secured a unique hit for the series in the United States of America and made the film the number one box-office draw in British cinemas for 1959. The *Carry On* series was here to stay.

With Bill Owen, Brian Oulton, Susan Stephen, Susan Shaw, Michael Medwin and Norman Rossington. Written by Norman Hudis. Directed by Gerald Thomas, 1959.

★ *Carry On Teacher*

In many ways the 'forgotten' *Carry On*, this little ramble through the British educational system holds no great influence in the films' initial success, nor changed the style radically from the opening two efforts, but there is an irresistible, dark, damp Wednesday afternoon off-school feel to the comedy, conjuring up a repeated collection of glorious eccentrics in the bemused and bewildered teaching staff of headmaster Ted Ray.

The old gang is back with a vengeance but this time, instead of playing the teaching lark for incompetent laughs, there is a modicum of talent in science master Kenneth Connor, physical education mistress Joan Sims and maths mistress – complete with flowing cloak and mortarboard hat – Hattie Jacques.

The childish bickering at the centre of the staff room is gaily and gamely supplied by a delicious two-handed battle between Kenneth Williams and Charles Hawtrey. Distressed at the wealth of the schoolchildren's organized pranks which throw up everything from stink bombs and itching powder to destroyed pianos and mass destruction, the ultimate headlong conflict results in a disastrous staging of *Romeo and Juliet*.

With Williams obsessed with the rhythm of the language and Hawtrey equally protective of the rhythm of his especially composed music, this is an artistic clash guaranteed to cause fireworks. However, the teachers contrast with the idealist, calculated and moralistic school-children – including young hopefuls Richard O'Sullivan and Carol White – who only cause the problem in order to stop beloved head-master, Ray, leaving for a super-duper new school.

In an age of rock 'n' roll riots, *The Blackboard Jungle* and Bill Haley's 'Rock Around the Clock' as a soundtrack for cinema seat ripping, this school film is a time warp back to the pre-*St Trinian*'s era, with an almost Billy Bunter-styled affection for learning and learners. It's an inner city school with an outer limits setting.

With Leslie Phillips, Rosalind Knight and Cyril Chamberlain. Written by Norman Hudis. Directed by Gerald Thomas, 1959.

★ *Please Turn Over*
Something of a celebrated scandal on the West End stage at the time, this jolly romp through teenage imagination, sexy literal achievements and maturity in the public gaze was actually based on the play, *Book of the Month*, by Basil Thomas. A sub-level *Carry On* – even the music was by Bruce Montgomery and photography by *Constable*'s Ted Scaife – the headlining star was, again, Ted Ray, before his Associated British Pic-ture Company (ABPC) contract resulted in Rogers being forced to drop him from his repertory company.

Margaret Lockwood's young daughter Julia was cast in the central role as the frustrated middle-class author of a sexy novel utilizing friends and family around her. The result? Angst and chaos in subur-bia. The film cleverly depicts the characters in normal circumstances, juxtaposed with the saucy elements from the book, with amazed reac-tions from the characters as they read about the secret lives of those closest to them. For some, it's a sort of back-handed blessing – mild-mannered doctor, Leslie Phillips, is revealed as a sex-mad Casanova, resulting in advances from glamorous patients which almost ruins his besotted love for assistant, June Jago. While for others it's a curse – Ted Ray's solid businessman is depicted as an embezzling, drunken failure, lavishing expensive gifts on his secretary (played with delicious relish by Dilys Laye), until the money has gone and his life is ruined.

Charles Hawtrey steals the limelight as the supercilious, sickly-smiling, money-grabbing jeweller, while that other *Carry On* stalwart, Joan Sims, is blessed with the brilliant double-edged role as housekeeper to the family. In reality, she's a fag-puffing, sour-faced harridan, but in Lockwood's fantasy world she's a frilly-knickered, ever-caring French maid.

The rather twee ending – love in the city with an angst-free, angry young man playwright – tends to let the comic side down somewhat, but it can be forgiven because of the truly inspired scenes featuring a cliché woman driver, Jean Kent, and terrified instructor, Lionel Jeffries.

Written by Norman Hudis. Directed by Gerald Thomas, 1959.

★ *Carry On Constable*
It may be *Carry On Sergeant* in different uniforms, but this fourth entry in the series marks a major turning point. Sid James – filling the vacated shoes of solid narrative focal point Ted Ray – is thrown into the deep end with truncheon, helmet and police whistle at the ready. A baptism of fire, he is surrounded by the central trio at the heart of the early *Carry On* incompetence – snobbish Kenneth Williams, ultra-superstitious Kenneth Connor and limp-wristed Charles Hawtrey – as well as the rakish charisma of Leslie Phillips, the steely efficiency of Joan Sims, and the loyal devotion of Hattie Jacques.

Episodic in the usual Hudis manner, moments of bizarre surrealism – a shared vision of ancient Rome – perfectly contrast with the fondly remembered comic interludes of bare-bummed coppers rushing from a freezing cold shower, mincing drag antics, flu-ridden anarchy, old-fashioned values and clumsy intelligence. Eric Barker – returning from *Carry On Sergeant* standing as the unpleasant face of authority in contrast to Sid's warmish attitude – scowls around in the background, while the usual *Dixon of Dock Green* terminology is ripped asunder by our struggling boys in blue.

The stirring final capture of a particularly nasty ring of crooks is packed with chest-puffing pride. Kenneth Connor finds love with Joan Sims, Leslie Phillips finds it with Jill Adams, and even Hattie Jacques has a peck on the cheek from the newly promoted Sid. This is the ultimate vintage *Carry On*, and one which, although heavily basking in the codes and conventions of the early films, clearly points the way forward.

With Joan Hickson, Cyril Chamberlain and Shirley Eaton. Written by Norman Hudis. Directed by Gerald Thomas, 1960.

★ *Watch Your Stern*

Kenneth Connor, having become almost by accident the headlining star of *Carry On* (the players were listed alphabetically and C beat most), was primed for big screen stardom with a collection of sub-Norman Wisdom romps. Usually cast as the diminutive do-gooder, whose eagerness to please and clumsiness always cause problems, Connor was cast in this right old navy lark, which recruited the familiar *Carry On* atmosphere without the *Carry On* title.

Radio's 'left hand down a bit ...' Leslie Phillips plays true to form as the bumbling naval officer, while Eric Barker's bluster and Noel Purcell, strolling across the deck with thick white beard bristling with admiralty rage, add clout to the proceedings. Basically, it's just a watered down *Carry On Sailing*, but there's also plenty of fun to be had with Hattie Jacques in full flow and Joan Sims as the ever-smiling love interest.

Sid James – looking every inch the John Player cigarette, archetypal seaman – is thrown in as a high profile guest star. Still, it's Connor's bumbling and bungles that make up most of the fun. A lowly man of the sea, with the confused brain of a scientific genius, he tackles improvements, espionage and other ill-fated escapades based round the navy's latest secret weapon – the Creeper Torpedo. Naturally, in the end his ability is finally recognized only to blow right up in his face and send the hapless central trio – Connor, Phillips and Barker – back to Civvy Street as bowler-hatted businessmen. Hardly a taxing piece of film comedy, but still chock-full with enough familiar faces and hilarious interludes to please the most fussy of *Carry On* admirers, and there's even a totally irrelevant and irreverent moment in the company of Eric Sykes and a blacked-up Spike Milligan. Pure bliss.

With David Lodge and Ed Devereaux. Written by Alan Hackney and Vivian A. Cox. Directed by Gerald Thomas, 1960.

★ *No Kidding*

In this bittersweet comedy, Leslie Phillips stars as David Robinson, who intends to sell his ancient family home before being persuaded by the gardener to turn it into a holiday home for the children of the rich. But Alderman Spicer, played by Geraldine McEwan, has other ideas – she wants it turned into a home for underprivileged children.

Written by Norman Hudis. Directed by Gerald Thomas, 1960.

★ *Raising the Wind*

In a film which really should have been called *Carry On Blowing*, Peter Rogers successfully mixes his familiar cast of *Carry On* favourites with the essence of his wife's popular *Doctor...* films. The third of the series, *Doctor in Love*, had just recruited Leslie Phillips to the medical fore and here, immediately reunited with barking, bombastic bully with a heart of gold, James Robertson Justice, the crossover edges are almost blurred away completely.

The screenplay, from regular *Carry On* composer Bruce Montgomery no less, happily tosses in a ragbag of student-based misadventures, musical nightmares and shared aspirations, with romantic leads Paul Massie – fresh from Hancock's *The Rebel* – and stunning Jennifer Jayne – earlier a hit in the ATV serial *The Adventures of William Tell* – struggling through education with a hard-done-by and hard-up sigh.

Buxom Liz Fraser, twittering Jimmy Thompson and self-important Kenneth Williams add hilarity to the endless charade of mucked-up lessons, shared digs, hapless performance and the like.

Another one of those cosy, open-fire type of pictures, which has the Rogers stamp all over it, Sid James – with quietly calculating Lance Percival in tow – is dragged in for yet another priceless cough and a spit as an unscrupulous songsmith. Reassuringly old-fashioned and packed with dozens of precious character actors, the film is perhaps best remembered today for introducing Jim Dale to the Peter Rogers and Gerald Thomas family. The comedian-cum-pop-star turned comic actor was signed up for the brief role of a cheeky trombonist for a disastrous conducting session led by Kenneth Williams.

With Eric Barker, Joan Hickson, Esma Cannon and David Lodge. Written by Bruce Montgomery. Directed by Gerald Thomas, 1961.

★ *Carry On Regardless*

This *Carry On* is a real curate's egg – the result of a ton of letters arriving at the office of Peter Rogers following the hugely successful release of four *Carry On* films. No one knew how long it could last, but many, many people wanted to be a part of the process. Thus, countless suggestions for new *Carry Ons* began pouring in and this is a hasty, rather disjointed attempt at addressing as many diverse topics, jobs and assignments as possible. However, whatever the film may lack in structure it more than makes up for in sheer unrestrained delight.

Sid James, sitting pretty in the catbird seat of the do anything, anywhere Helping Hands Agency, suddenly finds himself inundated with a horde of new recruits. The line-up is pretty much standard for an early *Carry On*. Kenneth Williams is typically petty, pompous and self-loving, Kenneth Connor is chirpy but uncertain – in particular when he's giving up smoking or enacting a train-based sequence from Hitchcock's *The 39 Steps*, and Charles Hawtrey is the incongruous boy-next-door type who looks like butter wouldn't melt, but seems more than content in having a bash at anything, including a boxing match.

Joan Sims had already been removed from the romantic lead position and usurped by the curvy blonde charms of the delicious Liz Fraser, while Leslie Phillips had moved on to pastures new and allowed a one-off, caddish return appearance for Terence Longdon. Bill Owen is simply happy to strut his cockney stuff, annoy Molly Weir's Scottish bird-fancier and play the tough man with the soft centre.

Some of the episodes are hilarious (Williams and the chimp; Hawtrey and the striptease joint) and others simply laboured, but the whole is a surprisingly pleasing and rewarding experience. It may be its writer's least favourite but it's an egg well worth tucking into, and Stanley Unwin's gobbledegooking landlord is a timeless joy.

With Jerry Desmonde, Freddie Mills, Victor Maddern, David Lodge and Nicholas Parsons. Written by Norman Hudis. Directed by Gerald Thomas, 1961.

★ *Twice Round the Daffodils*

If the Patrick Cargill and Jack Beale play *Ring for Catty* was simply used for the most basic of inspirations for *Carry On Nurse*, then the *Carry On* crew clearly returned with more reverence to the piece for this bittersweet amble through life in a men's ward. The pathos is far more to the fore this time around, with death and sadness undermining much of the less than carefree comedy. Set in a TB clinic – Pinewood Studios again, of course – nurse Juliet Mills (later recruited for *Carry On Jack* and *Nurse On Wheels*) spreads what little happiness there is around, and dashing Welsh hunk Ronald Lewis tries his luck.

It's all very sedate and emotive, but the spattering of *Carry On* favourites – particularly Kenneth Williams as a patient and Joan Sims as his loving sister – inject a healthy dose of humour into the film. The title, by the way, describes what each patient must achieve before finally being pronounced fit enough to leave – walk twice round the daffodils. An enchanting, dated, but heart-warming little movie, one senses that the writer felt more at home within the darker realities of life than with the frivolous world of the innuendo or the cheap jape.

With Andrew Ray, Donald Houston and Lance Percival. Written by Norman Hudis. Directed by Gerald Thomas, 1962.

★ *The Iron Maiden*

The age of steam may be dead and buried, but a keen and eager aircraft designer (played by a very keen and eager Michael Craig) spends all his spare time tinkering with his beloved traction engines. It's hardly the most promising of starting points for a comedy feature film, but there's enough sub-*Genevieve* nostalgia and romantic misunderstanding from Anne Helm to create some enjoyable moments. *Carry On Jack* guest star Cecil Parker is his typical gruff and disapproving self, while American star Alan Hale Jr turns on the brash Americanisms.

With Jeff Donnell, Noel Purcell, Ronald Culver, Brian Rawlinson and Jim Dale. Written by Vivian Cox and Leslie Bricusse. Directed by Gerald Thomas, 1962.

★ *Carry On Cruising*

It's a life on the ocean wave as the series ventures into full Eastmancolor for the first time and waves a cheery farewell to its original scriptwriter. The absence of the troublesome Charles Hawtrey is well documented, and Kenneth Williams only sailed because he initially believed rumours that the crew was going for a real Mediterranean cruise for the filming.

Many people's favourite of the early films, the script is literally dripping with wonderfully pretentious business about psychoanalysis and the like. However, for all its old-world charm, ensemble performance and catalogue of groanworthy interludes (the Kenneths – Connor and Williams – presenting a mini-bullfighting moment, Lance Percival cooking 'the Haines way'), there are some priceless clipettes on the journey.

Esma Cannon steals almost everybody's thunder as the 'mad little pixie' who traps Williams into a game of table tennis, leaps on to Connor in the ship's swimming pool and happily remains fairly sober as her body crumbles under the influence after a jolly drinking session with Liz Fraser and Dilys Laye.

Misdirected romantics and silly situations are, once again, milked for all their worth. There's plenty of time for pathos-driven emotion (it's Sid's 10th year as Captain and he's almost tempted to accept a new position) and, even more reassuringly, you can see the spectre of *Carry On Sergeant* and *Carry On Constable* in almost every frame. The opening crew discussion on deck, with Sid's suspicions arising with a whole host of new faces, sets the film in *Carry On* aspic straight away. A colourful delight, thanks to Connor's 'Bella Flo' guitar serenade, Sid's unflappability and the self-satisfied ego of Williams.

With Ronnie Stevens, Vincent Ball, Willoughby Goddard and Anton Rodgers. Written by Norman Hudis. From a story by Eric Barker. Directed by Gerald Thomas, 1962.

★ Nurse On Wheels

Juliet Mills returns as everybody's favourite nursing figure in this gentle rural comedy drama concerning the ups and downs of life as a district nurse. Thanks to the cast and crew, there are plenty of *Carry On* style moments but, akin to *Twice Round the Daffodils*, touches of sentiment are instrumental in the underlying sense of poignancy in the film.

Photographed by Alan Hume and with music from Eric Rogers, the film was based on the novel *Nurse is a Neighbour* by Joanna Jones.

With Ronald Lewis, Joan Sims, Raymond Huntley, Athene Seyler, Noel Purcell and Jim Dale. Written by Norman Hudis. Directed by Gerald Thomas, 1963.

★ Carry On Cabby

Probably the most important *Carry On* of all. It was the first *Carry On* without Kenneth Williams and the last with Bill Owen. The first *Carry On* for Jim Dale. The first scripted by Talbot Rothwell, and the first with music composed by Eric Rogers. But, ironically, this landmark entry started life not as a *Carry On* but as a product entitled *Call Me a Cab*.

A kitchen-sink *Carry On*, with dissatisfied wife Hattie Jacques facing the work-obsessed life of her husband, Sid James, with forlorn dismay. In a radical, feminist-geared stance against the working male, Sid's beloved taxi company is faced with leggy opposition from Hattie's flight of buxom beauties – the legendary Glam Cab drivers, with Amanda Barrie notable among their number. There is a real heart to the comedy, mixing Hudis's pathos and truthful emotion with the delicious barrel-scraping puns of the golden Rothwell era.

Esma Cannon's nerves of granite and Liz Fraser's sexy determination provide perfect allies for Hattie's plan, while Sid wallows in self-pity with his closest pal, Kenneth Connor. A real message for the early sixties – 1963 was the year that Britain discovered sex and the Beatles' first LP – this shows a beleaguered and unconfident middle-aged male race still entrenched in warm memories of battle together, but facing the battle of the home front in their women.

Charles Hawtrey, returning for the first time since *Carry On Regardless* and staying until 1972, is gleefully let loose in typical camp terms, undermining too much critical analysis of the narrative and contrasting moments of painful reflection with sparkling, boyish energy. Jim Dale's début as the chain-smoking expectant father is the cherry on the cake.

With Renee Houston, Norman Chapell, Peter Gilmore, Norman Mitchell and Michael Nightingale. Written by Talbot Rothwell. Based on an original idea by S.C. Green and R.M. Hill. Directed by Gerald Thomas, 1963.

★ *Carry On Jack*

The first script that Talbot Rothwell sent to the producer – the original title was *Poop-Decker RN* – became the very first costume *Carry On* and set the seal for most of the sixties' output. Surprisingly lacking in low-brow gags and spending far too much time building up the characters and historic context, there is still an impressive air of polished professionalism about this grandiose seafaring adventure.

Newcomer Bernard Cribbins turns on the embarrassed Englishness with gusto, and Juliet Mills does the cross-dressing, mission-fulfilling business alongside steady main-brace-slapping turns from Donald Houston, Percy Herbert and Cecil Parker. Indeed, at times, it's hard to imagine that this is a *Carry On,* with so few of the regular faces aboard, although a sickly, weak-as-a-kitten and twice-as-playful Captain Fearless – played with typical bravo by Kenneth Williams – and a slightly smelly cesspit cleaner, Walter Sweetly, brought to life with untypical subtlety by Charles Hawtrey, remind us of the film's *Carry On* roots.

The film was a major departure for the series, but still proved hugely popular. Thus, Rothwell was allowed to develop both the historic slant for the innuendo and, indeed, a more knowing, realistic style of narrative. There is a real battle going on here – the Armada, and pirates, Spanish villains and near-death experiences are all finely interlinked with the comedic situations of the main cast.

With Patrick Cargill, Peter Gilmore, Ed Devereaux, George Woodbridge and Marianne Stone. Written by Talbot Rothwell. Directed by Gerald Thomas, 1963.

★ *Carry On Spying*

A stunning and film-noirish innuendo feast basking in the hip and trendy cache of James Bond, via the elongated vowels and camp mannerisms of the almighty Kenneth Williams. Fully allowed to express himself with Snide-styled vocals and overblown performance, Williams minces his way through this beautifully tailored tale of espionage and foreign locations – all reassuringly filmed at Pinewood Studios!

Rothwell benefits from the companionship of a co-writer – the gags are brilliantly constructed in a way which milks every groan, wince and titter, while the narrative itself is tense and tightly constructed.

Williams – aided by the handsome hero Bernard Cribbins, the clod-hopping bag of nervous energy Charles Hawtrey and (in her first *Carry On*), the bubbly blonde bombshell of Barbara Windsor – rushes through the plot with gun at the ready, quick draws all over the place, outrageous smiles, bemused reactions and unrestrained laughter. His definitive screen performance.

As for the rest, with Bondian references piled high, there's time for *Casablanca* and *The Third Man* interludes, a stonking supporting cast (notably Eric Pohlmann's Fat Man and Eric Barker's M15 boss) and, the *Carry On*'s very own 007 – *Our Man in Havana* – Jim Dale, looking every inch the smooth secret agent continually usurped and disturbed by our intrepid quartet of mince spies. Lovingly filmed in black and white, rollicking along at the pace of a steam train, and packed with everything that makes the *Carry On*s great, this is a masterpiece of film comedy.

With Richard Wattis, Judith Furse, Victor Maddern, Dilys Laye and Norman Mitchell. Written by Talbot Rothwell and Sid Colin. Directed by Gerald Thomas, 1964.

★ *Carry On Cleo*

With Richard Burton and Elizabeth Taylor creating international headlines with their on-off relationship and the ultra-expensive cost of filming *Cleopatra*, it was only natural, with the series riding the crest of a wave, that the *Carry On*s have a cheeky little poke at the Queen of the Nile. The legal problems were rife (with everything from Twentieth Century Fox itself to Marks & Spencer having a bash), but with the confidence of one who feels invincible, the series battled through, bowed down to no one and delivered one of the undisputed classics.

Sid James returns to the series as the definitive bemused, bewildered and bedraggled Mark Antony; Kenneth Williams steals all the laurels (and rests on them) as the super-superior endangered Emperor

Julius Caesar; Charles Hawtrey does his usual bespectacled camp act, complete with a babe at every turn and some beautifully painful puns, while Kenneth Connor goes from zero to hero as the number one despatching clerk and defending angel for Williams, the nervous head of the organization.

The script is literally literal, packed with countless bucketloads of the sweetest corn around and played by the experienced cast like low-grade rep theatre. That is, all save Joan Sims, who twists, pauses and heightens her delivery with every Shakespearean trick in the book, spitting out her missives to Williams, cooing to her loving, cavorting daddy (Hawtrey), and storming through the narrative like a raging tigress.

Amanda Barrie plays the entire thing for laughs, turning on the huge, dewy-eyed innocence and defeating enemies and tempting Sid with a saucy giggle. Reassuringly steeped in sixties' terminology (Connor is mobbed *à la* Beatlemania, Williams lapses into a Harold Macmillan phase) this is timeless, hilarious and the benchmark for every *Carry On* that followed. For those few – such as *Carry On ... Up the Khyber* – that just usurped it, the praise is high indeed.

With Jim Dale, Julie Stevens, Victor Maddern, David Davenport, Norman Mitchell, Warren Mitchell and Jon Pertwee. Written by Talbot Rothwell. Based on an idea by William Shakespeare. Directed by Gerald Thomas, 1964.

★ *The Big Job*

And what a big job it is too. In the midst of *Carry On* fever, the team reverted to black and white production for this sparkling resurrection of a tired old format. In 1935, Flanagan and Allan had made *A Fire Has Been Arranged* and the plot was older still than that vintage caper. Basically, here, we have good old Sid James – as master criminal and bumbling incompetent George Brain leading his merry gang of crooks, Dick Emery, Lance Percival and Sylvia Syms, into the biggest bank robbery in the world... ever.

Well, not quite. The cops catch them, the loot is hidden in a tree and for a 15-year stretch the only thing on the old lag's mind is getting the ill-gotten gains back. There's just one problem – the area has been developed and the tree is smack bang in the middle of a police station's yard. That's the old, old hook on which a glorious movie is hung.

The gang work as an ensemble piece of effortless ease. *Carry On Cowboy*'s glam puss, Erica Ronay, turns up the heat and Joan Sims nags, fusses and terrorizes male guests with energetic conviction. Sid is reassuringly Sid, laughing at the right times, looking amazed at his gang's antics and coming up with a quick succession of idiotic plans to recover the loot. Jim Dale, in a strangled, sub-Kenneth Williams performance, keeps the less than impressive British police end up and Deryck Guyler is a constant delight as the desk sergeant who's more concerned with Gilbert and Sullivan than catching crooks.

With Brian Rawlinson. Written by Talbot Rothwell. Directed by Gerald Thomas, 1965.

★ *Carry On Cowboy*

Down in the lawless – well almost – dirt-track town of Stodge City, black-hearted and black-hatted Western baddie, Sid James, is running the place with lacklustre ease. Jon Pertwee's ill-fated Sheriff bites the dust, Kenneth Williams rants and yells his way through his role as Judge Burke, and the kindly, bumbling quack doctor (Peter Butterworth) does little but have his less than wicked way with the wife of Williams… allegedly. Enter young, keen and eager Jim Dale as the English sanitation engineer who is instructed to 'clean up' the place.

A wonderful mishmash of British bulldog spirit, the essence of the American West and a chance to wallow in the fine *Carry On* actors actually doing some choice character acting, makes for a rip-roaring Western adventure. Sid James is stunning as the villain who will do anything to anyone to get his way, while Joan Sims slinks round the place like Mae West, squeezed into a skin-tight dress, blonde hair piled high and that wiggle in the walk and giggle in the talk that turns your legs to jelly. Angela Douglas is pretty hot as well.

Every code and convention of Hollywood Westerns is effortlessly embraced, and each cliché given its own *Carry On* slant to enhance the pun-packed screenplay to the full. And for those who like their *Carry Ons* reassuringly similar, Charles Hawtrey is on hand with a cough, grin and plenty of firewater, as the charming Indian brave, Big Heap. Casting aspersions on the acting profession, apologizing for his poor manners and gently being led into full-blown battle against the white intruders by the cunning and conniving Sidney, Hawtrey is brilliantly aided and abetted by Bernard Bresslaw as the fearless, aggressive and realistic warrior, Big Heap.

A classic romp with a healthy cast and an even healthier-looking budget – every penny of which is clearly visible on screen. A bluffer's tip: look out for Richard O'Brien – creator of *The Rocky Horror Picture Show* and host of *The Crystal Maze* – as one of Hawtrey's Indian gang.

With Percy Herbert, Margaret Nolan, Davy Kaye, Michael Nightingale and Edina Ronay. Screenplay by Talbot Rothwell. Directed by Gerald Thomas, 1965.

★ *Carry On Screaming!*

With both fear and laughter, the crew tackle the teeth, fangs and claw of Hammer horror's finest. As a bumbling antidote to Sherlock Holmes and Dr Watson, Harry H Corbett and Peter Butterworth stagger through a mystery involving waxwork dummies, man–made monsters, vampires, werewolves, mad scientists, spooky woods and murder. Every glorious Bray Studios cliché is mercilessly thrown into the mixture from the stunning, murky colour photography to a less than friendly mummy who comes to life. Only the *Carry On*s could call this great Egyptian figure Rubbatiti.

Fenella Fielding dishes out the camp vamp attitude, smouldering around in a red velvet dress and seducing the powers of good without taking a breath. Kenneth Williams – the ashen, undead Dr Watt – minces about the place with hare-brained schemes, some priceless, schoolyard one-liners and a real sense of mysterious evil underlying the innuendo. Meanwhile, Bernard Bresslaw – in full Boris Karloff mode – clops around the eerie Bide-A-Wee rest mansion, emotionless, expressionless and with a voice booming down with monosyllabic mournfulness.

Everything comes together perfectly to create one of the very finest films in the *Carry On* canon, and while contemporary critics condemned it as dreary and even unfunny in the light of the much-praised *Carry On Cowboy*, this is pretty much the best way to introduce the novice viewer to the delights of Pinewood camp. It's just a pity that Sid James wasn't available for a cameo role.

With Joan Sims, Jim Dale, Charles Hawtrey, Jon Pertwee, Billy Cornelius and Tom Clegg. Written by Talbot Rothwell. Directed by Gerald Thomas, 1966.

★ *Don't Lose Your Head*

They seek him here, they seek him there, those Frenchies seek Sidney everywhere. Moving the game from Anglo to Rank, everything remained intact save the *Carry On* title for this hilarious, polished and beautifully played French Revolution romp. Sid James is incongruously cast as the dashing, flamboyant and adventurous Sir Rodney Ffing (with two 'F's), a foppish, mincing English aristocrat who masquerades as the brave Black Fingernail in his attempts to rescue the French nobs from the dreaded guillotine.

Jim Dale provides perfect support as his right-hand man and constant companion, Sir Roger D'Arcy, while Kenneth Williams and Peter Butterworth team up as the incompetent, manipulative and darn right seedy villains of the piece. Dany Robin adds plenty of Gaelic charm to this costume spectacular, and Joan Sims fumes, scowls and flirts her way through high society as the slightly common sister of the big cheese, Williams.

The goodie Sid versus the baddie Williams which would inform the best of the series – including *Khyber* – is brilliantly brought into play and the narrative has real structure to hold dozens of corny gags and situations together. Besides that, the regular team members benefit from stolid, authoritative supporting turns from Peter Gilmore and Leon Greene – outstanding as the simpleton executioner – and Marianne Stone as the buxom wench who runs the local hostelry.

Action-packed, laughter-filled and eternally patriotic, this has long since been acknowledged as one of the finest films in the *Carry On* series.

With Hugh Futcher, Valerie Van Ost and Michael Ward. Written by Talbot Rothwell. Directed by Gerald Thomas, 1966.

★ *Follow That Camel*
'Bilko joins the *Carry On* legion' as the original publicity shouted and, indeed, although another one of those Rank productions which initially refused to be part of the series, this is clearly a *Carry On* from start to finish. Phil Silvers, Broadway legend, vaudevillian and Bilko star, is drafted in as a replacement for Sid James, as the lazy, aggressive, womanizing Sergeant Knocker, while vast swathes of the regular *Carry On* team surround the one-off top-liner with finely etched supporting turns.

Jim Dale, the film's real star, plays his Beau Geste type with boyish, energetic, embarrassed bemusement while playing the fields of Eton respectability. Peter Butterworth – his second-in-command and little bit of England in a foreign land – keeps the niceties in place with baths, dressing assistance and cricket practice.

The rollicking climax, when Bernard Bresslaw's evil tribe is defeated thanks to Jim's stunning skill with a cricket bat, sums up the *Carry Ons'* attitude to Englishness and the English abroad – it's his God-given right to live and play where he damn well pleases. Joan Sims slinks around in the background while 'she who handeth it out on a platter' – Zig-Zig Anita Harris – makes every red-blooded male pulsate with an exotic belly-dance, and Angela Douglas dishes out delightfully endearing portions of English-rose sweetness.

A sort of dry run for the spectacular glory of *Carry On ... Up the Khyber*, this is, nevertheless, a brilliant *Boy's Own* adventure movie with plenty of sweet innuendo, a stunning cast and a sweeping direction that fooled an entire generation that Camber Sands, Sussex could in fact, double for the soulless desert of Africa.

With Kenneth Williams, Charles Hawtrey, John Bluthal, Julian Holloway and Peter Gilmore. Screenplay by Talbot Rothwell. Directed by Gerald Thomas, 1967.

★ Carry On Doctor

A spellbinding return to the profitable bedpans and bowel movements of *Carry On Nurse*. Even one of this film's alternative titles, 'The Death of a Daffodil', is a cheeky reminder of that film's best-loved gag. Flamboyant guest star Frankie Howerd is surrounded by an almost full roster of *Carry On* legends, all playing brilliantly to type and all milking the medical madness for all its worth.

On the patient side there's Sid James, almost totally bedridden, smoking, drinking and holding court; Charles Hawtrey suffering the ultimate camp fantasy, a phantom pregnancy; Bernard Bresslaw with a foot in plaster and Peter Butterworth suffering after an unmentionable operation. Kenneth Williams parades the ward with spiteful authority as the house doctor, Hattie Jacques is 'surprise, surprise' the harridan Matron, Joan Sims sobs, mutters and whispers as Frankie's timid assistant, and Jim Dale turns on the Jack-the-lad cool as the likeable doctor who keeps everybody cheerful until facing his Waterloo, thanks to the jealous angst of Williams.

It's basically a comedic addressing of every medical drama known to man – whether that be *Emergency Ward 10* or bang up-to-date *Casualty*. There are familiar elements dripping from every frame. Packed with in-jokes, out-jokes and in-between jokes, this is by far the best of all the medical *Carry On*s and a timeless encapsulation of what makes the contemporary comedies so funny, beloved and, above all, current.

With Julian Holloway, Julian Orchard, Marianne Stone and Deryck Guyler. Written by Talbot Rothwell. Directed by Gerald Thomas, 1967.

★ *Carry On … Up the Khyber*

The jewel in the *Carry On* crown. Everything comes together to form the perfect embodiment of all that is great about the series. We have the definitive head-to-head battle against workshy, sex-mad hero Sid James and turbaned, nostril-flaring, snotty villain Kenneth Williams. Bernard Bresslaw, towering above everything and barking his way through a power-house performance of pure energy, plays true to his role until the legendary 'That will teach them to ban turbans on the buses!' remark.

Charles Hawtrey – complete with dangler warmer – unobtrusively plays for the British side, while cowardice meets religious passivist via sexual monster in the bumbling, crumbling missionary of Peter Butterworth. If the British empire is, indeed, falling about our eyes and, in 1968, with the Common Market and independence becoming a reality it certainly was, then the *Carry On* team play home truths for larger than life pantomime.

The direction is peerless, the Welsh countryside looks every inch the Indian backdrop, the cast – including Roy Castle's last-minute Jim Dale replacement – is spot on and the atmosphere is of an all-conquering series of films knowing it's reached a peak. In a way, there was no other direction but down from then on, but, thankfully, it took a further 10 years to take full effect.

The closing dining-room sequence is probably the finest moment in the entire series. Arguably the Peter Rogers masterpiece, this is the one *Carry On* that can justifiably and proudly find itself cropping up on the all-time great British movie lists from even the most cold-hearted, anti-*Carry On* critics.

With Joan Sims, Angela Douglas, Cardew Robinson, Julian Holloway and Peter Gilmore. Written by Talbot Rothwell. Directed by Gerald Thomas, 1968.

★ *Carry On Camping*

The epitome of cheap and cheerful and classic *Carry On* film-making. The horrendous filming conditions – in the middle of a bleak, bleak winter – are legendary, and Barbara Windsor's bra-popping exercise sequence has passed into our collective national consciousness. Beyond criticism, this is, admittedly, a ramshackle run through a load of tent gags and outrageous outdoor situations, but only the most humourless person could fail to crack up at the credentials.

Kenneth Williams and Hattie Jacques are perfect as the authority figures in charge of Barbara and the teenage birds; Sid James and

Bernard Bresslaw are the randy mates on the razzle in the campsite, and Joan Sims and Dilys Laye their long-suffering, much ignored girl-friends. Charles Hawtrey is the beanpole loner who wanders through the movie in a continual daze, while Terry Scott and Betty Marsden come straight from sitcom land and playfully milk the loveless marriage relationship for every last laugh. Peter Butterworth, muttering and cluttering in the background, money-pinches for England, protects his hens from any off-putting nocturnal business and effortlessly undermines Sid's randy flights of fancy with an air of bemused innocence.

A hopelessly dated, late sixties hippie invasion that still manages to remain sort of contemporary, and the brilliant 'beautiful people' time-scale is worth the cringes and long-haired weirdos just for Sid donning his John Lennon, National Health specs. Priceless.

With Sandra Caron, Julian Holloway and Trisha Noble. Screenplay by Talbot Rothwell. Directed by Gerald Thomas, 1969.

★ *Carry On Again Doctor*
A hasty and healthy return to the profitable business of ill health. Jim Dale is back as a sort of parallel universe version of his *Carry On Doctor* physician and Kenneth Williams, yet again, turns on the pompous self-importance with a hint of a pleasing, likeable underbelly.

Basically a film of two halves, the first recreates the atmosphere of *Carry On Doctor* and allows the scriptwriter to toss in all the gags he didn't have room for the first time round. Charles Hawtrey scores as the rather unpleasant, jealous and conniving Dr Stoppidge, Joan Sims takes life easy as the wealthy widow in the financial-gain sights of Williams, and Patsy Rowlands – making her series début – suffers at the hands of her disinterested employee.

The second half is even more fun, with our hapless hero, Jim, being sent off to the out of the way medic mission in the Beatific Islands, and meeting up with Sid James, the ever-cheerful medical orderly, witch-doctor, man of six wives, fags and bottles of whisky, Mr Gladstone Screwer. The hut-based scenes of sexual frustration, loneliness, amazement and sheer emotive despair between the ever-sinking Jim and the happy-as-Larry Sid are arguably the most underrated, most fun moments in the *Carry On* series. The tennis ball of laughter never touches the floor between these two past masters of the art.

Back at home, Sid's weight-reducing potion makes Jim both rich and famous, long-lost glam girlfriend, Barbara Windsor, gives our man a hard time, and even Williams and Hawtrey (in drag) get in on the act. It's hardly earth-shattering stuff, but, thanks to a stunning central turn from Jim Dale (his last until *Carry On Columbus*), this remains one of the best *Carry Ons* of the decade.

With Peter Butterworth, Peter Gilmore, Wilfrid Brambell and Patricia Hayes. Written by Talbot Rothwell. Directed by Gerald Thomas, 1969.

★ *Carry On Up the Jungle*

It's all innuendo guns at the ready in the deepest, darkest depths of Pinewood Studios, with mincing bird-fancier (the feathered kind) Frankie Howerd and raging bird-fancier (the other kind) Sid James, leading an expedition to track down a rare, specially gifted exotic bird and the long-lost son of dignified aristocrat, Joan Sims.

The long-lost son turns out to be a full-grown Terry Scott (Jim Dale politely declined the role) as a Tarzan clone complete with loin-cloth, dagger and a dreaded track record in negotiating his way round trees. Jacki Piper, making her series début, goes from plain Jane to bikini babe; Kenneth Connor – back for the first time since *Carry On Cleo* – adds facial contortions and little-man bemusement opposite Howerd's full-on delivery, and a blackened-up, browned-off Bernard Bresslaw opens the tinned corned beef.

Again, there is a little bit of every foreign clime which shall be forever England, and the ensemble cast walk their way through the jungle-based clichés with great skill. The scene with Joan Sims being playfully mucked about by a frisky snake is legendary. The fun really starts cooking when Sid discovers heaven in a settlement populated entirely by women. Charles Hawtrey is the reigning 'queen' – sorry, King – and, as it turns out, the long-lost husband of Joan Sims. She was amazed – and so was he.

The dodgy, studio-based jungle, stock wildlife footage and an air of padding doesn't affect the fact that this is a classic entry in the *Carry On* series. Hey, it looks cheap and, my goodness it was cheap, but the laughter generated is beyond price.

With Valerie Leon, Reuben Martin and Nina Baden-Semper. Written by Talbot Rothwell. Directed by Gerald Thomas, 1970.

★ *Carry On Loving*

Everybody wants to do it, but only a select few can imagine it in this, the ultimate 'it' picture. The 20th *Carry On* and a belated stab at introducing a new crop of talent (Richard O'Callaghan, the ill-fated Imogen

Hassall) to counterbalance the established favourites. Randy joker Terry Scott dominates most of the funniest scenes, staggering through polite society with a bumbling, ill at ease attitude, but it's the really old guard who act as the innuendo cement.

Sid James and Hattie Jacques battle behind the closed doors of their ultra-naff marriage agency, Charles Hawtrey – in the briefest of brief supporting turns – camps around men's toilets and railway stations in his dogged pursuit of Sid's alleged womanizer, and Bernard Bresslaw growls, grimaces and generally chews up the scenery as the jealous wrestling boyfriend of Joan Sims.

Situation comedy, French farce, Shakespearean mistaken identity, and some of the most groanworthy puns in the history of mankind are a jolly funny mix and one of the biggest box-office successes in the series. The chaotic bun fight climax – something of a tradition by now – ends the loosely connected madness on a high, and launches the series into a new rocky decade. The seventies may have been saucy but, by the close, sauce had been pretty much replaced by scandal – and the *Carry Ons*, as a working entity, were consigned to the wastepaper bin.

With Patsy Rowlands, Peter Butterworth, Jacki Piper, Julian Holloway and Joan Hickson. Written by Talbot Rothwell. Directed by Gerald Thomas, 1970.

★ Carry On Henry

A right royal *Carry On* for the 21st in the series, and a truly majestic central role for good King Sid James, wenching, moaning, fighting, eating and boozing, literally, for England. Everybody bows down to this power-house comic creation, and priceless supporting pillars of strength from politically corrupted Kenneth Williams, religiously corrupted Terry Scott and sexually corrupted Charles Hawtrey, add spice to the every-day goings-on at Windsor Castle.

Patriotic pride and delicate relationships with Europe form the basis of the point, but Sid seems at his happiest wooing the local talent and desperately trying to deceive tasty garlic-crunching queen, Joan Sims, in the wedding bed. Beautiful to look at and featuring Barbara Windsor's most refreshing, enchanting *Carry On* performance, the location filming in Windsor and Pinewood adds lustre to the stunning costumes, colour photography and relentlessly hilarious screenplay.

A bluffer's point is that, pre-fame seventies pop singer and heart-throb, David Essex, featured as a cheeky young man in a tax-debating rally sequence, but this ended up on the cutting-room floor. Relish the chillingly funny final exit of Williams and Scott, as well as Sid who was born to be King.

With Patsy Rowlands, Peter Butterworth, Margaret Nolan, Julian Holloway, Peter Gilmore and Alan Curtis. Written by Talbot Rothwell. Directed by Gerald Thomas, 1971.

★ *Carry On At Your Convenience*

Toilets toilets everywhere, but not a drop to drink. This right-wing, capitalistic and rather naive comic assessment of the unions and the attitude of the workers was the first sign that *Carry On* comedy wasn't infallible. A box-office disappointment, it wasn't until 1976 that the production costs were recovered and some of the stars – Richard O'Callaghan included – felt uneasy and unhappy about the contents.

Ironic then, that 30 years later, the film seems to sum up exactly what was so cool and groovy about the series in the first place. True, everything seems wildly overplayed, the endless assembly line of lavatories seems like a wry comment on the endless assembly line of *Carry On* films and the entire cast seems to have a tongue firmly stuck in their (left, upper) cheek.

Sid James, as the works foreman, gambles, flirts, smokes his pipe and laughs at every opportunity; Kenneth Williams is the definitive figure of British industry, blindly sitting back as his mini-empire crumbles; Charles Hawtrey flits through the fun in an outrageously garish shirt, and Bernard Bresslaw is at the rock bottom of his moronic gentle giant characterization. Newcomer Kenneth Cope is ideal as the bolshie, play-by-the-rules shop steward, and Jacki Piper raises the temperature as the miniskirted canteen girl.

In a picture packed with delights, Hattie Jacques and the horse-betting budgie scenes stand out a mile, but there's something reassuringly and historically important and just darn fun about the climactic day trip to Brighton. Even the fact that a supporting turn from Terry Scott was exorcized from the final print can't bring this classic down.

With Renee Houston, Margaret Nolan, Patsy Rowlands and Marianne Stone. Written by Talbot Rothwell. Directed by Gerald Thomas, 1971.

★ *Carry On Matron*

In a more permissive age and with practically every medical joke exhausted, the sights were changed to a maternity hospital with a whole Pandora's box of unmarried mother and contraception pill gags with 'the bottomless stomach' of Joan Sims and the paranoid Madeline Smith causing the staff maximum grief.

The medical business relies heavily on the sweet and cheerful, larger than life figure of Hattie Jacques to smooth the edges, while Kenneth Williams goes totally into hypochondriac overdrive as the flustered, flamboyantly camp medico, Sir Bernard Cutting. Coming late to the action, but stealing every scene in which he appears, Charles Hawtrey delivers a rich tapestry of undermined psychoanalysis, throwaway one-liners and bewildered innocence at the fuss caused by his secret TV-watching with dear old Matron.

Barbara Windsor strips off again, Terry Scott – resurrecting the fresh-faced, randy doctor persona of Jim Dale – turns in his last *Carry On* performance, and newcomer Jack Douglas twitches into view with a record-breaking baby delivery. Sid James and his hapless band of bumbling criminals – Bernard Bresslaw, Bill Maynard and Kenneth Cope dragged up as a nurse to case the joint – form the sub-plot which pushes the film forward.

It's just an excuse for a load of really tired old medical gags, but there's some wonderfully bizarre moments – the frantic gang discussion about London bus routes stands out – and this is much more than just your average tale of hopeless crooks pinching hordes of the pill. Well, how could it not be?

With Kenneth Connor, Jacki Piper, Margaret Nolan, Derek Francis, Bill Kenwright and Valerie Leon. Written by Talbot Rothwell. Directed by Gerald Thomas, 1972.

★ *Carry On Abroad*
In the days when the traditional family holiday by the British coast was being replaced by cheap, tacky and badly organized package trips abroad, the *Carry On* crew embraced just the smallish pinch of satire for this 'Brits on the razzle in the Med' romp. Arguably the last truly classic film in the series, the departure of Charles Hawtrey after this film sounded one of the most important death knells. Thankfully, it's a gleeful final hurrah for everybody's favourite camp tippler, as he leap-frogs with stunning glam girls Sally Geeson and Carol Hawkins, chats up Barbara Windsor, and immediately dispenses his bowler-hatted busi-nessman look once the sunshine reflects off his glasses.

Sid James and Joan Sims as the definitive married couple struggling to get away from each other, enjoy the tongue-in-cheek comments and, ultimately, find renewed sexual interest via the collapsing hotel climax; Kenneth Williams is simply Kenneth Williams as the energetically eager tour operator; Kenneth Connor staggers into frustrated old age as the henpecked Mr Blunt, and Ray Brooks, the voice of Mr Benn, delivers an outrageous but joyful Continental lover.

Patriotism, disgust at foreign attitudes, alcohol and sex seem to be at the forefront of most people's minds, while the game of cricket once again comes in handy, this time as a defence against Olga Lowe's clapped-out ladies of easy virtue – and Alan Curtis gives a stunning cameo as the shifty, easily corrupted Chief of Police. However, it's the frantic, foreign angst of hotel workers Peter Butterworth and Hattie Jacques who perfectly contrast the stock *Carry On* characters with flamboyant disregard for presentation, equity or social code. Bernard Bresslaw is also pretty cool as the monk who kicks the habit.

With June Whitfield, Jimmy Logan, Patsy Rowlands, Derek Francis and Hugh Futcher. Written by Talbot Rothwell. Directed by Gerald Thomas, 1972.

★ *Bless This House*

Sid James – leading a double life as lecherous dude on film and family man on telly – saw his domestic sitcom smash-hit turned into this enjoyable spin-off feature film. Thanks to the *Carry On* crew, there's a slightly more risqué, slapstick-heavy emphasis to the plot, but fundamentally nothing has changed – except it is Robin Askwith, not Robin Stewart, playing his son while Peter Butterworth is his new best friend, and Terry Scott and June Whitfield have moved next door.

Basically a comedy of the generation gap, Sid is bemused by his teenage daughter, Sally Geeson, frustrated by his wife, Diana Coupland, and pretty much outraged about most aspects of modern living. The situations are familiar, cosy and family-based, with the emotive climax – his son's wedding to Carol Hawkins – allowing for frantic, last-minute dashes, illegal whisky-making and a happy-ever-after ending.

With Norman Mitchell, Frank Thornton, George A. Cooper and Marianne Stone. Written by Dave Freeman. Directed by Gerald Thomas, 1972.

★ *Carry On Girls*

Feminism, itching powder, female wrestling, Brighton locations and a rip-roaring beauty contest – what took the *Carry On*s so long to address the ultimate lad's fantasy, and have a 60-year-old Sid James in a cool dude suit and with a mentality turned to babe-watching?

The screenplay and performances force the casual viewer on to the side of good-natured, good-fun smut as radiated by Sid's chuckling, bum-pinching, super-smooth operator. The rest of us were on his side from the outset anyway. Barbara Windsor leads the glamour-girl brigade with a fiery cockney independence, while long-suffering Joan Sims faces an extended, romanceless relationship with the sharpest man in town – Sid, of course.

The jokes are all rounded, prominent and come in pairs. The old team survivors (notably Peter Butterworth and Kenneth Connor) contribute supports of withering male impotence, and Bernard Bresslaw's eyes stick out on stalks at the fascinating sight of Margaret Nolan, Angela Grant and the other stunners who populate the fun in the minimum of clothing. A perfect summer season movie, it may play uncomfortably frankly and 'in yer face' at times, but this is still a classic seventies contemporary comment from the *Carry On* crew.

With Jack Douglas, Valerie Leon, David Lodge, Jimmy Logan and Sally Geeson. Written by Talbot Rothwell. Directed by Gerald Thomas, 1973.

★ *Carry On Dick*

A return to the comic costume romp and, indeed, the fundamental narrative structure of the classic *Don't Lose Your Head*. Here we have a distinguished Sid James donning the black mask and huge weapon of notorious highwayman Dick Turpin. Kenneth Williams, with flaring nostrils and supercilious comments firmly in place, is in hot pursuit, with his bumbling, occasionally sharp-witted and frequently disobedient sidekick, Jack Douglas, not hanging about as the legendary dubbed Jock Strapp.

The old gang go through the motions with flintlocks fully cocked, the essence of a very merrie olde England is well captured, and although the script, thanks to the master's failing health, is patchy on occasions, there are enough truly barrel-scraping puns to lift the most jaded of spirits.

Bernard Bresslaw booms out instructions as the head of the Bow Street Runners, Kenneth Connor turns in a delightfully crusty constable performance, and Joan Sims saddles posh French with fruity cockney as the ultimate travelling glamour-girl show owner. There's time for a Sid James drag sequence, a flash of Barbara Windsor's breasts, the bare buttock cheeks of Bernard Bresslaw and free and easy sexual couplings all over the place. A colour-by-numbers *Carry On*, but one designed by a Turner.

With Peter Butterworth, Patsy Rowlands, Margaret Nolan, Marianne Stone, David Lodge and Penny Irving. Screenplay by Talbot Rothwell. Based on a treatment by Laurie Wyman and George Evans. Directed by Gerald Thomas, 1974.

★ Carry On Behind

Carry On Camping II – or 'Who Needs a Tent When You've Got a Caravan?' With Sid James out of action and Kenneth Williams given full reign to mince about the back lot at Pinewood Studios, international star Elke Sommer was drafted in for a bit of hilarious foreign misunderstanding in this enjoyable archaeological comedy. If you are pondering over the title, its cheeky connotations are purely by chance – oh, yes! – as it refers to the caravans and holiday home comforts that the holiday-makers carry *behind* them. So, now you know.

Critics and non-admirers may dismiss this as a load of old fossils, corny gags and embarrassing domestic situations in the great, damp, muddy outdoors and, yes, for a lot of the time that is a fair point of view. The saving grace is that among those old fossils are such priceless delights as Kenneth Connor's randy old Major and Peter Butterworth's decidedly odd odd-job man. Jack Douglas and Windsor Davies take on the mantle of Bernie and Sid from *Carry On Camping*, escape from their wives (for a short time at least), ponder a bit of fishing, and then reckon that a bit of fun with bikini babes Sherrie Hewson and Carol Hawkins would be much more like it, wouldn't it? A string of only slightly connected sketches, built round a common theme, and a strip-tease, bum-exposing climax which pulls out all the stops for farcical laughs.

With Bernard Bresslaw, Patsy Rowlands, Ian Lavender, Adrienne Posta and Liz Fraser. Written by Dave Freeman. Directed by Gerald Thomas, 1975.

★ Carry On England

It was back to the barrack-room fun and games that had started the series for this 28th *Carry On* effort in the immediate wake of Sid James's death. Things were never going to be the same again – and this wartime army romp brought a whole crop of newcomers into the fold who couldn't quite cut the mustard.

The script is fairly workmanlike and the direction lacks sparkle, but there's no denying that bombastic son of a gun, Kenneth Connor, makes more than an impressive mark as the central authority figure,

Captain S Melly. (Work out his nickname for yourselves!) Connor's character may not be a likeable one, but for admirers of the actor this is a stunning, startling piece of work.

Joan Sims and Peter Butterworth are tacked on to the military-based frolics just in case you forget you are watching a *Carry On* and it's really down to a twitching, bumbling Jack Douglas to keep the comedy flags fully flying. Windsor Davies and Melvyn Hayes are on hand to capitalize on the popularity of the BBC sitcom *It Ain't 'Alf Hot, Mum*, and the incompetent training session perfectly updates and rearranges similar frantic moments from *Carry On Sergeant*. But dwindling interest, a decline in cinemas and diminishing confidence in the product as a whole signposted this as the start of the last few gasps for the series.

With Patrick Mower, Judy Geeson, Julian Holloway, Diane Langton, Larry Dann and Peter Jones. Written by David Pursall and Jack Seddon. Directed by Gerald Thomas, 1976.

★ *That's Carry On*
After a defeat what do you do? Well, if you are Peter Rogers and Gerald Thomas you pick yourself up, brush yourself down and start all over again. This glistening compilation of the 'best gags from the *Carry On* series' – one waggish critic commented that that would last all of ten minutes – plunders the priceless archives of the entire series from *Carry On Sergeant* to *Carry On Behind*.

With our innuendo-mongering hosts, Kenneth Williams and Barbara Windsor, linking the vintage footage with terrible puns, facial contortions and a long-running gag concerning Kenneth's desperate need for a toilet, the history – for better or worse – of a British film institution is laid out before the viewer. Naturally, everybody's favourite bits are included – be it the dining-room climax of *Khyber*, the exercise sequence from *Camping*, or Frankie's energetic ambulance arrival in *Doctor* – and as a social document of a true cinematic success story, this is very hard to beat. No analysis, no intellectual commentary, no historical context, just laugh after laugh, and with a couple of hosts like those two, who's complaining?

With the entire Carry On *gang in archive material from the first twenty-seven* Carry On *films, the linking material was written by Tony Church; and the archive material was written by Norman Hudis, Talbot Rothwell, Dave Freeman and Sid Colin. Directed by Gerald Thomas, 1977.*

★ *Carry On Emmannuelle*

For 20 years the *Carry On* gang had been banging on about sex and very rarely getting any. The times, however, were very much a-changing, and that most permissive of foreign imports was let loose into the cosy, self-contained environment of Pinewood Studios. Suzanne Danielle makes the perfect sex kitten opposite the limp-wristed, bum-flashing, weak-willed French Ambassador, Kenneth Williams.

The upstairs and downstairs relationship between house-owners and housekeepers makes up the richest vein of comedy. Butler, Jack Douglas, cook, Joan Sims and boot-boy, Peter Butterworth, stagger, stumble and slide their way through duties, play around with the mistress, and generally keep the rocky comic content on the *Carry On* straight and narrow.

These beautifully played pieces may be written in a rather lacklustre style, but the performances keep the laughs coming. They certainly contrast the eventually boring and repetitive sexual conquests. The last hurrah for a series that made a producer's fame and fortune may be disappointing, but there's a certain something – and that's not just the chance to ogle Danielle in the raw.

With Beryl Reid, Larry Dann, Eric Barker, Claire Davenport, Victor Maddern and Norman Mitchell. Written by Lance Peters. Directed by Gerald Thomas, 1978.

AS EXECUTIVE PRODUCER

★ *Cat Girl*

A supernatural horror with a higher than usual degree of plausibility. A beautiful girl becomes obsessed by a curse on her family, whereby successive members develop the instincts of wild animals.

The film tells the story of the battle for the girl's sanity by her psychiatrist with whom, prior to his present marriage, she was in love. This tale of horror with future Hammer Queen, Barbara Shelley, its moody direction and tense atmosphere make this economically made chiller a cut above the rest.

With Robert Ayres and Kay Callard. Directed by Alfred Shaugnessy, 1957.

★ *The Flying Scot*

Dissatisfied with the small profits shown by his petty crimes, Ronnie Cowan decides to make an attempt at pulling off the most sensational robbery of all time. He has learned that the Bank of Scotland periodically sends half a million pounds in one-pound notes to London for destruction. The money is transported on the famous passenger train, *The Flying Scot*. An above average second-feature thriller.

With Lee Patterson, Kay Callard and Alan Gifford. Directed by Compton Bennett, 1957.

★ *The Tommy Steele Story*

The definitive cheap and cheerful biopic, with the rock star having just burst on to the public scene and his brief rise to super-stardom proving a perfect money-spinning vehicle. From life on the ocean waves to singing sensation in London's fashionable Soho coffee bars and on to performing at the Café de Paris, Tommy Steele – playing himself – revelled in relating the truth of his amazing start in the business. The ultimate cash-in movie, rock 'n' roll may have been a flash in the pan, and the producer wasn't hanging around to find out.

With Lisa Danieli, Hilda Fenemore, Cyril Chamberlain and Charles Lamb. Written by Norman Hudis. Produced by Herbert Smith. Directed by Gerard Bryant, 1957.

★ *Ivanhoe*

Popular 1950s' swashbuckling television series from the familiar ATV stable.

★ *Carry On Christmas*

This first venture for a *Carry On* into the very different world of television allowed the team to tackle Charles Dickens' *A Christmas Carol* and that meanest of misers, Ebenezer Scrooge. Sid James is the defini tive money-pincher, thrown into turmoil, thanks to three visits from merry Christmas spirits. There's a bedraggled Charles Hawtrey, sex-pot Barbara Windsor and hippie dude Bernard Bresslaw, highlighting the poor miserable souls that heartless Sid's dastardly deeds have affected.

Hammer horror is touched with Terry Scott's Dr Frankenstein, a toothy Dracula from Peter Butterworth and a wordless creature from Bernard Bresslaw. Frankie Howerd holds court as the impoverished poet Robert Browning and returns as the limp-wristed Fairy God-mother of poor Cinderella, Barbara Windsor. Peter Butterworth and Terry Scott score top points as the ugliest, most hilarious ugly sisters in television history and Charles Hawtrey fumbles about as a misplaced, camp as a row of tents, Aladdin. Christmas viewing would never be the same again.

Written by Talbot Rothwell. Produced by Peter Eton. Directed by Ronnie Baxter, 1969.

★ Carry On Again Christmas

It's that time of year again and the old gang return for a black and white rendition of Long John Silver and the *Treasure Island* story. Sid James is perfectly cast as the peg-legged pirate, hopping round the place complete with parrot, crutch and desire to track down hidden treasure. Charles Hawtrey turns on the ultra-camp, Barbara Windsor makes a less than convincing Jim Hawkins, and Terry Scott hams it up brilliantly as the Squire in this sparkling seasonal romp through Robert Louis Stevenson's familiar tale.

With Kenneth Connor, Bernard Bresslaw, Bob Todd and Wendy Richard. Written by Dave Freeman and Sid Colin. Produced and directed by Alan Tarrant, 1970.

★ Quest for Love

Resurrecting elements of the 1933 Leslie Howard melodrama, *Berkeley Square*, and latching on to the source sci-fi romantic material of John Wyndham's *Random Quest*, this was a unique and challenging project directed by Ralph Thomas. The story tells of a young physicist (Tom Bell) who is involved in a serious explosion, jumps into a parallel universe, falls in love with a dying girl (Joan Collins) and rescues her back into his own reality. Ethereal, mysterious and beautifully filmed.

With Denholm Elliott and Laurence Naismith. Written by Terence Feely. Music composed by Peter Rogers & Eric Rogers. Produced by Peter Eton. Directed by Ralph Thomas, 1971.

★ Revenge

A country community takes the law into its own hands when two children are raped and then murdered by a mentally deranged man. Joan Collins and Kenneth Griffith give eye-catching performances in this disturbing and very well-made psychological thriller. *Carry On* composer Eric Rogers wrote the musical score.

With Sinead Cusack, James Booth and Ray Barrett. Written by John Kruse. Produced by George H. Brown. Directed by Sidney Hayers, 1971.

★ Assault

A further collaboration with directing/producing team Sidney Hayers and George H Brown resulted in this grim and gruesome twist on a familiar police investigation thriller plot. Suzy Kendall stars as the distraught art schoolmistress helping the local village bobbies track down a ruthless serial rapist. The musical score was composed by *Carry On*'s Eric Rogers.

With Frank Finlay, James Laurenson, Lesley-Anne Down, Freddie Jones, Tony Beckley and Anthony Ainley. Written by John Kruse from the novel by Kendal Young, 1970.

★ *All Coppers Are*

Twelve years earlier, Peter Rogers had upheld the cosy, warm and safe world of *Dixon of Dock Green*-styled policemen in *Carry On Constable*. This far more hard-hitting drama starred Nicky Henson as a no-good crook and Martin Potter as a dutiful copper, both of whom find themselves in love with the same girl – Julia Foster.

With Ian Hendry. Written by Allan Prior. Produced by George H. Brown. Directed by Sydney Hayers, 1972.

★ *Carry On Christmas*

The third small screen Christmas *Carry On* recruited less of the old team than usual, and set them down in an eighteenth-century dining-room discussing questions of historic song, pantomime and haunted houses. Perhaps the stand-out moment reflects the success of *Carry On Henry*, with aged Peter Butterworth introducing a selection of madrigals sung at the Hampton Court home of good King Hal.

Kenneth Connor enjoys himself hugely as the naval hero trapped in a spooky house and the show finishes with a rollicking, tongue-in-cheek and very risqué pantomime, with Jack Douglas slaying them as a tatty Demon King. Norman Rossington and Brian Oulton were recruited at the eleventh hour to replace an absent Charles Hawtrey.

With Hattie Jacques, Joan Sims, Barbara Windsor, Billy Cornelius, Valerie Leon and Valerie Stanton. Written by Talbot Rothwell and Dave Freeman. Produced by Gerald Thomas. Directed by Ronnie Baxter, 1972.

★ *Carry On London!*

The very first *Carry On* stage show and a rousing success from its opening night in Birmingham. Hastily transferred to the Victoria Palace, in London's West End, it was a revue format headlining Sid James, Barbara Windsor, Kenneth Connor, Bernard Bresslaw, Jack Douglas and Peter Butterworth in a series of silly songs and even sillier sketches.

Notoriously, according to his published diaries, Kenneth Williams considered the entire thing a crass waste of time, but he would, wouldn't he? The sketches resurrected memories of *Carry On Cleo*, *Carry On Camping* and the medical classics, while seasoned pros, such as Connor and Douglas, could ham, corpse and ad-lib to their hearts' content.

Written by Talbot Rothwell, Dave Freeman and Eric Merriman.
Additional material by Ian Grant. A Louis Benjamin Production, 1973-1975.

★ *What a Carry On!*

As part of a lucrative deal with ATV, Peter Rogers allowed cameras into the London opening night of *Carry On London!*, and this exclusive selection of sketches from the show was the result. Introduced by *Police 5*'s Shaw Taylor and featuring interviews with the six team members who starred in the stage show, it also included clips from many *Carry On films* and sound-bites from famous people in the audience such as Eric Sykes.

Programme associate Tony Hawes. Produced and directed by Alan
Tarrant, 1973.

★ *Carry On Christmas*

Sid James is the archetypal department store Santa Claus in this cracking seasonal television special. Reflecting on the spirit of the season and recalling Christmases from long ago, a series of historical sketches recreates the 25th of December as seen through the eyes of the caveman, a sophisticated dining-room, the time of Robin Hood and the trenches of the First World War.

Stand-out contributions come from Jack Douglas and Peter Butterworth as a couple of outrageous German soldiers, Bernard Bresslaw as the overgrown baby caveman, Bean Podkin, and Kenneth Connor as the slick, bespectacled store manager, Mr Sibley. Sid and the gang throw in some wonderfully unsubtle star turns in the comic vignettes, and there's even time for a drag ballet sequence which is guaranteed to bring a tear to the eye.

With Joan Sims, Barbara Windsor, Julian Holloway and Laraine
Humphreys. Written by Talbot Rothwell. Produced by Gerald Thomas. Directed
by Ronald Fouracre, 1973.

★ *Carry On Laughing*

Two seasons of self-contained, 25-minute chunks of new *Carry On* comedy were filmed at ATV's Elstree studios from the end of 1974. Many of the familiar current film team – with the exception of

Kenneth Williams – were drafted into low-brow laughs and high-octane entertainment that were all set in historic context. Several remain as some of the rarest and finest examples of Rogers' television work. Speaking in 1977, he claimed that the shows 'hadn't achieved what he set out to do', namely to resurrect the flagging fortunes of the films at the cinema, but despite some dodgy interludes these are packed with fine carrying on.

Directed by Alan Tarrant. Produced by Gerald Thomas, 1975.

Series 1

★ *The Prisoner of Spenda*
Sid James is caught up in a comic slant on the old *Prisoner of Zenda* tale, while Peter Butterworth and Jack Douglas do their best to protect the political future of their country.

With Barbara Windsor, Kenneth Connor, Joan Sims and Diane Langton. Written by Dave Freeman.

★ *The Baron Outlook*
Sid James stars as Baron Hubert in this romp of French crusaders, castle inspection and mistaken identity.

With Joan Sims, Barbara Windsor, Kenneth Connor, Peter Butterworth and Linda Hooks. Written by Dave Freeman.

★ *The Sobbing Cavalier*
In the days of the Roundheads versus the Cavaliers, landowner Jack Douglas is pulled from pillar to post in an attempt to protect his flamboyant brother-in-law, Sid James. Peter Butterworth steals the honours as a humourless Oliver Cromwell.

With Barbara Windsor, Joan Sims and David Lodge. Written by Dave Freeman.

★ *Orgy and Bess*
Hattie Jacques – in her only appearance in the series – gets stuck into her meaty part as Queen Elizabeth I, and Sid James is a perfect Sir Francis Drake in this right royal rave-up. Kenneth Connor is quite outstanding as the Spanish King.

With Barbara Windsor, Jack Douglas and Victor Maddern. Written by Barry Cryer and Dick Vosburgh.

★ *One in the Eye for Harold*
Jack Douglas and Kenneth Connor lug a mysterious secret weapon through the countryside on their way to the Battle of Hastings.

With Joan Sims, Diane Langton, David Lodge and Linda Hooks. Written by Lew Schwarz.

★ The Nine Old Cobblers

The show's crowning glory, with Jack Douglas elegance personified as ace detective Lord Peter Flimsy, and Kenneth Connor as his right-hand man, Punter. Here the duo investigate the mysterious affair of murderous goings-on when an ancient bell rings.

With Barbara Windsor, Joan Sims, David Lodge, Victor Maddern and Patsy Rowlands. Screenplay by Dave Freeman.

Series 2

★ Under the Round Table

Kenneth Connor reigns supreme as good King Arthur, with Jack Douglas providing the camp element and Bernard Bresslaw the beefcake.

With Joan Sims, Peter Butterworth and Victor Maddern. Written by Lew Schwarz.

★ The Case of the Screaming Winkles

That detecting duo, Jack Douglas and Kenneth Connor, are back to look into sudden death and disorder in a seaside hotel and funfair.

With Joan Sims, Peter Butterworth, David Lodge and Sherrie Hewson. Written by Dave Freeman.

★ And in My Lady's Chamber

Kenneth Connor is the head of the *Upstairs and Downstairs*-fashioned town house, with sexpot Barbara Windsor moving in for the matrimonial kill and Peter Butterworth turning on the slinky sleaze. Jack Douglas and Joan Sims steal the honours as the household staff.

With Bernard Bresslaw, Sherrie Hewson and Carol Hawkins. Written by Lew Schwarz.

★ Short Knight, Long Daze

More Arthurian antics in the court of Kenneth Connor and Joan Sims. Peter Butterworth again leaves a mark as the bumbling, eccentric wizard, Merlin.

With Bernard Bresslaw, Jack Douglas and Susan Skipper. Written by Lew Schwarz.

★ The Case of the Coughing Parrot

High-society sleuths, Jack Douglas and Kenneth Connor, return to solve the riddle of an exotic bird with a tickly throat.

With Joan Sims, Peter Butterworth and David Lodge. Written by Dave Freeman.

★ *Who Needs Kitchener?*
Back to *Upstairs and Downstairs* parody with crusty Kenneth Connor, flirty Barbara Windsor, Scots butler Jack Douglas, and huffing house-keeper Joan Sims.

With Bernard Bresslaw, Sherrie Hewson and Carol Hawkins. Written by Lew Schwarz.

★ *Lamp-Posts of the Empire*
A sort of short version of *Carry On Up the Jungle*, with adventurous Kenneth Connor desperately trying to track down the elusive Dr Pavingstone – Bernard Bresslaw. Barbara Windsor adds some glamour and Jack Douglas the giggles as the hapless, twitching white hunter, Elephant Dick Darcy.

With Peter Butterworth, Oscar James and Reuben Martin. Written by Lew Schwarz. Produced by Gerald Thomas. Directed by Alan Tarrant 1975.

★ *Carry On Laughing with the Slimming Factory*
Summer season farce, staged at Scarborough's Grand Opera House, and starring Jack Douglas as bumbling hero, Jack Hardy. A standard comic romp from the writer who penned the Sid James stage favourites, *Wedding Fever* and *The Mating Season*. Here, old-timers Kenneth Connor and Peter Butterworth help raise the roof.

With Liz Fraser, Linda Hooks, Anne Aston and Danny O'Dea. Written by Sam Cree. A Don Robinson Production. Directed by Bill Roberton, 1976.

★ *Carry On Laughing*
Hugely successful, prime-time compilation of classic clips from the Rank *Carry On* films, covering the sixteen films from *Don't Lose Your Head* to *Carry On England*.

Written by Talbot Rothwell. Edited by Jack Gardner and Peter Boita. Directed by Gerald Thomas from 1981.

★ *What a Carry On*
Much more of the same, this was a crafty answer to the popular ITV compilations for the BBC. Again, Rogers and Thomas steered these profitable packages into production.

Written by Talbot Rothwell. Edited by Jack Gardner. Directed by Gerald Thomas, 1983.

★ *Carry On Laughing's Christmas Classics*
Recreating the atmosphere of the compilation film, *That's Carry On*, familiar hosts with the most, Kenneth Williams and Barbara Windsor, were dragged into a Thames Television studio to link this half-hour package for the Christmas schedules. Clips from *Carry On ... Up the Khyber*, *Carry On Camping* and *Carry On Behind* were linked with rough and ready camp discussions between the two stars, and the entire thing ended with Williams as the fairy atop the Christmas tree. It was that kind of show.

Written by Talbot Rothwell and Dave Freeman. Edited by Jack Gardner. Produced by Gerald Thomas. Directed by David Clark, 1983.

★ *Carry On Columbus*
After what seemed like an eternity of waiting, the remnants of a vintage cast were forced into Pinewood Studios with the prime names of the modern alternative invasion, and came up with this rag-bag of skits, smut and silliness. The script repeated a load of old favourites. Jim Dale strutted his stuff with total conviction as the great explorer and Keith Allen (probably the most stimulating of the new boys) played the deadening puns with the perfect amount of respect.

The plot revolves round Columbus heading off to find a better route for trade, but accidentally stumbling upon America instead. But the story doesn't really matter when you have Bernard Cribbins mumbling about Jewish persecution, Julian Clary dancing a flamenco, their royal heiresses Leslie Phillips and June Whitfield looking bemused and Rik Mayall flaring his nostrils in homage to Kenneth Williams. The mix, far better than many made out and continue to make out, didn't gel like the old days, the costumes got the biggest laughs, and life without innuendo seemed the best option for all of ninety minutes.

With Jack Douglas, Peter Richardson, Jon Pertwee, Maureen Lipman, Peter Gilmore, Alexei Sayle, Sara Crowe, Richard Wilson and Nigel Planer. Written by Dave Freeman. Produced by John Goldstone. Directed by Gerald Thomas, 1992.

★ *Just for Laughs*
Another compilation programme, for ITV this time, concentrating on other classic British comedy films of the 1950s, 1960s and 1970s. The *Doctor ...* series, *Bless This House* and the Leslie Phillips vet comedy, *In the Doghouse*, were included. Ten half-hour programmes were made.

Edited by Jack Gardner. Produced and directed by Gerald Thomas, 1988.

★ *Laugh With the Carry Ons*

A third and final clip-show from the *Carry On* crew. This time, the ITV network showcased a series of compilations from previously untouched films – namely Anglo Amalgamated classics from *Carry On Sergeant* to *Carry On Screaming!*, and the last of the original run, *Carry On Emmannuelle*. Severe style-jolting was the natural, frequent impression. This was the last project overseen by the great Gerald Thomas: he died before the shows were finally aired.

Written by Norman Hudis, Talbot Rothwell, Sid Colin and Lance Peters. Edited by Jack Gardner. Produced and directed by Gerald Thomas, 1993.

Index